D1542944

Graham Greene

Graham Greene

The Aesthetics of Exploration

GWENN R. BOARDMAN

University of Florida Press
Gainesville
1971

A University of Florida Press Book

COPYRIGHT © 1971 BY THE STATE OF FLORIDA
BOARD OF TRUSTEES OF THE INTERNAL
IMPROVEMENT TRUST FUND

All Rights Reserved

DESIGNED BY STANLEY D. HARRIS

Library of Congress Catalog Card No. 78–126425
ISBN 0–8130–0312–1

PRINTED IN FLORIDA

828.912
G799 z 6   C .1

PREFACE

In this discussion of Graham Greene's work, I have quoted extensively from the earlier Uniform Edition and other editions, to assist the reader wishing to make comparisons with *The Collected Edition* (published by Heinemann and Bodley Head). My discussion has not been revised to incorporate changes in the text or information contained in Greene's introductions, although the first volumes of *The Collected Edition* appeared while my book was being prepared for publication.

The introductions are a valuable source of footnotes to Greene's work. They include comments on the craft of fiction (e.g., his difficulties with "one lay figure" in various novels), as well as his evaluation of his work (e.g., his judgment that the last sixty pages of *It's a Battlefield* are "as successful as anything I have written since" and his "soft spot" for *England Made Me,* along with comments on a critic's difficulties with the incestuous relationship of Anthony and Kate). Some introductions provide amusing glimpses of journeys linked with Greene's fiction (e.g., his adventures in Cuba and West Africa and their relationship to *Our Man in Havana*).

Nevertheless, Green's allusions to James' prefaces offer a hint that we should not take the introductions as definitive. For instance,

the introduction to *Our Man in Havana* traces the origin of that
entertainment to a friend's request for a film script after World War
II. Yet Greene's review written in 1936 shows that the idea was in
his mind ten years earlier.

I wish to express my gratitude to the following for permission to
quote material: to *Renascence* for portions of my essay *"Under the
Garden*: Graham Greene's Aesthetic Explorations" which first appeared in that journal; to W. H. Auden and Random House for lines
quoted from W. H. Auden's *The Orators*, and to Faber and Faber
for use outside the United States; and to Mr. Diamuid Russell for
lines from A. E.'s "Germinal."

I have quoted from a personal communication of Graham Greene
of August 1971.

CONTENTS

KEY TO SYMBOLS

INTRODUCTION

GRAHAM GREENE is an inveterate explorer, whether making a *Journey without Maps* or giving an amusing account of *Travels with My Aunt* more than thirty years later. He has found in his own travels that discovery is much more than a physical progress, and that the imagination has its own geography. He has said, "The explorer has the same creative sickness as the writer or the artist. . . . To fill in the map as to fill in the character or features of a human being, requires the urge to surrender and self-destruction."[1]

The artistic quest is expressed in Greene's fiction through his central metaphor of the map—a metaphor stretching from his first novel *The Man Within* (where the lost Andrews seeks an actual path) to his account of Absurd Man, Querry, in *A Burnt-Out Case*. Querry tells a "fairy story" about a boy living "once upon a time in the deep country" who grew up to become a Jeweller continually traveling but "always [coming] back to the same place where the same things happened," back to the joyless world of dead spirit, filled with men suffering from leprosy of the soul. Through his experiences with the lepers of the Congo, Querry ultimately finds his own way back to a world of feeling and laughter.

1. "Books in General," *New Statesman*, June 21, 1952. See Bibliography for full information on Greene's works.

The story "Under the Garden" can serve as a footnote to *A Burnt-Out Case* and to Greene's lifetime of actual and fictional travels, for it reveals that ultimately each man must go back to the creative sources, facing hidden fears and uncritically accepted ideas until he is ready to return, as Wilditch does in "Under the Garden," to "the world of choice." For the questing artist is not simply a traveler and map-maker. He looks at the world with the fresh eyes of childhood, ultimately tempering this vision with essential maturity and experience. The artist confronts the world labeled (unsatisfactorily) by others, by men using the dead language of convention. He must learn to make his own maps, and to scorn the clichés and sentimentality of the "popular" writer.

Greene has recorded his own explorations in terms of psychological as well as aesthetic exploration, and the reader discovers links between the stages of Greene's artistic growth and his actual journeys through Liberia, Mexico, Indo-China, and the Congo. His first conscious examination of "the region of the imagination," *Journey without Maps* (1936), tells of travels in unmapped Liberia, a "heart of darkness" appropriate both to Greene's "African fixation" and to his debt to Joseph Conrad, a writer who "impressed Africa as an imaginative symbol on the European mind." Greene could also take up the threads of life "very far back," in the innocence of racial childhood, where he hoped to discover at what point civilization, and his own work, had gone astray. He mapped the creative process and constructed a guide for travelers lost in the confused territory of the 1930s.

The religious "Limbo" of Africa and its ancient magical Power led to *Brighton Rock* (1938). But they were inadequate sources of inspiration for a Catholic writer. Hence Greene journeyed to Mexico, along *The Lawless Roads* (1939), where he could observe a land of perpetual adolescence, in which the Power had become secular and the Glory of God was in the hands of a whisky priest. From this region Greene returned to a Europe that was entering World War II, a civilization of hate that reminded Greene how far we were from learning "the most difficult lesson of all"—the lesson of Love and of the Creator upon the Cross.

Out of the war years, Greene brought novels and plays in

which he charted the confusions of love, pity, and hate. With *The End of the Affair* (1951), he reached his finest expression of man's love and God's. Yet Catholicism sometimes seemed an obstacle rather than a key for the reader trying to understand Greene's novels. Perhaps because of his recognition of this difficulty, Greene prepared to write "a kind of morality," a suitably simple story for those readers who were contaminated by popular culture, men living in that "empty, graceless, sinless chromium world," where Catholicism had lost its old "mystique." From his journeys to Indo-China, Greene brought a "guilty" European representative of the Old World and an "innocent" American symbolic of the New Adult: *The Quiet American* (1955).

"An Indo-China Journal" (1954) records Greene's recognition that "under the enormous shadow of the Cross it is better to be gay," an idea developed in the three amusing self-parodies, *Loser Takes All, Our Man in Havana,* and *The Complaisant Lover.* None of these works, however, showed a truly mature acceptance of today's Absurd existence. Greene had to make another journey, "In Search of a Character," looking for a man coming to terms with contemporary life. Once again he traveled to the heart of darkness, Africa, this time through Conrad's own region, the Congo. Greene came back to England with a new journal charmingly reporting absurdities as well as serious observations. He had found his character, Querry, a representative man coming to terms with the Absurd. Greene then put together the dissected map he had first referred to in *Journey without Maps*: his "properly connected whole" picture of man and artist is *A Burnt-Out Case* (1961).

Thus Liberia, Mexico, Indo-China, and the Congo exposed new levels of artistic consciousness and provided metaphors for Greene's artistic development. We must, however, keep in mind that Greene identifies the "truth" he sought on the journeys of his geographical explorations as "a question of style" rather than a philosophical equation. Yet it is also the truth of "eternal values," the relation of man's soul to God—an essential dimension of the fictional as of the real world.

Greene has often denied that he is a Catholic novelist. He says only: "Quand on est catholique, il ne faut pas chercher à faire du 'catholicisme.' Tout ce que l'on dit ou écrit respire inévitablement le catholicisme."[2] Greene also speaks of the lost religious sense of today's world as a loss to the world of fiction. He regrets the reduction of characters to "cardboard," as they seem without "the solidity and importance of men with souls to save or lose." He regrets, too, the artist's lost primitive, unspoiled vision—the vision that he rediscovered on the first of his own journeys. The reader can follow Greene's exploration of the stages of psychological perception and literary growth, reliving childhood and adolescence and sharing in the existence of flawed modern man. This is the way to learn to laugh at our own Absurdity and to recognize with Greene that "we are all Comedians." The first step to this discovery is taken on the confusing paths of a *Journey without Maps.*

2. "Propos de table avec Graham Greene," p. 136. Greene's comments on the lost religious sense appear in discussions of Henry James and references to T. S. Eliot and in his essays on Mauriac (*LC*, p. 69) and on Fielding and Sterne (*LC*, p. 64).

Chapter 1 JOURNEY WITHOUT MAPS

SURELY ONLY a fool would undertake such a journey—a trek on foot into unmapped Africa, accompanied by a white woman and a string of assorted African tribesmen, none of whom could adequately understand or be understood by their employer. This explorer, however, was Graham Greene, who later admitted that he had been "a complete amateur at travel in Africa . . . [with] no idea of what route to follow or the conditions [he] would meet" (*JM*, p. 46). His apparent folly in spending four weeks carefully and painfully walking through the heart of darkness actually proved to be a very profitable "smash-and-grab raid into the primitive" (p. 140). Greene's exploration—begun in terms of Conradian mystery— led him to new understanding of the sources of the creative spirit, understanding reflected in his artistic growth.

When Greene sailed from Liverpool shortly after Christmas 1934, he was a journalist and novelist of limited accomplishment. His writing ranged from a book of poems, *Babbling April* (1925), to an "entertainment," *Stamboul Train* (1932). He had also edited letters to the London *Times*, and written reviews and essays for *The Spectator*. Of Africa, however, he knew little beyond the romantic adventures of *King Solomon's Mines* and other boyhood reading,

the speeches made by weary missionaries on school lecture plat-
forms, and the dark mystery of Joseph Conrad's Africa.

Greene has since pointed out the relation between the romantic
world of *King Solomon's Mines* and the actual continent of Africa:
they belong to "the same region of the imagination—the region of
uncertainty, of not knowing the way about."[1] In his early novels,
Greene clearly did not yet know his way about as a writer. For in
spite of the resemblance of themes and characters to those in his
later work, Greene was often guilty of what he calls "nib-deep writing,"[2] an uncertainty of purpose rather than a craftsman's artfully
structured ambiguity of meaning.

All of Greene's early novels are marred in varying degrees by
lack of subtlety in characterization, metaphor, and structure. There
is often a naïveté of attitude as well, not to be found in such later
stories as *Brighton Rock* (1938), *The Heart of the Matter* (1948),
and *A Burnt-Out Case* (1961). Greene had not yet found his way
to the imaginative "mystery" he began to comprehend in Africa.
For instance, man's fragmented self is oversimplified, expressed
quite clumsily as divided personality in *The Man Within*, where
Andrews is torn between his good and bad "angels" ("There's another man within me that's angry with me"); as twins in "The End
of the Party" and *England Made Me*; and as brothers in *It's a
Battlefield*. Journeys in these early novels are too narrowly confined,
staying close to the railroad tracks of *Stamboul Train* or following
a fugitive in *The Man Within*. Each of these novels ends in a
situation reminiscent of Greene's own sensation, described in "The
Lost Childhood," of being lost in wild jungle country without a map.
Andrews, Conrad, Coral, Kate, and Anthony are also like the men
described in the epigraph of *It's a Battlefield*: isolated in individual
conflict and confusion, lost in one sector of experience, and out of
touch with the world.

When *Journey without Maps* was published in 1936, it revealed
that Greene's journey to Africa had been much more than geographical exploration. It is a record of Greene's exploration of the
creative process itself, showing the stages by which he moved

1. *The Lost Childhood*, p. 15.
2. "A Novelist's Notebook," *Spectator*, October 1, 1937.

toward his artistic discoveries. In its pages, Greene refers to natives, witch-doctors, villages, and jungle paths, but the subtitle "A Travel Book" is misleading. Close reading reveals that, rather than being a traveler's journal like his cousin's book, *Land Benighted*,[3] Greene's is a guide to the novelist's awakening imagination.

Scarcely concealed beneath the description of one inexperienced explorer's African journey lies the real heart of Greene's four uncomfortable weeks. We can follow the trail from the artist's first— and often incorrect—response to his environment, through his quests for meaning and his shifting evaluation of experience, to an ultimate point of view from which he can create his world. Greene himself began the journey with a vague dissatisfaction about the world of superficial values and easy sentiment. He sought some kind of solution in Africa's "quality of darkness . . . the inexplicable"; he wished to discover "at which point we went astray" (*JM*, pp. 9–10). To his inexperienced eye the coast of Africa had all the innocence and beauty that a boy's romantic imagination would expect: he saw natives walking hand in hand, seeming to like each other, and giving "a sense of warm and sleepy beauty, of enjoyment divorced from activity and the weariness of willing." Soon he found that this impression was not the true Coast, that a swarm of natives could also resemble "flies on a piece of meat" (pp. 26, 28).

Greene had yet to discover, through the subtleties and disappointments of Africa, that life was not simply divided into the polarities represented by Conrad's world and T. S. Eliot's.[4] Only at the end of his creative journey, after he was back in the familiar English scene, could Greene begin to evaluate and apply all that he had learned in Liberia. Waiting at the English Customs shed with his African "loot," Greene would at last hear an English child's cry as an echo of African innocence, of African virginity and "graves not opened for gold." This cry was to be his symbolic link between

3. Barbara Greene was the white woman who accompanied Greene on his journey, although he never mentions her by name in his book. Her *Land Benighted* includes a frank picture of Greene and amusing details of the trek.

4. Usually Greene underscores ironic comment with lines from Eliot, as in his description of Major Grant "Having to construct something upon which to rejoice," i.e., "Ordering a woman, as one might order a joint of meat, according to size and cut and price" (*JM*, pp. 76, 75). Greene uses Conrad's words to emphasize the romantic aspects of Africa.

Africa's contrasts of darkness and "blinding sunlight" and England's
cold April mist. For it is the very sound of innocence, and Greene
has written in one of his essays, "The creative spirit has remained
tied to innocence" (*LC*, p. 138).

THE MAP OF THE CREATIVE PROCESS

"The Way to Africa," the first section of Greene's *Journey without Maps*, may be used as a pocket guide to his trek. He began by
"going astray" at a Conradian "tall black door" in a narrow London
street. This allusion to Greene's literary going astray under Conrad's
influence remained obscure for twenty-six years, until the publication of *In Search of a Character* in 1962.[5] Greene's difficulties in
finding the way to Africa similarly hint at his difficulties in finding
the way to more perceptive writing. He failed to find the Liberian
consul at first and had to ask directions of someone who knew the
way—a woman working nearby in St. Dunstan's Church. The questing writer would scarcely have anticipated enlightenment in such
a setting, yet St. Dunstan's does help the blind (St. Dunstan's
Lodge served as a rehabilitation center for the blinded veterans of
World War I). Thus it was appropriate for Greene to be given as-
sistance by the patron saint of new vision.

The novelist must begin his work by confronting the raw material of daily existence. For Greene, this confrontation began at the
Liberian Consulate, where he observed a group of men finishing
their lunch at three o'clock, in a tiny room incongruously furnished
with old telephone directories, school textbooks of chemistry, and a
basin stuck in the top of a wastepaper basket. Greene found a Conradian simile for this group: they were like a shabby caravan held

5. In this journal Greene describes the extraordinary power of Conrad's
work over his own. He explains that he consciously abandoned Conrad "about
1932" (i.e., not long before his journey) because Conrad's influence was "too
great and too disastrous" (*SC*, pp. 31, 33). Greene notes a trick that he had
picked up from Conrad: comparing concrete to abstract. He comments on Conrad's weakness of taking an episode from his own life and trying to lend it "for
the sake of 'literature' " a greater significance than it could sustain. (Greene
himself had obviously used far too many untransformed memories in his early
work.) He also suggests Conrad's wider influence: "Conrad's *Heart of Darkness* impressed Africa as an imaginative symbol on the European mind"—"Fiction," *Spectator*, February 10, 1933.

up for a moment. Their strange appearance did not, however, discourage Greene from continuing his quest and trying to follow the puzzling clues. He did not solve all the mysterious hints offered by the unfamiliar setting of the Consulate—for instance, the nature of the "bast-like threads" floating on their dishwater, or the contents of the "bursting parcels of what looked like stones"; but he rapidly made one important discovery. Although these men were "very kind," their kindness was not the romantic reflection of tribal dignity suggested by even a shabby caravan. On the contrary, these men mirrored the perverse values of the civilized world; their kindness "all came down to a question of paying money."

In *England Made Me*, Greene's creativity did not carry him beyond journalistic mockery of such commercial values. But the questing artist Greene accepted these seedy neo-Africans, men of "uncertain" nationality who apparently had not explored Africa themselves. He simply looked at their blank map, told an expedient lie, and signed their papers.

The apparently trivial action of looking at an inadequate map is actually a highly significant gesture, the symbolic action expressing Greene's central metaphor of the map. This is the artist confronting the world that has been labeled by others, in order to discover the errors of conventional views of "right" and of "justice" (in *Brighton Rock*, the errors of Ida's outlook), or of "love" and "hate" (in *The End of the Affair*, the discovery made by Bendrix). Often of course, as Greene suggests in "Subjects and Stories," the popular novelist substitutes commonplace imaginative distortions and sentimental clichés for "life as it is and life as it ought to be."

In an unfinished story, "The Other Side of the Border," Greene shows the symbolic value of the map even more clearly. Danvers recognizes that "there are no reliable maps" of Africa and says, "We'll have to make our own" (*19S*, p. 220), as Greene does in his novels. The map in this story is "like a crystal in which men see many different things—success and failure, suicide in a second-rate hotel and a government contract, perverse loves and strange homes, a snake in a lavatory." These associations recall Greene's interest in psychoanalysis and dreams. In contrast, Morrow—imagining that he "understands" the map which represents "a whole obscure state of mind"—merely responds to it with sentimental feelings about "home" and "school" (p. 197).

Greene abandoned this story based on his African exploration (but not published until 1947) in favor of *Brighton Rock,* a novel in which the map metaphor extends to a specific account of the territory "entre le Bien et le Mal." Yet Greene's post-journey map metaphors are often reminiscent of earlier ones. Even in his first published novel, *The Man Within,* Greene wrote of Andrews finding scents and sounds "jumbled together like the pieces of a puzzle . . . half forgotten because of his fatigue and fear" (p. 4). These phrases anticipate the epigraph of *Journey without Maps* and Greene's personal battle with fatigue and fear in an African hut (the section "Rats," discussed in detail later). The plot of *Stamboul Train* turns upon a map in Dr. Czinner's guidebook. In *Its a Battlefield,* Milly's bed is a map "waiting to be explored" (p. 76). Yet even in this 1934 novel the map metaphor is forced. The Assistant Commissioner has a vague memory of "someone" who had mapped hell in circles and sees his own world as being "only the outer circle." Greene concludes this description with: "At each station on the Outer Circle [a literal reference to the London Underground Railway] a train stopped every two minutes" (pp. 19–20).

Anthony and Kate of *England Made Me* (1935) are literally in a strange country; Greene emphasizes Anthony's weakness by saying that he had "lost the knack of map-reading" (p. 248); Kate was as weary as "a traveller who discovers that his maps again are faulty" (p. 191). Gradually Greene's metaphor picks up additional meanings. By 1951, in *The End of the Affair,* it quite clearly suggests the territory both of this world and the next when Bendrix is "lost in a strange region" and says, "I have no map" (p. 56). In *A Burnt-Out Case* (1961) Greene adds to his map metaphor his recurrent allusions to lepers; Dr. Colin owns "the atlas of leprosy."

Clearly Greene's metaphor is much more than the common simile he used in 1939 as epigraph to *The Lawless Roads*: "Man's like the earth." In the much more elaborate epigraph of *Journey without Maps,* Greene quotes Oliver Wendell Holmes:

> The life of an individual is in many respects like a child's
> dissected map. If I could live a hundred years, keeping my

intelligence to the last, I feel as if I could put the pieces together until they made a properly connected whole. As it is, I, like all others, find a certain number of connected fragments, and a larger number of disjointed pieces, which I might in time place in their natural connection. Many of these pieces seem fragmentary, but would in time show themselves as essential parts of the whole. What strikes me very forcibly is the arbitrary and as it were accidental way in which the lines of junction appear to run irregularly among the fragments. With every decade I find some new pieces coming into place. Blanks which have been left in former years find their complement among the undistributed fragments. If I could look back on the whole, as we look at the child's map when it is put together, I feel that I should have my whole life intelligently laid out before me. . . .

But of course no man ever enjoys this privilege. More often he is faced, as Greene was, with the mess we have made of ourselves, as individuals and as a "civilization."

Before his African journey Greene had been guided by the artistic paths of Joseph Conrad, Henry James, and Percy Lubbock. Their explorations, however, provided no more reliable guidance for Greene's own craft of fiction than that offered by the Liberian maps of the British General Staff and the United States War Department. These African maps further symbolized the polarities of ignorance and imaginative invention: a British map blandly confessing ignorance while carefully indicating several nonexistent towns, and a United States map so inaccurate that "it would be useless, perhaps even dangerous to follow it, though there is something Elizabethan in its imagination" (*JM*, pp. 43–44). Even the British Blue Book that seemed to provide a "satisfyingly complete picture" of Liberia reflected only a rather superficial and inadequately evaluated official journey down the Kru Coast.

On his own journey Greene found that African porters could follow paths already worn through the jungle, but they rarely knew the names of the villages. Distant places were as foreign to them as to Greene. A family of educated Liberians might own "a map of the whole of Liberia" (p. 284), but it was only a sketchy chart of the coastal towns. Even Europeans who thought they knew the routes led Greene astray. Or they were as ignorant as Mrs. Croup, the missionary's widow, who had always traveled in a hammock; her carriers explored as far as Bamakama, while she journeyed without ever becoming aware of the territory through which she moved. Greene also found that indications of distance were unreliable, for European time had been left behind at the coast and "three hours distant" could never measure the appalling hardships of walking unfamiliar paths. Ironically, the only traveler who could tell Greene the "whole" route was a figure reminiscent of the European scene, a Mandingo trader riding from the interior with the regularity of "a traveller in silk stockings who catches the Brighton Belle once a week" (p. 126).

At all these levels Liberia became a symbolic representation of the "Dark Age of scholarship and civilization"[6] that existed in Europe. It was a country in which to look for the stage at which civilization had lost touch with ancient perceptions and creative vigor, for it contained both the primitive pure terrors and pleasures and the partly civilized and corrupt Coast on which Greene saw life as a caricature of European and American failures. The inaccuracies of its sparsely dotted charts further reminded Greene of his own childhood, a time that he describes as "fourteen years in a wild jungle country without a map" (*LC*, p. 16).[7]

Of course Greene was well aware that no map can reveal everything about the country it claims to show. Any thoughtful explorer will discover for himself whether a village is infested with cockroaches or rats, whether the chief will offer a gift ("dash") of a basket of excellent rice or a basket of rotten eggs. This is the per-

6. "The Cinema," *Spectator*, May 8, 1936. This condition is the result of "centuries of cerebration" (*JM*, p. 10).

7. This sensation reflects Greene's dissatisfaction with conventional accounts of his world. He was born in 1904, in Berkhamsted—a small town not far from London. Its Georgian houses, scattered Elizabethan buildings, and miles of watercress beds all seem very pleasant and peaceful. Its houses climb up the hills from the valley through which run the railway and quiet canal; beyond the houses lie green meadows, beech woods, gorse-covered common, and the "big house" set in its park. There is no hint of the horrors of suicidal and pregnant poor, of the squalid incidents Greene includes in his various references to Berkhamsted in *Journey without Maps*, "Twenty-four Hours in Metroland," "The Innocent," and *The Lawless Roads*. Nor does the school of which Greene's father was headmaster appear to be either more ugly or more evil than other such minor public schools. Greene himself even admits in *The Old School* that it was in many ways superior.

sonal experience, serving as a reminder that Greene's novels are no more a manual of instruction for daily life than the map serving as frontispiece to the latest paperback edition of his *Journey without Maps* is a practical chart for a traveler in Liberia. Comparison with Greene's text makes it clear that the spot marked as "Dagamai" on this map is the village of Duogobmai, a place he found only after many difficulties. He referred to it as the "horrible village," the "worst village" of his trek. Yet Nicoboozu, which Greene said was the "high point" of his travels, is not marked on this map at all.

Such discrepancies emphasize that Greene is not offering a formal philosophical guide of the sort suggested by Paul Rostenne's title, *Graham Greene: Témoin des temps tragiques*. Nor does Greene write apologetics, for "L'apologète écrit pour une certaine catégorie de lecteurs, le romancier s'adresse à tous."[8] Greene's fiction is the result of a journey continually enlivened by humor, as on the African journey his weariness and sickness were countered by his satiric perception of whites afraid they would be "done," yet hastening out to see whom *they* could "do" (p. 88), and by the whimsical picture of Greene and his strange companions: "One really needed to be a minor prophet to emerge suddenly like this, almost unaccompanied, with two harps and a monkey" (p. 138). Greene also recorded scenes of extraordinary and unexpected beauty, moments at which the line and movement of a Negro woman, the delicacy of a cloud of butterflies, the slender Oriental grace of Liberian egrets, lifted his spirits or erased the preceding ugliness of setting, of event, or of personality. He saw always with the eye of the artist, although his pen was guided by the mind and hand of an unusually thoughtful and analytical writer.

Analyzing and re-examining the puzzling sections of experience, Greene reconstructed its parts until he really began to "see life whole." Slowly he felt his way toward an awareness of human complexity and a consistent perspective on human experience, until he could make "the direct statement, which demands some insight into the way men really act."[9] Such a statement is the core of creative expression, the result of a novelist's successful probing of the per-

8. "Propos de table avec Graham Greene," p. 136.
9. "The Cinema," *Spectator*, December 1, 1939.

sonal and racial subconscious. In order to mark the guidelines by which the parts of this puzzling picture must be fitted together, Greene personally walked the paths of Liberia. There he experienced the sensation described in Auden's lines from *The Orators* serving as one of the epigraphs for *Journey without Maps*:

> "O do you imagine," said fearer to farer,
> "That dusk will delay on your path to the pass,
> Your diligent looking discover the lacking
> Your footsteps feel from granite to grass?"

Since Africa provided both literal and symbolic examples of this lacking, it was natural that Greene eventually returned to the African continent for his picture of man faced with Absurd existence— Querry, the "burnt-out case," a man who had turned "at bay" (see Chapter 7).

The Heart of Darkness

In spite of the opening suggestions of Conrad's world and continuing allusions to characters and scenes from Conrad's novels, Greene was not looking for "the heart of darkness" in a precise Conradian sense. When Greene described Africa as "roughly the shape of the human heart," he was using the heart as a symbol of man's essential nature, a nature that he continues to view in the context of eternal values. Greene used a quotation from Kurt Heuser's *The Inner Journey* to amplify his meaning: "The interior: that might signify the heart of the continent, but also the heart of things, the mystery: and finally, the comprehension of himself in nature and in Time."[10] This comprehension includes the understanding of others and of one's self; another writer's perceptions will not suffice. Only through personal discovery can the author achieve artistic growth that is based on really new perceptions of the relationships between political, social, and religious parts of life.

10. "Analysis of a Journey," *Spectator*, September 27, 1935. Greene uses slightly different words in *Journey without Maps*: "One is willing to suffer some discomfort for the chance of finding—there are a thousand names for it, King Solomon's Mines, the 'heart of darkness' if one is romantically inclined, or even more simply, as Herr Heuser puts it in his African novel, *The Inner Journey*, one's place in time, based on a knowledge not only of one's present but of the past from which one has emerged" (p. 8).

Religion is obviously only one segment of this dark center, although the mystery at the heart of religious experience is crucial in Greene's creative process. "Lack of religious enthusiasm . . . diminishes . . . artistic talent" (*JM*, p. 103); the writer without such enthusiasm cannot create characters. Roman Catholic Greene, however, found none of his own adult religious values in Africa. Instead, he rediscovered the old dark forces or Power that he recollected from his childhood.[11] He found also primitive religious observances suggesting the ancient link between magic and religion, and ranging from the "Big Bush Devil" to a simple reduction of combined Christian and Pagan symbols: cross, clay, and youngest mother (p. 97). Reviewing Etta Donner's *Hinterland Liberia* in 1939, Greene suggested the nature of Africa's appeal to the European: it has a religious fascination, offering the "opportunity of living continuously in the presence of the supernatural. . . . [Secret societies] sacramentalise the whole of life."[12]

Most of the natives in Africa nevertheless provided only limited lessons for a Catholic writer. In a review of the film *Dark Rapture* in 1940, Greene wrote: "This is as near as we can get to what Africa was before the white man came. . . . One carries away from the cinema a sense of innocence, of human dignity reduced to its essentials, no robes or decorations. . . . The pygmies go wandering deeper and deeper into the heart of darkness . . . wandering in a kind of theological Limbo."[13] Limbo is the region of unbaptized children and therefore not an adequate source of instruction for the questing Catholic.

Nor was the peculiar Protestant Christianity of Liberia, the

11. "In a Christian land we have grown so accustomed to the idea of a spiritual war, of God and Satan, that this supernatural world, which is neither good nor evil but simply Power, is almost beyond sympathetic comprehension. Not quite: for those witches which haunted our childhood were neither good nor evil. They terrified us with their power but we knew all the time that we must not escape them. They simply demanded recognition: flight was a weakness" (*JM*, p. 213).

12. "Three Travellers," *Spectator*, December 8, 1939. In *Journey without Maps* Greene refers to the secret societies as a particular part of the heart of darkness (p. 209).

13. "The Cinema," *Spectator*, February 16, 1940. Also, "Religion [in West Africa] has a very Kafka air" according to Greene's review "West Coast," *Spectator*, April 12, 1935, p. 622.

state founded "as an example to all Africa of a Christian and self-governing state" (p. 6); it only served to remind Greene of the degeneration of Christianity in Europe. In Liberia as in Europe, he found the church reduced to serving as an arbiter of social graces and as a form of political or financial expediency. Missionaries— Lutheran, Methodist, Episcopal, Catholic—were on the whole more concerned with health and education than with the spiritual experience of the natives. Catholicism in the bush might even appear in the disappointing form of Sanoquelleh's "crooked" and interfering priest (p. 209). Finally, in the African responses to all forms of Christianity, Greene found disappointing ambiguities: the black government distrusted the missions, the Mohammedan District Commissioner hated Christians, and the natives continued pagan practices that were ill concealed by nominal Christianity.

Africa's heart, then, was not a source of narrowly religious inspiration. At first reading, the section of *Journey without Maps* entitled "The Shape of Africa" (pp. 29–32) might even suggest that for Greene the "heart" was as hopelessly sentimental as "that great soft organ with its unreliable goodness and easy melancholy and baseless optimism" described in one of his film reviews.[14] The section begins with a girl weeping as she walks across a square that is littered with fallen leaves. But she rejects the cinema and walks into a bar. Through associative recall Greene adds to this scene his own memories of Berlin appearing below his plane "like an illuminated Underground map," but revealing a world of violence as he looks at it more closely. He remembers a painful Easter spent in Paris in 1924, when he had seen "a man and woman copulating . . . under a street lamp, like two people who are supporting and comforting each other in the pain of some sickness." Next, Greene records his childhood and adolescent memories, including an awakening sense of cruelty. But of his earliest memory, a dead dog at the bottom of his pram, Greene declares, "There was no emotion attached to the sight. It was just a fact."

In praising the "admirable objectivity" of that earlier period of

14. Greene used this definition in criticizing the sentimental heart of popular fiction and cinema, in "The Cinema," *Spectator*, November 11, 1938. This is the sentimental heart characteristic of Ida's nature in *Brighton Rock,* or of Amy's in "Jubilee."

life, Greene was formulating one of his recurrent themes: the child's freedom from the stultifying clichés of adult experience. Greene made another reference to "the objective light of childhood" in "Herbert Read," the essay in which he spoke of the creative spirit as being "tied to innocence" (*LC,* p. 138). Only if the writer looks at his world as a child does can he preserve the freshness of his creative imagination. At the same time, and like an explorer, the author records his discoveries with a child's "virgin sensibility" (*LC,* p. 138). This is the idea underlying Greene's assertion that there was neither horror nor sentiment in the child's view of the dead dog: for the adult, the very terms "child" and "dog" would have been obscured by sentimental connotations. Later, young Greene had seen a man running out of a house, but the child was unhampered by the adult's recognition of the "meaning" of the incident. For the child, the episode represented only movement and excitement; for the adult it was reduced to, "He wanted to kill himself."[15]

Greene was beginning to examine the perspective given by time and maturity, as he was to realize later on his journey that Kailahun had become in memory a clean village, although "what impressed me at the time was the dirt and disease" (p. 63). In concluding his survey of the "shape" of Africa, Greene again looked at the girl, weeping and isolated in her bar, a symbol of lost happiness: "I thought for some reason even then of Africa, not a particular place, but a shape, a strangeness, a wanting to know. The unconscious mind is often sentimental; I have written 'a shape,' and the shape, of course, is roughly that of the human heart." To the cliché-ridden bar patrons, the girl was merely someone who made them uncomfortable, so that no one sat near her. Yet Greene observed,

15. Greene refers again to this incident in "The Innocent" (1937), a short story in which the narrator returns to his childhood home, Bishop's Hendron, a place that appears ugly and drab to his unimaginative companion Lola. The narrator remembers that the dirty pile of sand had seemed to be "the seaside" when he was a child. And he discovers a drawing that he had made as a boy trying to express his love for a little girl. To his adult eyes it seems an obscene picture, the work of a "dirty-minded stranger on a lavatory wall." After he has returned to his pickup Lola, the narrator observes, "I had believed I was drawing something with a meaning unique and beautiful; it was only now after thirty years of life that the picture seemed obscene." In referring to childhood associations, the narrator speaks of "the smell of innocence" (a phrase suggesting Greene's exploration of African innocence).

"You don't weep unless you've been happy first; tears always mean something enviable" (p. 29). As a writer, he was trying to look behind the stereotypes of speech and gesture and to uncover their emotional springs.

Memories like these scattered impressions recorded in *Journey without Maps* are really "a form of simile" (*SC*, p. 31n3). To uncover appropriate similes, Greene probed the unconscious heart as the psychoanalyst would probe a patient's unconscious mind. Going "very deep" into the racial childhood that so often paralleled his own, Greene was following the ancestral threads described by Freud. Africa revealed to him a world of childhood's earliest half-memories as well as that libido whence dreams come to life and present themselves to the conscious adult writer. Greene's technique is explained in his little-known essay "Analysis of a Journey," in the *Spectator* of September 27, 1935. Here, Greene set himself up as a psychoanalyst probing the reasons for a journey "X" had just completed. He decided that "any journey, like a form of dreaming, is an attempt to express the pain [of the past] in harmless images, slipping it past the censor in the shape of a casino, a cathedral, a *pension* at Rapallo." In the slightly different version of the "Analysis" included in *Journey without Maps*, Greene preserved the reference to dreams, which are a recurrent device in his novels and have inspired some of his plots and incidents (*SC*, p. 52n1).

"Psychoanalyst" Greene discovered from X that his patient responded to "Africa" with images of "death and forest and maps and school and dust and darkness, unhappiness and the Gare St. Lazare . . . the face of an unpleasant boy and evensong and a pair of dividers." These are more personal symbols than those listed in *Journey without Maps*: witches and death, unhappiness and the Gare St. Lazare, the huge smoky viaduct over a Paris slum (p. 9). In each catalogue, however, the "disorderly" crowd of words is very different in emotional value from the clear-cut images associated with specific areas of Africa, such as South Africa, which suggested "Rhodes and the British Empire and an ugly building in Oxford and Trafalgar Square" (p. 9). The writer is not satisfied with these stereotyped images of "South Africa"; yet he must not be restricted by intensely personal symbolism. Hence the need for the writer to become his own psychoanalyst and bring the patient—himself as well as the sick world from which his fictional action is drawn—"back to the idea which he is repressing: a long journey backwards without maps, catching a clue here and a clue there . . . until [he] has to face the general idea, the pain or the memory" (pp. 109–10).

Liberia proved especially suitable for Greene's probing of unconscious and preconscious memories, since it was literally without maps and thus forced the writer to do his own probing for direction. Faced with a country that was supposed to be "a byword for corruption and slavery" (p. 90), Greene found instead "the timelessness, the irresponsibility, the freedom of Africa" (p. 160), qualities that invited him to appreciate our remote tribal memories. Released from the accustomed literary and social constraints of Europe, he could let himself "drift with Africa" (p. 71). Without civilization's interference (symbolized in *Journey without Maps* by the various authorities—French and British as well as Liberian—who placed obstacles in Greene's paths), Greene could gradually discover the primitive world in which imagination had not yet been stifled.

Even the surface dirt of monotonously recurring African landmarks of village, palaver-house, and forge could not hide the essence of civilization:

> . . . the sense of a small courageous community barely existing above the desert of trees, hemmed in by a sun too fierce to work under and a darkness filled with evil spirits—love was an arm round the neck, a cramped embrace in the smoke, wealth a little pile of palm-nuts, old age sores and leprosy, religion a few stones in the centre of the village where the dead chiefs lay, a grove of trees where the rice birds, like yellow and green canaries, built their nests, a man in a mask with raffia skirts dancing at burials. This never varied, only their kindness to strangers, the extent of their poverty and the immediacy of their terrors. Their laughter and their happiness seemed the most courageous things in nature. Love, it has been said, was invented in Europe by the troubadours, but it existed here without the trappings of civilization. . . . One was aware the whole time of a standard of courtesy to which it was one's responsibility to conform (pp. 86–87).

In this perception, Greene acknowledged that purity of motive and gesture are more desirable than the chromium and cellophane covers of civilized hypocrisy. As he has observed, breaking this tribal framework leads "straight to the gadget world of the States," where even Catholicism no longer includes any "mystique" (*SC*, p. 17).

Sometimes, even in Africa, Greene found "civilized" government and politicians in "the Tammany Hall manner" (*JM*, p. 121) destroying the tribal dignity. Nevertheless the reversal of the customary roles of ruler and ruled still left some advantage with the Liberian neo-Africans in Monrovia: "There was less discrimination against the white than there was against the black in most white colonies. . . . A fair observer would have been astonished at the moderation of the black rulers" (p. 295).

A fair observer would also have to admit that the "noble savage" a European might have expected to find in unexplored Africa did not exist, even in the relatively uncontaminated "communal life beyond the clearing." Greene himself recognized that this ideal savage had probably never existed. Only occasionally could he glimpse in the very young, "among the few who are not disfigured by navel hernia," the old perfection of "something lovely, happy and unenslaved, something like the girl who came up the hill that morning, a piece of bright cloth twisted above her hips, the sunlight falling between the palms on her dark hanging breasts, her great silver anklets, the yellow pot she carried on her head" (p. 65). Here, Greene's pained awareness of the loss of innocence was soothed by his delight in beautiful form and movement, in striking color that seemed to dramatize his response to the sense of freedom suggested in his use of the words "happy and unenslaved."

Greene responded to the lovely swooping flight of small bright rice birds, fragile transparent primrose-yellow flowers with red centers and black stamens, butterflies, and the graceful black women. He carried this beauty into new country as an emblem of "an instinctive simplicity, a thoughtless idealism" (p. 112). The beauty of the vision made Greene anticipate disillusion, yet for the first time he was not disappointed; soon afterwards he found at Kolahun a girl with slanting eyes and a quality of deep repose, "the loveliest thing I saw in Liberia" (p. 121). This girl's loveliness provided appropriate counterpoint to the "Stuart air" of the Liberian government that surrounded her.

Occasionally, Greene found himself unable to respond to similar beauty. In time he learned to recognize the source of his dulled perceptions in his own physical weariness, as weariness later led him to observe that Mexico was "a state of mind," and beauty only "an emotion in the observer" (*LR*, pp. 185, 197). To the exhausted traveler, Africa's swallow-tailed butterflies seemed no more worth watching than black ants, a realization foreshadowing Greene's technique—in *Brighton Rock*, for instance—of letting the reader see Brighton ocean as sun-speckled or slimy green according to the nature and mood of the observing character.

As he traveled, Greene learned to analyze his own failures of response and to reach that "comprehension of himself in nature and in time" that Kurt Heuser had described. A particularly clear example of Greene reaching such comprehension is his account of "Rats" (pp. 155–58), in which we can actually see him in the process of turning about the jigsaw pieces of experience, memory, and information in order to construct a picture of himself in his world. He had been worrying about rats on the eve of his entry into Liberia from Sierra Leone; he continually remarked on the rat-infested huts of various villages. And then, amid the dirt of Duogobmai, the very worst village, unable to "drink away" his fear, Greene at last came to terms with it. First, he asserted with his customary casualness, "Rats indeed take some getting used to." He reflected on the inadequacy of "facts" in providing understanding: the knowledge that every person passing in Piccadilly Circus had a rat counterpart in the tunnels underneath scarcely constituted "experience" of rats. On the other hand, Greene in Africa—in spite of his experience of the damage done to his clothes and food by the rats—had still not seen one. He was at first no closer to understanding in Africa than he had been in England.

These similes of memory, however, provided clues. Greene recalled the incongruous image of a Parisian rat "lalloping" up the stairs of a fashionable hotel some years before. This humorous image led to a terrifying one: the "reconnoitring" rat reminded Greene of Uhlans marching across a Belgian country road. These grand terrors in turn recalled the petty horrors of another countryside, of an occasion when homely people had fearlessly offered the appalled Greene a flea-infested dead rat. Further memories—this time literary ones, accounts of rat-borne diseases—scarcely reassured the uncomfortable traveler. Finally, however, his general reflections and specific memories faded before the vivid scene that had been created in a well-told anecdote: a nun's recollection of a rat sniffing at her hair. Faced with this confusion of facts, disordered memories, and fears, only the writer who knows how to examine the pieces of his puzzle, how to organize them into a single significant image, can reach a satisfyingly complete picture. In this instance, Greene recognized that it was not, after all, "unreasonable" to fear a rat. Returned to the actuality of rats and dirt in his African hut, Greene could discover "a curious lightness and freedom. . . . One was happy all the same; one had crossed the boundary into country really strange; one had gone deep this time" (p. 158).

Going deep into the racial childhood, and following Africa's insistence that he "take a long look" (p. 110) at his own primitive fears, Greene discovered that the actual world of African childhood contained its own varieties of pain and grief. Often the adult natives displayed the cruelty more typical of children, tormenting each other, conscious only of immediate sensations of pleasure or fear or hunger. Nevertheless, Greene found also "gentleness, kindness, an honesty which one would not have found, or at least dared to assume was there, in Europe" (p. 87). Although the natives teased their monkey, "sometimes they were kind to it" (p. 137). More important, the carriers' childlike behavior illuminated Greene's own responsibilities as adult and as writer. In their response to his forcing of the pace, to his insistence that they press on to the dreadful Duogobmai (an insistence based on a white man's wrong "information," black men's ignorance, and his own false confidence), they were "like children who have caught a grown-up lying to them" (p. 152).

Africa also brought Greene back to memories of his English school, to recollections of its prefects, cracked bells, lonely walks, stone stairs—the memories that he had used in their crude state in *England Made Me* to describe the school life of Anthony Farrant.

The bush school imposing the mysteries of African culture, as well as more subtle (and perhaps more depraved) fears, on the children of Liberian villages reminded Greene of the English public school lying "grimly . . . between childhood and manhood" (p. 100). Attempting to organize his carriers, to discipline them, to keep them working, to feed them, Greene felt like a prefect, or like a new master whose discipline was being tested by his students. Greene even found in his two boys, Laminah and Alfred, typical "bullies at school with a new boy who couldn't hit back" (p. 137).[16]

In spite of these unpleasant memories, the journey succeeded in reawakening "a kind of hope in human nature," that led Greene to wonder whether the "bareness, simplicity, instinctive friendliness, feeling rather than thought" might not suggest the way for his contemporaries to start again (p. 234)—as he was to make a new start with Raven and Pinkie. The consistently high rate of spontaneity, honesty, and enthusiasm seemed to him just those qualities that were missing from the contemporary European scene. If he also found craftiness, he was reassured by encounters with a candid childlike African politician, by simple music and dancing and the innocent intoxication of his carriers, as well as by the ready hospitality continually offered even by impoverished villages.

Always "the real native was someone to love and admire" (p. 55), although in British Sierra Leone, Greene met only two "perfectly natural" Africans, Mr. Jones and Mr. D. Unfortunately, the full account of these gentlemen has disappeared from the Uniform Edition of Greene's works.[17] This omission is particularly unhappy, since the episode in which Greene invited the black Mr. D to lunch offered a splendid commentary on the faults of the "civilization" he was criticizing. Greene's friendship with Mr. Jones, the Customs inspector, similarly suggested where London's newspapers had lit-

16. Greene's personal recollection of two bullies at his own school who "perfected during my thirteenth and fourteenth years a system of mental torture based on two aspects of my rather difficult situation—my father was headmaster and my elder brother was head of my house . . ."—"The Revenge," *Commonweal*, January 14, 1955.

17. The original version appears in the Compass reprint, p. 48. Apparently a London newspaper columnist had been heavily humorous at the expense of the black mayor of Freetown. Mr. Jones commented to Greene, "Of course we are mere children," in a way that revealed that the Africans of Freetown were more adult than their childish European critics.

erally "gone astray" in their supercilious reports on African "childishness."

Comparing Africa with Europe in order to find out the precise
point at which we had "gone astray," Greene spoke again and again
of the contamination that had resulted from the white man's "civilization."[18] At the outset of his African journey, Greene commented
that the English had "planted their seedy civilization and then escaped from it as far as they could. Everything ugly in Freetown
was European . . . if there was anything beautiful in the place it
was native" (p. 33). His first realization was that there were different levels of European behavior. On the one hand there were pros-
pectors, merchants, and others "simply out to make money"; on the
other there were the hypocritical white men who gave garden par-
ties and were supposed to be in Africa for the good of the ruled. It
was these, "the real rulers," with their short tours of duty and fre-
quent leaves, who had so much to answer for in Africa. The plate-
layers, for example, were exploited—paid sixpence a day but
docked one day's pay every month for food they had actually been

18. Similarly in "The Waste Land," *Spectator,* June 7, 1935, Greene
wrote, "It is hopeless to pretend that the civilization we offer the African in return for his own is the superior civilization of Crome and Vaughan, of Cotswold
manor houses and Suffolk churches; it is the civilization of the big commercial
companies . . . not the civilization of art but of finance." He expanded this view
in *Journey without Maps* (pp. 64–65). Greene found the simplicity of French
Guinea "a little tarnished by the touch of white rule" (p. 189); the people who
had been "touched by civilization" were those who had "learnt to steal and lie
and kill" (p. 278). Coastal drunkenness was "crude" in contrast to the happy
palm-wine intoxication of interior Africa. The seedy edge of civilization continually "pushes up from the coast"—symbolized in the posturing of a young girl
"conscious of her nakedness" (p. 265). Greene further distinguished between
the seediness of Liberia's black coastal government and that of Sierra Leone's
white rulers. Monrovia was a "beginning," where a newer, more scrupulous
Liberia was just coming into existence and there were signs of primitive but
genuine aestheticism. In contrast, Freetown was "a spectacle of decay," displaying the worst of European artistic influence in cheap, gaudy fabrics, and in
imitations of genteel English "style." Greene contrasted the "interference" of
white colonial rulers with the black rulers of Liberia who at least left the villagers to "their devils and secret societies and private terrors, to the paternal
oppression of their chiefs" (p. 124). Nevertheless, "after a trek of more than
three hundred miles through dense deserted forest, after the little villages and
the communal ember, the great silver anklets, the masked devil swaying between the huts, it was less easy to appreciate the civilization of the coast" (p.
304). Later (e.g., in *In Search of a Character*), Greene qualified his criticism
of Sierra Leone. He returned to Freetown in 1968 and adds footnotes to the
earlier African experiences in "The Soupsweet Land" (see Bibliography).

required to buy for themselves. Again, Greene detected a difference between the whites—doctors, storekeepers, gold smugglers,
shipping agents, consuls—who frankly worked for money, and the
Americans of a nearby Firestone plantation who concealed their
objective with their "commercial idealism." Firestone "leased" a
million acres of Liberian land in a deal that forced native employ-
ees to buy at company stores where even the staple rice was always
more expensive than in Monrovia itself.

Yet whenever he looked more closely at the white man's contamination of the black, Greene was forced to recognize that the
Africans themselves revealed a range of behavior as great as any
he had known in Europe. It was not merely that the boundaries of
the bush were "as distinct as a European boundary" (p. 66). There
were more important and more subtle distinctions. The natives of
the interior of Liberia never had a good word for the politicians in
Monrovia—the "innocent" black children obviously could think for
themselves. Even the witches came in gradations reminiscent of
the levels of development in Greene's youthful dreams. At one extreme was the witch of Landow making wild rushes, wearing a
great crude muzzle, and at the other was a woman's devil with
"simpering, silly, sinister gait." Landow's was a mask of childish
fancy running in the vein of nightmare, while the woman's devil recalled the witch of Greene's childhood, although it was a work of
conscious art in the service of a belief (p. 132). Greene found also
in Africa dishonest Negro officials, the descendants of ex-slaves,
aping white customs ("painfully playing the white man"), or consciously degrading themselves with the self-mockery epitomized by
Freetown's businessman with his motto of "That's Bungie all Over."
Sometimes Greene found that the African was a precise equivalent
of some European type. In the Buzie tribesman, Bubu, smoking his
clay pipe, Greene detected a familiar figure: "One could imagine
him a season-ticketholder, the reliable support of his mother and
sisters in a remote sad suburb" (p. 128). Vande resembled "an English foreman, cheerful, unexciting, a pipe-smoker" (p. 117); the
headman of Kpangblamai in another race would have been "one of
those elderly men who pinch girls' bottoms on buses in a friendly,
harmless way" (p. 130).

Gradually Greene perceived areas in which the touch of white civilization could not be blamed for the Africans' own spoiled childhood. He learned that the Buzies differed from the easygoing, lazy, not very religious men of the Bande country (p. 101); it was typical of the Bassa tribe to promise and then to fail (p. 269), although perhaps this fault resulted from the "contamination" of the nearby Liberian coast. African political figures such as the old puppet chief at Mosambolahun could be as ineffectual and as surrounded by corruption as their European counterparts. The filthiest, most disease-ridden, and least hospitable of the African villages was Duogobmai —a community so little known to civilization that few people had even heard its name (Greene never discovered its possible relation to the "Dagamai" he sought), and Greene reached it only by accident, after much confusion and misinformation. Villages far from the familiar paths displayed crafts that resembled the tasteless gim-crackery of European cities or the false "artiness" of church bazaars. In the farthest corner of one of the least-known colonies, French Guinea, Greene found a commercial sense, tourist baits, and an industrial center.

Slowly Greene learned to accept these anomalies. He accepted the presence of such Africans as Mr. Reeves, a Mohammedan with seal-grey skin, dark eyes revealing "cruelty and sensuality . . . gross, impassive and corrupt" (p. 94); or the black man in a European suit who covered his "hard mean face" with a defensive expression of "silliness and subservience" and, like Mr. Reeves, "kept his brother blacks well in hand" (p. 139). Everything was strange. But it was also strangely familiar, like the clay-daubed widows whose appearance recalled one of Greene's forgotten memories. Greene was gaining the understanding that brought a universal significance to his novels in contrast to his earlier provincialisms of "queer" foreigners, solid working types, and the stereotyped eternal schoolboys.

It was essential that Greene should bring back such understanding from his explorations of darkness and racial beginnings. For although the way forward at the Liberian frontier was "as broad as the primrose way," it was also "as open as a trap" (p. 74). And if the way back was "narrow, hidden, difficult," it yet led to the English scene, the scene to which Greene must eventually find his way. His map must show easy and difficult paths, the ancestral threads to original innocence as well as the navel-strings to the sins of the world. "The Way Back" section of *Journey without Maps* suggests this range through its frank picture of England's civilization.

Greene here recalls Major Grant's visits to a brothel in Savile Row, ordering his meat ("Something rather lean"); Miss Kilvane, the disciple of prophetess Joanna Southcott, whose Maori disciples gave her a car she could not drive; and Charles Seitz, whose frozen and verminous body was dragged head-first down the stairs. He also remembers a gypsy's tribal magic—the ancient Power, perhaps —and a ploughman in a distant field (this last image echoing the Preface to *The Nigger of the Narcissus,* Conrad's comparison of the motions of a laborer in a distant field and "the workman of art"). Greene concludes: "We turned away from Major Grant and Miss Kilvane, from the peace under the down and the flat off the Strand, from the holy and the depraved individualists to the old, the unfamiliar, the communal life beyond the clearing" (pp. 81–82).

But it was only a temporary turning. Later, as Greene came back from his journey down the primrose way of Liberia, he saw the Coast ahead. He reflected, "We were all of us back in the hands of adolescence, and I thought rebelliously: I am glad . . . [to be] home, where we will soon forget . . ." (pp. 280–81). Yet in writing about Mexico, Greene was later to describe "a way of life we have hopelessly lost but can never quite forget" (*LR,* p. 215). Thus the paths continually led from civilization to darkness and back to civilization again. Sometimes the iced beer, fresh beef, and hideous churches of the coast lured Greene back to civilization as much as the religious sense, the masks, and the mystery had drawn him into Africa. There is a similar tension in Greene's novels: on one side are the comforts of the false mother Ida with her easy life and certainty of "right"; on the other lies the power of God in combat with the evil force of a divinely damned Pinkie. Characters are continually torn by the dual appeals of supernatural pain and natural comfort. They journey in today's jungle, while Greene maps their incredibly difficult routes, the "labyrinthine ways."

The "seedy" coast of Africa is perhaps the closest to African innocence that any European can really approach. There is certainly a resemblance between the "navel-string" of dissatisfaction that kept Greene's officers in *Journey without Maps* tied to the Coast (p. 311) and the "ancestral threads" by which the unconscious mind can lead man back to the communal life, the terror, and the gentleness of the dark interior. It was in this seedy coastal area that Greene found a place appropriate as a stage for supposedly civilized men. He commented: "La nature humaine ne s'y déguise pas."[19]

Perhaps Greene's choice of the shabby side of civilization to stand between the conflicting demands of knowledge and innocence is related to the rare truth he found on the coast: the moment of perceiving innocence ahead in the interior and corruption on the way back. The closing paragraphs of *Journey without Maps* make this clear. Greene recalled figures from "The Way Back" section—Major Grant and Miss Kilvane—and compared them with his African memories:

> Major Grant ringing up the brothel . . . the Old Etonian in
> Kensington Gardens, the Nottingham "tart" and the droshky-
> drivers of Riga dwell on that rim of land which is known all the
> world over as the Coast, the one and only coast. They are not,
> after all, so very far from the central darkness: Miss Kilvane
> listening to the ghost of Joanna just as the circle of blacks in
> Tailahun listened to the enigmatic speech of Landow; the
> Catholic priest saying, "And now the Immaculate Conception"
> as the bus drove through the market, the tangle of stalls and
> overhead wires, the neo-Gothic hotels under the black
> overhead Midland fog. This may explain the deep appeal of
> the seedy. It *is* nearer the beginning; like Monrovia it has

19. "Propos de table avec Graham Greene," p. 127. Greene was explaining his choice of a setting for *The Heart of the Matter*. In novels, essays, and reviews Greene repeatedly uses the term "seedy," and it is not surprising that critics have picked upon "seediness" as the characteristic quality of Greene's fictional world. But when he uses the word, Greene does not merely refer to a condition that could as easily be described as "shabby" or "grubby" or "frayed"—although he uses those terms also. When Greene describes a man or a region as seedy, he is remembering Africa and the infinite possibilities still to be found in a world poised between the darkness of creative innocence and the false brilliance of chromium-plated clichés.

begun to build wrong, but at least it has only begun; it hasn't reached so far away as the smart, the new, the chic, the cerebral (pp. 311–12).

Nevertheless, "smart," "new," and "cerebral" are unfair generalizations.

For Greene had discovered that the white man's touch on Africa sometimes resulted not in seediness, spoilage, and contamination, but in improvements of native existence. Even at school Greene had found it "a little hard to reconcile the popular idea of missionaries with the thin tired men who used to stand on a platform rapping with a small stick while the starved-looking bodies of black children slid across the screen" (*JM*, p. 203). In Africa he discovered further refutation of European "nonsense" about missionaries. Seeing the devotion of the American Episcopal monks of Bolahun, Greene was "for the first time unashamed by the comparison between white and black. There was something in this corner of a republic said to be a byword for corruption and slavery that at least wasn't commercial. One couldn't put it higher than this: that the little group of priests and nuns had a standard of gentleness and honesty equal to the native standard" (p. 90). When the English nuns of Bolahun served tea, Greene was reminded of an English cathedral town: "It was an English corner one could feel some pride in: it was gentle, devout, child-like and unselfish, it didn't even know it was courageous" (p. 92). Greene found in these devoted nuns and priests a fitting and heartening contrast to the English of Freetown, who enjoyed European comforts yet continually pitied themselves and despised the natives.

All these aspects of African life contributed to Greene's new awareness of "the way men really act." For his discoveries were never limited to personal or psychological revelations; they always included new aesthetic exploration. Even in perceiving the beauty of "flat black breasts" Greene was discovering the relativity of beauty. He was finding the aesthetic springs of unexpected pleasure.

Even more important, Greene discovered "A thing I thought I had never possessed: a love of life" (p. 206). This discovery should not, however, be taken as literally as some critics have accepted it. Greene was not "jolted alive" by primitive violence;[20] his awakening to life was a symbolic one, similar to his discovery in Mexico: "I suppose the love of life . . . was returning" (*LR*, p. 185). In Africa, Greene wrote: "I had made a discovery during the night which interested me. I had discovered in myself a passionate interest in living. I had always assumed before, as a matter of course, that death was desirable. . . . [My discovery] was like a conversion, and I had never experienced a conversion before. (I had not been converted to a religious faith. I had been convinced by specific arguments in the probability of its creed)" (*JM*, p. 263). Greene's "intellectual" conversion to Catholicism had been celebrated at a brief baptismal service that left him feeling that he "had taken up the thread of life from very far back, from so far back as innocence" (p. 116). His "love of life" was the euphoria that resulted from facing one's fears, as he later faced the Liberian rats; it was a conversion that left a "sediment" of comprehension. When Greene said "conversions don't last," he meant only that the temporary emotional response, in life as in religious experience, is not enough for the thoughtful novelist. Moreover, "a passionate interest in living" is a very desirable quality in any writer: sharp observation, accurate dialogue, faithful rendering of "life as it is," and the intense awareness of a skilled craftsman.

One of the perceptions that followed Greene's tracing of the Freudian ancestral threads was the value of facing suppressed memories such as his own fear of "the idea of eternal life and damnation" (p. 109). As he followed Africa's urging to "take a long look"

20. The importance of "violence" in Greene's life has been generally overrated, partly as a result of his own statements. In his essay "The Revolver in the Corner Cupboard," Greene described his experiment with Russian roulette as part of his "war against boredom" after psychoanalysis had left him "wrung dry" and unable to enjoy beauty. In an interview Greene referred to his dread of boredom and described his method of combatting this "ennui" by journeying: "D'ailleurs je voyage trop. C'est une espèce de névrose. J'essaye de me restreindre. . . . Mais j'aime l'incertitude des voyages. . . . J'aime être incertain chaque jour de vivre encore le lendemain." (See Tanneguy de Quénétain, "Faut-il brûler Graham Greene?" in *Réalités*, décembre 1962.) Greene's remarks suggest that it was not so much the "violence" of Russian roulette as its uncertainty that appealed to him. But the "uncertainty" is that of the artist "wanting to know" and seeking newer and finer perceptions.

at himself and his time, Greene was reminded of the period when he faced his childhood terrors. Greene had replaced the witches of his recurrent childhood dream with new imaginative creations. He dreamed of the Princess of Time and of a series of obviously juvenile romantic characters ranging from sinister Chinese to sensuous black maidens. Fortunately his adult facing of the primitive terrors was a more profitable source of literary growth. The primitive African world, where dream and reality were so readily interchangeable, further taught Greene how to cover up his tracks so that "the process of creation is complete."[21]

Emerging from Africa, Greene reflected: "This journey, if it had done nothing else, had reinforced a sense of disappointment with what man had made out of the primitive, what he had made out of childhood. . . . It isn't a gain to have turned the witch or the masked secret dancer, the sense of supernatural evil, into the small human viciousness of the thin distinguished military grey head in Kensington Gardens with the soft lips and the eye which dwelt with dull lustre on girls and boys of a certain age" (pp. 278–79).

Certainly it is not a clear gain to have made these changes. But Greene was well aware that the solutions—artistic, personal, universal—did not lie in a return to Africa's primitive depths. He concluded his account of the journey, "I have no yearning for a mindless sensuality, even if it were to be found there: it is only that when one has appreciated such a beginning, its terrors as well as its placidity, the power as well as the gentleness, the pity for what we have done with ourselves is driven more forcibly home." Greene added T. S. Eliot's lines on "fishing in the dull canal . . . round behind the gashouse" to express his sense of all that we have done but ought not to have done, and all that we have left undone.

Yet Greene's conclusion was essentially optimistic. He has said, "Pessimiste, moi! Je me croyais au contraire débordant d'opti-

21. "Fiction," *Spectator,* June 29, 1934. On the journey Greene rediscovered the essentials of literary form, including the good story as one that does not "go too far and tell too much" but casts a light in many directions—"the satiric, the social, the psychological"—while individual experience adds color to the facts (*JM,* p. 57). At a stopover on the voyage to Africa, Greene watched his own *Stamboul Train* in its transformed Hollywood version and concluded that the cinema would invariably expose the weaknesses of the stories from which it had drawn its material.

misme."[22] This optimism is not a facile conviction that everything will turn out well, that every man is basically endowed with primitive innocence or virtue. Nor is it a conviction that justice will triumph, or an echo of Ida's "I know what's right." Such easy optimism is indeed satirized in the person of Ida Arnold, Greene's delightful composite of ancient superstition (the Greek goddess μήτηρ ἴδη), Victorian self-righteousness, and contemporary colorless Christianity.[23]

Greene's optimism is the result of his acceptance of human nature in Africa, where men are complex and troubled and "living in this world," yet under the shadow of religious power. Greene discovered the symbol of his optimism as he stood in the empty Customs shed with the "loot" of his African souvenirs. Through the cold April mist of England he heard the sound that brought him a realization of the value of Africa's darkness and "blinding sunlight."

The symbol Greene found was the cry of a tenement child, a cry echoing the ancestral fear, the devil dancing in the child's sleep. He took it as the focal point of his reawakened "hope in human nature," the fresh start that might come from returning to the "bareness, simplicity, instinctive friendliness, feeling rather than thought" (p. 234) of Africa. There, in the child's cry at Dover, "was as far back as one needed to go, was Africa: the innocence, the virginity, the graves not opened yet for gold, the mines not broken with sledges" (p. 313). Significantly, it was an English slum child, Raven, who appeared as the first of Greene's lost children in the three entertainments that began with *This Gun for Hire* (1936). Another slum child served as Greene's first great character creation, Pinkie, the heart of *Brighton Rock* (1938).

22. "Propos de table avec Graham Greene," p. 129.
23. Ida represents "the new paganism of the West which prides itself on being scientific but is often peculiarly neurotic . . . [and shows a] sentimental lack of consistency" (*JM*, p. 92). Also, her name recalls the many allusions Greene makes to Arnold of Rugby, including "A masked devil . . . a headmaster with rather more supernatural authority than Arnold of Rugby ever claimed" (p. 99), and Greene's satiric self-criticism, "as the ghost of Arnold of Rugby addressed his head prefect [the young chief] through my lips" (p. 230). Presumably Matthew Arnold's "Christianity" would be a further source of annoyance to Greene. In addition to these religious and cultural associations, Ida's name offers a group of mother-images (see Ch. 2n15).

Chapter 2 MAPS OF LOST CHILDHOOD

A T HOME in England, Greene began to fit together the fragmentary experience of his African journey. First he wrote a short story, "The Basement Room" (1935), which he had "conceived on a cargo steamer on the way home from Liberia to relieve the tedium of the voyage." This was the first story in which Greene used the lines he has so often quoted from A.E.'s "Germinal": "In the lost childhood [sic] of Judas / Christ was betrayed."[1] Greene's first example of lost childhood was Philip, a boy who "felt a stranger in his home." The adult world prematurely forced upon Philip a sense of responsibility and an awareness of the horrors of violent ac-

1. Greene took these lines for the theme of his title essay in *The Lost Childhood*, where he quotes the verse in full:

> In ancient shadows and twilights
> Where childhood had strayed,
> The world's great sorrows were born
> And its heroes were made.
> In the lost boyhood of Judas
> Christ was betrayed.

Greene's essays, stories, and travel journals are rich in allusions to this verse. The figure of Judas moves through many of his novels; betrayal and self-betrayal are recurrent themes. But the idea of lost childhood is strongest in the three stories closest to Greene's African journey: "The Basement Room," *This Gun for Hire*, and *Brighton Rock*.

33

tion. After the death of Mrs. Baines, a figure reminiscent of Greene's African and childhood witches (even her voice was like one "in a nightmare"), Philip "betrayed" his only friend, the butler Baines. As "an old Coaster," Baines was clearly intended to represent that narrow strip of civilization described in *Journey without Maps*; he marked the point at which the fresh perceptions of a child were replaced by an adult's dulled sensibilities.

The significance of the African allusions in "The Basement Room" would not be clear without the key provided by *Journey without Maps*. Greene was apparently finding it difficult to convert his African journey into appropriate fiction. "A Chance for Mr. Lever" (1936) was only superficially indebted to the Liberian setting; and the unfinished novel "The Other Side of the Border" lacked the proper African atmosphere.[2] As direct records of his journey Greene also published several essays in the *Spectator*; these were later incorporated into *Journey without Maps*.

In order to construct his map of lost childhood—a guide to the qualities lost from contemporary civilization—Greene had to find a more satisfactory setting than his mysterious continent. One of the remarks he had made on the journey provided his clue: "You couldn't talk of darkest Africa with any conviction when you had known Nottingham well" (*JM*, p. 115). Then Greene would return to England for his scene, as he had returned to England after his trek through Africa. And out of his own depressing memories of Nottingham lodgings and his first job Greene constructed "Nottwich," where the detective Mather learned to "humanize" a map by walking the city's streets as Greene had walked the paths of Africa.

Mather's quarry was Raven, a lost child emblematic of all those wailing in England's tenements. Neglected by the society in which he had grown up, corrupted by the ugly adolescent Cholmondeley, and cheated by the Nottwich munitions king, Raven carried a sym-

2. In an explanatory note to the volume *Nineteen Stories*, Greene said that he realized this novel's main character had already appeared in *England Made Me*; also, *Brighton Rock* was "more insistent to be written." Although he was dissatisfied with the African atmosphere of "The Other Side of the Border," Greene did consider his rendition of Denton the "right" view of his childhood town, Berkhamsted. One of the characters in the unfinished novel is Colley, a man who held jobs "up and down the seedy margins of strange continents"—suggesting Kolley Kibber, Hale's role in *Brighton Rock*.

bolic "chip of ice" in his breast. This chip suggests both the pain inflicted by civilization and the imagination stifled by empty existence. As an image it is doubly appropriate, for it is drawn from "The Snow Queen," and Greene has described detective stories as "modern fairy tales."[3]

Greene had discovered in the fairy story, in which primitive violence is as common as in Africa, the most suitable form for the adventures of lost children. Man and child are always faced with a mystery in the fairy-tale world. Its terrors and punishments are nightmare versions of those in the civilized world; its pleasures and rewards are the eternal dream fantasies. At the same time, this shocking fantasy world appeals to unimaginative people who would not otherwise be awakened to the brutality of twentieth-century life. Finally, Greene has suggested that stories of violence satisfy "that moral craving for the just and reasonable expression of human nature left without belief" (LC, p. 190).[4]

The detective story is also a simplified narrative that appeals to readers living in our confused world. "There is a touch of nostalgia in the pleasure we take in gangster novels, in characters who have so agreeably simplified their emotions that they have begun living again at a level below the cerebral" (JM, p. 10). The thriller is a story of action, and as Greene pointed out in his essay "Bombing-Raid," action has "a moral simplicity which thought lacks."[5] This very quality makes the thriller doubly appropriate: it reaches our understanding in complex ways at subconscious levels, while its narrative reduces the complexities of contemporary existence to more comprehensible form.

Greene commented in his report on "The Catholic Temper in Poland": "It sometimes seems as though our whole planet had

3. Greene first described detective stories as "modern fairy tales" in a book review, "The Entertainments of A. E. W. Mason," The New Statesman, October 4, 1952. This Gun for Hire (1936) was Greene's second "entertainment"; the first was Stamboul Train.

4. Greene has offered many comments on the function of violence. In 1949 he said: "Si nous voulons faire éclater la miséricorde de Dieu aux yeux des incroyants, il faut qu'on la voie au-dessus des êtres les plus dégradés" ("Propos de table avec Graham Greene," p. 128). Such individuals live in a world most dramatically represented by the cruel setting of the "thriller."

5. Spectator, August 18, 1939. Reprinted as "Bombing Manœuvre" in The Lost Childhood.

swung into the fog belt of melodrama."⁶ The detective melodrama
thus becomes an analogue of our search for the way out of confusion. Greene has even suggested: "Murder if you are going to take
it seriously at all is a religious subject: the interest of a detective
story is the pursuit of exact truth."⁷ Thus the thriller reveals all the
levels of exploration with which Greene is concerned. We might
even say that "the pursuit of exact truth" is a search for "the heart
of the matter" of religious experience as it is in Scobie's quest, in
"The Hint of an Explanation," and in *A Burnt-Out Case*. Because
the detective's pursuit of truth leads to the solution of a mystery,
the detective story can serve as a symbol of the way to God's truth,
to the solution of the "equation" that Bendrix demanded in *The
End of the Affair*.

The detective story, however, always simplifies both quest and
solution. Its mysteries are ultimately resolved, and even its misleading clues usually provide only temporary obstacles to the clever detective. Often the popular detective story is marred by what Greene
refers to as "intellectual childishness," although ideally it will reveal "a certain accumulative poetic effect of an undefeatable justice."⁸ Greene in his own detective stories never loses sight of either
the Divine Judge or the dramatic irony of "poetic justice."

This Gun for Hire meets all the criteria for Greene's special
variety of "fairy story." Raven is a fitting quarry for Greene's ideal
detective because he seems at first to possess "the completely callous
brain and the hopelessly lost soul."⁹ Raven regards murder as "just
a new job" and curses his harelip as "a serious handicap in his profession" (p. 3). Yet beneath his ugliness and behind his conventional villainy, Raven is the lost child demanding our attention and
our understanding. As Greene puts together the puzzle of Raven's
life, we see the pathetic emptiness of this childhood: his parents
were a murderer and a suicide, and Raven's childhood memories included the sight of his mother's blood-soaked body sprawled across

6. *Atlantic*, March 1956.
7. "The Cinema," *Spectator*, June 17, 1938.
8. "Fiction," *Spectator*, May 18, 1934.
9. Greene's description of a criminal in "The Cinema," *Spectator*, June
12, 1936. Greene prefers the violent detective story to "the English school of
scholarly detection and Wimsey psychology."

the kitchen table—"She hadn't even thought enough of me to lock the door" (p. 109). Raven's only "home" was an orphanage where education consisted of inappropriate facts and inconsistent religion. Christianity was "practiced" (foreshadowing that superb practicing Catholic Rycker) in the saying of prayers "twice a day and before meals too" (p. 106). It was a Christian "home" that suspended punishments on Christmas day, but saved these beatings until the day following.

No wonder that Raven mocks the idea of anyone having a "Christian" name or that he sees the Christmas fir tree and crib as "junk." Raven's confused view of these symbols of love and goodwill emphasizes one of the common weaknesses in contemporary religious experience. Greene implies that Raven's antipathy for the sentimental tinsel and plaster of Christmas scenes is less reprehensible than the empty sentimental "religion" of Ida with her planchette and her Bible "in the cupboard" beside "the Warwick Deeping, *The Good Companions*" (*Brighton Rock*, p. 213).

Raven himself strives to discover the truth of the religious mystery. He declares, "They twisted everything, even that story. . . . They made him a god because they could feel fine about it all; they didn't have to consider themselves responsible for the raw deal they'd given him. He'd consented, hadn't he? . . ." (p. 76). Raven here anticipates Scobie's view of Christ's "suicide." However faulty his solution, Raven at least looks at the puzzle and ponders the relation of its parts. Actually, his view is correct according to his experience. For Raven, home has indeed been "solitary confinement for a kid that's caught talking in the chapel, and the birch for almost anything you do" (p. 104). In comparison with Raven's "home," Minty's in *England Made Me* seems a place of exquisite luxury: a brown woolen dressing gown, cocoa and water biscuits in the cupboard, a little Madonna on the mantlepiece, a spider under his toothglass. Made by hatred, much as Minty had been formed by infinite rejections, Raven nevertheless evolves a limited morality: It is evil that "people of the same class should prey on each other" (p. 78).

The limitations of Raven's life are expressed in the recurrent line "Ah, Christ that it were possible." Already lost, Raven's peace is not possible; in his drab world it is impossible even to learn the language of survival. He cannot communicate with the willing Anne; their friendship is doomed by the circumstances and customs of their world just as inevitably as the ancient primitive goodness and tribal dignity had been tarnished by the coastal bureaucracy Greene discovered in Liberia. "Ah, Christ that it were possible. . . ." But God has not so willed it. The Divine context suggests a promise beyond Raven's earthly tragedy and urges the reader to look beyond the political and social questions that had limited Greene's earlier novels. Raven's vague longing, however, lacks the more specific Divine promise expressed in Pinkie's similar line, "Between the stirrup and the ground," which refers to the final moment of repentance in which man can ask for God's mercy.

Raven's "lost childhood" is not intended to stigmatize him as a Judas. He is not the betrayer. Instead, "he had been marked from his birth for this end, to be betrayed in turn by everyone until every avenue into life was safely closed" (p. 146). Although at first Raven might seem to betray the war minister who like himself is an orphanage boy, this action results from Raven's ignorance of the truth rather than from an "evil" nature. Raven's harelip is his sign of Christ's pain; it reveals him as the first of Greene's symbolically marked heroes, simultaneously carrying the scar of Original Sin and the wound of Christ's pain.[10]

10. As Greene uses the symbol of the scar it is both a sign of man's sin and a reminder of God's grace, reflecting "the ugly wounded face of God" (*LR*, p. 260), i.e., the face of Christ who died to save us from our sins. There is a further suggestion in Greene's marked heroes of "faces the world has corrupted" (*LR*, p. 289); Pinkie has such a face, for he carries Nelson Place with him "like a visible scar" (p. 251). According to Roman Catholic belief, Adam was wounded in his natural endowments; wounds have been suffered by our human nature primarily as a result of Original Sin, but also in consequence of every actual sin committed. Even when the wound of sin is healed, it leaves a scar. Sometimes in Greene's stories the scar becomes a birthmark: Sarah identifies Richard Smythe's birthmark as "the mark of pain," clearly God's mark, since she envies Richard "seeing You in the glass every day" (*EA*, p. 147); the birthmark is "almost like a mark of distinction" (p. 94). The priest's faith in *The Power and the Glory* is "like a birthmark" (p. 47), and the lieutenant's scar is "perhaps . . . the relic of an escape" (p. 19). Even Greene's early stories include scars of at least marginal significance. There are Jews with scarred and altered noses (e.g., in *Stamboul Train*) reminding us of the role of the Jews in condemning Christ. Anthony's scar in *England Made Me* marked an actual moment of going astray in childhood. But with Raven's scar Greene begins to move toward the final symbolic mutilations of *A Burnt-Out Case*. The scar of

Perhaps Greene was already formulating his question "What is innocence?" Later, to Scobie, "guilt and innocence were as relative as the wealthy" (*HM*, p. 12). In Raven's case, guilt and innocence are part of poverty, for Raven is a poor boy in a threadbare coat, tentatively responding to the affection he had not known as a child, seeking responses from a scrawny kitten and a hump-backed girl. At first he cannot believe in the friendship that is offered by a pretty girl, Anne; yet her friendship, falsely based on her romantic misreading of Raven's activities, is actually a prelude to betrayal. We are not, however, permitted to judge her "guilty" of betraying the marked boy. Her action is inevitable, the "right" one, according to the standards of justice in her society.

Where then does justice lie? Raven can be judged as an evil murderer, his guilt increased by his action in shooting the minister's dithering secretary. The war minister himself carries a load of guilt for murders resulting from his official position, yet according to the common morality he is an innocent man. Greene further stresses the difficulty of passing judgment by showing that the minister's childhood had resembled Raven's (the minister's father was a thief, and his mother a suicide by drowning). The old man and the boy both make some gestures commonly judged as marks of goodness. The minister would like to help the poor; he has lived a frugal domestic life with gas ring and boiled eggs. Raven attempts to give his crippled girl a dress that has "class." Nevertheless, both are condemned to death by their world.

In contrast, the "civilized" world accepts the respectable veneer of the munitions king and his henchman Cholmondeley. The apparently respectable old industrialist sips a glass of milk and nibbles a biscuit, he is physically as helpless as a baby, and yet he controls

---

Pinkie's world can be misinterpreted as a "mark of manhood, of potency," however (p. 146). Even in *The Quiet American*, Fowler's "wounds" are sexual, the marks of his alienation from his wife. In *The Heart of the Matter* and the related "The Hint of an Explanation," the word "accident" conveys the idea of "death and wounds," although the religious context refers to the "accidents" of transubstantiation. Bendrix' scar has a double nature that fits the theme of love and hate in *The End of the Affair*. It is "part of his character as much as his jealousy" (p. 131), but it also signifies his unselfish protection of another man's body from a falling wall. Finally, Greene describes Querry's wound as "secret" (*BC*, p. 9), carrying us back to the association of "accident" with the "secret" of the Mass.

a factory that deals in mass murder. The fat Cholmondeley is an eternal adolescent, delighting in rich desserts, sticky candy, and bright jewelry, and enjoying all kinds of cruelty. Cholmondeley also takes chorus girls to Acky's horrible "house," passes stolen money, and tries to commit murder. A solid citizen of Nottwich, he travels first class while the police hound the marked and threadbare boy and the ascetic war minister lies murdered. Here is a confused picture of the chaos of values that had driven Greene to Africa.

Greene had found communication difficult in Africa; he shows that it is just as difficult in Nottwich and in London. Men neither listen to one another nor understand the words they do hear. Even at the most simple literal level, the London café-owner talks of war ("It's good for business"), unaware of the counterpoint of Raven's criticism of Christmas tinsel and red berries ("Sentiment"). The novice reporter with an Oxford accent can find no response from the experienced newsmen. He is told to keep still about his interest in a petty bank-note crime, for these newsmen are only interested in the "important" crime of a murdered war minister and the threat of war. The reader, however, has seen these puzzle pieces from several angles. He knows that the two stories are in fact one. Fitted together correctly, these disparate elements will provide new knowledge. Yet only God has complete knowledge. When the detective eventually reconstructs the puzzle, he formulates only a partial truth.

Once again, Greene's metaphor of the child's dissected map helps us understand his artistic purpose. Each part of the puzzle must be looked at from many angles, the pieces must be continually compared and rearranged, and the writer must have some idea of the completed picture. In Greene's work this map-making process begins with exploration that is reported as "fact" (e.g., *Journey without Maps*, which in turn is made out of fragments or essays). In the second stage, ideas, events, and people from the journey reappear in short stories (e.g., "The Basement Room" and "A Chance for Mr. Lever"). A novel—sometimes preceded by an entertainment—comes last.

In *This Gun for Hire* the process of reconstruction is clear; the reader is continually given pieces of information that must be turned around and re-examined before their significance appears. An air-raid practice becomes a medical students' "rag," while the "rag" in turn serves as cover for Raven's murderous revenge and the death of the munitions manufacturer who would certainly share the responsibility for deaths in a real air raid. Mr. Cholmondeley's "weak" stomach is no obstacle in his attempt at murdering Anne with his "hands strong and sticky with icing sugar." To Mather, "those fellows over there" are incompetent; to the reader Mather is at fault. Anne's record is much more than a sentimental song, "A snowflower / A man brought from Greenland." For her, it is protection against the flight of stairs, the lonely supper, the uncertainty of a chorus girl's life. For Raven, the tune is a symbol of his inner feeling, a chip of ice that ultimately breaks in his heart "with great pain." Mather sits in judgment on Raven's "moll," not knowing that he is passing judgment on Anne, his own fiancée.

If the reader wonders how to reconstruct this map, he must seek clues not in the "truth" of the familiar whodunit but in the ironically "happy" ending of Greene's fairy story. Close examination of Anne's "unshadowed" happiness as she cries "We're home" is actually a way of discovering her unhappiness. She does not yet see the picture of her life "whole," but the reader has seen its parts from a different angle. Rather than being united in a happy, fairy-tale ending, Anne and Mather are just across the border from strange territory. An immense distance separates their worlds: "London had its roots in [Anne's] heart; she saw nothing in the dark countryside." But Mather is specifically "a countryman" (p. 160).

Brighton Rock resembles *This Gun for Hire* in being a story of action; it too deals with the detection of truth. But the law is no longer represented by a proper policeman, Mather. Instead, Ida is detective, judge, and jury. Pursuing "fun" rather than the justice she overtly seeks, Ida reveals the weaknesses of our secular society. Not only does she take to herself the function of Divine Justice (part of the mistake later made by Scobie); she also substitutes her own values for Divine Truth. Ida assumes that she knows what is "Right" and "Wrong." But she has no concept of good and evil, no perception of the borderland between this world and the next.

In interpreting Ida's function and the action of *Brighton Rock*,

the reader soon discovers why Greene has classed it as both novel
and entertainment. Like *This Gun for Hire*, it deals with crime in
a sordid setting; it too is an exciting narrative of pursuit. The American publication of *Brighton Rock* as an "entertainment" was justified. It also belongs with the novels that follow Greene's journey
through Africa: its action is bound up with the problems of Catholic values in a secular world. The story's final classification as
"novel" is the correct one.

The theme of justice in *Brighton Rock* also reveals the improvement of Greene's artistry after his African exploration. In *It's
a Battlefield*, Greene had attempted to expose the injustice of man's
justice, but he selected crude labels. The naïve Assistant Commissioner believed that in the East there was no interference with justice by politicians or businessmen; he was a romantic believer in
the perfection suggested by Africa's "dark mystery." The philan-
thropic Caroline spoke gravely of social injustice, while her own
comfortable life tended to negate Greene's attempt at social commentary.[11] Furthermore, Greene's use of the prison chaplain lacked
subtlety. The chaplain's criticism of the arbitrariness and incompre-
hensibility of human justice was awkwardly explicit, especially
when the commissioner claimed that human justice is "much the
same" as divine justice and the chaplain replied, "One can't hand
in a resignation to God" (p. 231).

Instead of such oversimplifications, Greene presents in
Brighton Rock two clearly but subtly interrelated views of justice.
On one side is Ida's view, a reflection of the sort of Right and Wrong
described in the popular press. On the other side is Divine Judgment, often seen through the eyes of the two lost Roman Catholic
"children" Pinkie and Rose. Many critics have asserted that Rose's
"good" complements Pinkie's "evil." Pinkie certainly feels that she
completes him: "What was most evil in him needed her; it couldn't
get along without goodness" (p. 167). Yet Rose's apparent virtues
are not true examples of goodness. Sometimes she is set against the
negations of Pinkie's perverse nature; she at least attempts to go to

11. Greene himself was distressed by the awkward handling of "justice"
in *It's a Battlefield* and deleted some passages on that theme from later editions. However, he finally restored them when he discovered that they were
essential to the characterization.

Confession before their marriage, and her Catholic training has some bearing on her reluctance to commit suicide. Nevertheless, she wills herself toward damnation. Her earthly punishment is the cruel epithalamium of Pinkie's recorded voice crying, "God damn you, you little bitch, why can't you go back home for ever and let me be?" (p. 236). This is the beginning of God's justice, a punishment that will make her recognize her earthly choice: "Why this is hell."

But we can go no further. Greene's characters continually demonstrate that we cannot comprehend God's ultimate verdict, because we cannot know what goes on in a single human heart. Only God can truly judge and dispense punishment or mercy. Greene hints that God will be merciful to Rose: she has at least the promise of a child, and she has gained time in which to repent "between the stirrup and the ground." Since God's is "such an odd sort of mercy, it sometimes looks like punishment" (*EA*, p. 178), Rose's earthly punishment—her sense of loss—may be no more than a prelude to eternal salvation. It may also, of course, be a prelude to damnation. It may even foreshadow Purgatory. Yet God's ultimate heavenly mercy would ensure Rose's eternal separation from Pinkie; to Rose, this might seem the worst punishment of all.[12]

Pinkie's attempted betrayal of Rose is another manifestation of Christ's betrayal in the lost childhood of Judas. The wail of the tenement child that Greene had heard when he returned from Africa now becomes the wail of two children from Brighton's tenements, Rose and Pinkie. Both had been baptized as Roman Catholics, but Pinkie had not "howled the devil out" (p. 169) at his baptism. Instead, Pinkie learned only to make loud protests of cruelty and withdrawal, culminating in the screams of his final pain as he literally leaped into the abyss. Greene had written of the crying Dover child that it was "too young to have learnt what the dark may conceal in the way of lust and murder" (*JM*, pp. 312–13).

---

12. Greene is quoted in a *Time* interview (October 29, 1951), p. 103, as saying that *Brighton Rock* is about a man who goes to Hell, *The Power and the Glory* about a man who goes to Heaven, and *The Heart of the Matter* about a man who goes to Purgatory. Within the novel, Greene does not make such a foolish assertion, for he follows his conviction that the novelist's task is to pose, not to answer, questions.

Pinkie had learned fast enough about both. Rose's childhood had left obvious scars, but Pinkie soon scarred her with the terrible additional marks of love and hate.

"Childhood" is a term entirely lacking sentimental connotations in *Brighton Rock* and in Greene's other novels. Childhood innocence is not synonymous with primitive perfection.[13] In his essays, Greene stresses that the world of childhood is one of "moral chaos, lies, brutality, complete inhumanity . . . the more than human evil of the lying, sadistic child."[14] But the child's baptism provides a "stock of innocence," making of childhood a time of "virgin sensibility" (*LC*, p. 138). The baptized child has the privilege of drawing on a "bank of sanctity" (*LR*, p. 202). Pinkie's story, however, shows that the bank is inadequate for our violent world. Pinkie's baptism did not "take" (p. 169)—a symbolic expression of his freedom from blame. He is not a villain but the product of an impoverished environment, of a world that drains away his goodness faster than he can accumulate an adequate store. As a Catholic adult he should make his own deposits in the bank of sanctity in order to avoid supernatural bankruptcy. But Pinkie has been spiritually stunted by the Brighton slum. In spite of momentary spiritual awakening, his goodness cannot grow in the world of racetrack toughs, Colleoni's organization, Prewitt's law, and Spicer's or Dallow's odd friendship.

Pinkie's childhood is also the particularly crippling kind that Greene later identified with Mexico: "The pistol shot and the crooked judge and the cock-fight and nobody caring for another's life" (*LR*, p. 84). He had known Hell personally, in the ironically named Paradise Piece. But the Catholic tradition recognizes the proximity of good and evil, of Heaven and Hell. Pinkie is a tragic figure because he had almost taken the right path. He can look

13. Greene writes of the terrors of childhood, as in "I Spy" or "The End of the Party." Childhood is a time of "anarchy . . . cruelty and unhappiness" as well as of happiness (*LC*, p. 75). It is also "life under a dictatorship, a condition of perpetual ignominy, irresponsibility and injustice," according to a review, "Fiction," in *Spectator*, June 30, 1933. Even in the superbly entertaining *Our Man in Havana*, childhood is "cruel and inexplicable." Nevertheless, in childhood the creative spirit is still "alive."

14. "The Cinema," *Spectator*, May 1, 1936. Here, Greene was writing of "the dark side of childhood."

back to the territory of Catholic consolation; he can still ask for Divine mercy. He has prayed, and his heart has been open to God.

In contrast, Ida in spite of all her "comforts" has no awareness of the spiritual Comforter, no sense of anything beyond the moment, little perception beyond her amoebic love of pleasure and her instinctive response to "fun." Her easy sexual pleasures are explicitly equated with the common pleasures of the pub and the Brighton excursion. To Hale, this trippers' world at first has the appearance of a glistening and pure Victorian scene, but it is actually no better than the sucking green sea and the littered beach of Pinkie's territory.

Ida's "good" bears no relation to Divine values. Greene uses her to define the weaknesses of our commonly accepted moral clichés about justice, order, and right. Her face is "like the map of a campaign marked with flags" (p. 267), but these cliché-flags only lead their followers astray. Ida knows nothing of either the "purer" terror or the "deeper" pleasures of primitive darkness and religious power. She knows only the comforts of Ouija board and neatly shelved Bible; she is reassured by the tidy flames of a crematorium. For eternal life she substitutes this life: a good time symbolized by brass bedposts, creamy chocolate éclairs, and ruby port. Instead of Christ's spiritual Communion she offers the communion of pier, pub, and bed. Hale receives "the taste of port wine on his tongue" (p. 19) in a bitter parody of communion; instead of receiving eternal life through the body of Christ, he receives instead death through Ida's.

Greene has created Ida as a cheap, shallow, and ignorant mother-image[15] to serve as fitting goddess for our corrupt civilization. She typifies the false values that Greene most dislikes. The deepest expression of her philosophy is "I like fair play" (p. 99), and Ida's mind works "with the simplicity and the regularity of a

---

15. Ida, "the old and vulgarised Grecian name" (p. 17), suggests the myth of Zeus' wet-nurse (ἴδη) or one of Rhea's names (μήτηρ ἴδη). Greene's Ida is also a Freudian mother-image, with her big breasts and moist mouth, a woman who makes Hale think, "Back to the womb"; for Hale she is also a symbol of "darkness" and of "knowledge" (p. 9). But her heart is of the empty, sentimental kind. As already noted (Ch. 1n23), Ida also represents the new paganism of the West.

sky sign" (p. 44). Her mothering offers no compensations for the lost childhood. Her good nature ("a touch of the nursery and the mother," p. 17) cannot save Fred Hale, although she seems like "life itself" (p. 6). Carrying her compassion "like a rank cheap perfume" (p. 314), she reveals her spiritual aridity in the words "It's going to be exciting, it's going to be fun, it's going to be a bit of life" (p. 55); Greene underscores her fault with such phrases as "enjoyable distress" and "merciless compassion" (pp. 43, 160). Ida concedes, "If you believed in God, you might leave vengeance to him"; but she really believes that vengeance is hers, and "Vengeance and reward—they both were fun" (pp. 44, 45).

These are the limitations of a homely heart that is "touched" by the word *tragedy* (p. 38), that responds to a funeral with the same thrill of horror as for a ghost story (p. 43), that knows no pity for something Ida does not understand (p. 94). Once again, Greene's map metaphor charts Ida's weakness: "It was as if she were in a strange country: the typical Englishwoman abroad. She hadn't even got a phrase book. She was as far from either of them as she was from Hell—or Heaven. Good and evil lived in the same country, spoke the same language, came together like old friends, feeling the same completion, touching hands beside the iron bedstead" (p. 168). Rose may be "a stranger in the country of mortal sin" (p. 253), but she can stand beside Pinkie, she can communicate with him—however inadequately—and she can recognize the markers on the route to God.

In this spiritual territory, Pinkie and Rose are at home, as they are at home in the actual, shabby world of Brighton. Yet Greene never implies that the Brighton underworld or any other "seedy" setting is the only country in which to discover the roads leading to God.[16] Of course Brighton stands for all the false values typified by

16. Greene believes that such a setting exposes human nature more fully to the novelist's pen (see Ch. 1n19). Also it is the region in closest proximity to the old innocence of vision: it is a place where civilization has only just begun to go astray, where the writer has only begun to substitute clichés for imagination. Unfortunately, some readers misinterpret the seediness of Greene's settings: "Quant aux incroyants, ils ne sont pas scandalisés, mais montrent une incompréhension presque totale, même les critiques les plus intelligents. Ils sont si loin de toute vue chrétienne de l'homme qu'ils ne peuvent entrer dans mon univers" ("Propos de table," p. 128).

Ida. It is Greene's personal symbol of our superficial civilization, and allusions to Brighton recur throughout his writing: even his children's book *The Little Horse Bus* includes a trunk labeled Brighton-on-Sea and two posters urging "Come to Brighton." But Pinkie claims allegiance to the "real Brighton"—a world of "all the cheap amusements, the Pullman cars, the unloving week-ends in gaudy hotels, and the sadness after coition" (p. 295). This is the familiar trippers' world that lies before Hale at the opening of *Brighton Rock*: "With immense labour and immense patience they extricated from the long day the grain of pleasure: this sun, this music, the rattle of the miniature cars, the ghost train diving between the grinning skeletons under the Aquarium promenade, the sticks of Brighton rock, the paper sailors' caps" (p. 3). Pinkie's earthly territory is also "the populous foreshore, a few thousand acres of houses, a narrow peninsula of electrified track running to London, two or three railway stations with their buffets and buns" (p. 173).

Pinkie knows yet another territory—the invisible world that gives importance to the visible, ugly, and painful one. The "common geography" he shares with Rose would never take him along Ida's fun-filled ways. He does not thrill to a sense of adventure ahead. He looks forward to "peace"—"a grey darkness going on and on without end, a country of which he hadn't seen as much as a picture postcard, a place far stranger than the Grand Canyon and the Taj Mahal" (p. 200). Nevertheless he can picture this strange country more accurately than men see Christ drawn in "the image of their own sentimentality," and more precisely than Cubitt, who is "a professor describing to a stranger some place he had only read about in books" (p. 247).

Pinkie has gained his intuition from an almost mystical perception, from "thirsting in the desert" (p. 247). Unfortunately his experience has not led to the true purity that follows a saint's fast. He does not share Ida's mistaken belief that confession and repentance are "just religion" (p. 266); he understands their importance. But he cannot give himself up to God's demands. Once, Pinkie had sworn to be a priest; now, in a phrase reminiscent of Greene's essay on "Frederick Rolfe," Pinkie has changed his belief: *"Credo in unum*

Satanum" (pp. 219, 220). Perhaps this creed is superior to Dallow's simple one: "The world's all right if you don't go too far" (p. 220). Yet Pinkie's vision has been permanently distorted by his crippling childhood, so that religious and secular values have been jumbled into a false picture of life. He sees the shooting gallery dolls as "Virgins in a church repository" (p. 24); he sees Rose as "one of the small gaudy statues in an ugly church" (p. 221).

Although Pinkie is a traveler lost in a country he does not see accurately, he retains vague memories of "a whole lost world" (p. 66) that is very different from Ida's vacant one. From his childhood he has brought terrors that color his judgment of Hell, of which he says, "Of course it's true." But of Heaven he says only, "Maybe." The "purity" of Pinkie's lost innocence is a false condition that prohibits drinking, or betting, or taking a girl. It is a misdirected asceticism in which the pain inflicted by nails, splinters, and razor blades is a source of pleasure.

Yet as Pinkie travels he is moved by "a faint nostalgia" for his lost Faith. His tears reflect memories of church music; his emotion is an "enormous" feeling as of a force about to cause "huge havoc—the confession, the penance and the sacrament . . ." (p. 322). Pinkie is weary from his journey, however, and lacks the "energy" to repent. He travels farther and farther down a road he had never intended to follow. Tired, Pinkie longs for escape, but "It was impossible to repent of something which made him safe. . . . When he was thoroughly secure, he could begin to think of making peace, of going home, and his heart weakened with a faint nostalgia for the tiny dark confessional box, the priest's voice and the people waiting . . . to be made safe from eternal pain. Eternal pain had not meant much to him: now it meant the slash of razor blades infinitely prolonged" (pp. 143–44).

Pinkie cannot see the country accurately because he is so firmly "bound in a habit of hate" (p. 311). He is also bound by a "habit of thought" (p. 143), an inability to repent that bars his way to salvation. Comforting himself with the delusion "One confession when . . . [I'm] safe to wipe out everything" and "I'll give a statue" (pp. 144–45), Pinkie sometimes resembles Greene's numerous characters afflicted with the "habit" of piety. In *Brighton Rock* this resemblance is occasionally an artistic flaw: Greene is too insistent in his underscoring of Pinkie's kinship with the pious, as well as with the saints and the good Catholics. Moreover there is a weakness in *Brighton Rock*'s repeated juxtaposing of the "good" evil of Pinkie and the evil "good" of Ida's world.

There are of course obvious advances in the technique of *Brighton Rock*, for instance its single pursuit in contrast to the multiple and involved pursuits of *Stamboul Train*. Greene has replaced the old-fashioned movie scene of the car chase, the melodramatic rooftop escape, the attempt to "crucify" Czinner and nail him to the front page of Mabel's paper, with a new kind of pursuit. Easy and false morality in the person of Ida pursues tortured but true evil in the person of Pinkie. Ida loses her quarry as he leaps over the cliff edge. Ironically, her arrival perhaps salvages the good in Rose: she may have helped drive Rose toward the soul's salvation in God.

Before he was able to assemble a more valid picture of the territories of good and evil, however, Greene had to make his second major journey, the trip to Catholic Mexico. In the Catholic context of *The Power and the Glory*, it would be appropriate for a character such as Pinkie to assert that he had taken Rose's goodness "like you got God in the Eucharist—in the guts. God couldn't escape the evil mouth which chose to eat its own damnation" (p. 238). But in *Brighton Rock*, Pinkie's statement seems forced.

There is also a difficulty in the character of Rose. If she were truly marked by God we might accept her as a tragic figure. She has unfortunately been "stamped" with the image of Pinkie, not of God; Pinkie is part of her, as his voice is firmly stamped on the vulcanite of his terrible record. Rose's belief that Pinkie is "wonderful" is not a response to his virtue: at this moment in the action he has just purchased her from her parents. Moreover, in spite of claiming that she knows "a lot," Rose forgets her Roman Catholic lessons. She even declares, "I'd rather burn with you than be like Her [Ida]" (p. 151). These errors follow from Rose's lost childhood. She went astray in a home that smelled like a lavatory, a home whose mother lacked even the false warmth of the bosomy Ida. Rose had no chance to escape from her "ancient shadows and twilights." Without becoming "evil" like Pinkie, she still has been crippled.

Rose is a stranger who has few clues to Pinkie's world. She cannot fully understand the customs of his territory, where money is kept in a soap dish, "meals" consist of canned sardines and milk, and the fire remains cold. The reader is often similarly confused. When Pinkie carries the shooting-gallery doll as though he were "holding the Mother of God by the hair" (p. 25), the meaning of the figure is obscure, illuminating neither the religious nor the secular truths. Roman Catholicism appears to be falsely imposed on the scene. Fortunately, Greene found a scene in which Catholicism was natural: Mexico, where the civilized and the primitive existed side by side and the secular power had only recently rejected the old Catholic "magic." In journeying through Mexico, Greene found "seedy" settings and characters whose decayed Catholicism still showed traces of God. Here was a world where Greene could trace the labyrinthine way on which the wandering man could find both himself and his God.

Chapter *3* FILLING IN THE MAP

G REENE'S JOURNEY to Africa had molded him into a writer sensitive to the values of his world and to the artistic possibilities of its conflicts and contradictions. His full development as a Catholic novelist,[1] however, came only after his travels along the lawless roads of Mexico. The "theological Limbo" that Greene had observed in Africa—the natives' primitive belief in Power, and even the various forms of Christianity—all appealed on the simplest terms "to the imagination" rather than to the intellect.

Novels and entertainments written before the Mexican journey

1. Greene has denied that he is a "Catholic" novelist. He describes himself as "a writer who in four or five books took characters with Catholic ideas for his material" (*SC*, p. 13n5). In a letter addressed to his former publisher, printed as preface to *The Comedians*, Greene asserts: " . . . even in the case of a novel laid in England, the story when it contains more than ten characters would lack verisimilitude if at least one of them were not a Catholic." Greene has also denied that he writes Catholic "apologetics." But he does admit: "Quand on est catholique, il ne faut pas chercher à faire du 'catholicisme.' Tout ce que l'on dit ou écrit respire inévitablement le catholicisme" ("Propos de table," p. 136). During an interview he claimed: "Mon attitude religieuse a changé depuis l'époque de *La Puissance et la Gloire*, l'élément émotionnel tend à disparaître" (see Tanneguy de Quénétain's interview "Faut-il brûler Graham Greene?" p. 123). Whatever the nature of Greene's own Catholicism, the Catholic elements in his novels do change in the direction of artistic wholeness: the artist's (Greene's) mind controls the personal intrusions.

have the imaginative appeal, but the "intellectual" appeal that had attracted Greene to the Faith is absent. Their religious allusions often lack point. Even in *This Gun for Hire* and *Brighton Rock,* Greene fails to offer his characters walking the dusty way of this world a discernible route to the next. It is true that Greene's characters "restent dans le monde avec toutes leurs passions et leurs faiblesses."[2] In the earlier novels, however, it is not easy to remember that his characters also dwell in a world created by God.

In Mexico, Greene found a landscape that could be simultaneously charted in its familiar, secular aspect and with his personal, religious symbols. His Mexican journey was a literary assignment in search of lost Catholicism rather than a personal safari in search of lost childhood. But once again the journey helped him to "see life whole" and to fulfill the novelist's duty "to tell the truth as he sees it." This truth is an accuracy that is "largely a matter of style," for literature has nothing to do with edification. Literature may present a moral, but the novelist has an obligation to present "the point of view of the black square as well as the white."[3]

Greene fully met this obligation in *The Power and the Glory.* In it he successfully linked religious belief and artistic creation. The novel expresses artistically the truth Greene discovered even at moments when he "loathed" Mexico: "Here were idolatry and oppression, starvation and casual violence, but you lived under the shadow of religion—of God or the Devil" (*LR,* p. 234). And God was a familiar figure in this world, while He had been a stranger in Brighton. The lost state of Tabasco was the perfect dramatic setting for the "importance of the human act"—the Catholic's problem as well as the novelist's. As Greene commented in a review, "Rob human beings of their heavenly and their infernal importance and you rob your characters of their individuality."[4]

2. "Propos de table," p. 133.

3. *Why Do I Write?* p. 30. Greene points out that the storyteller's task includes the awakening of sympathy, acting as devil's advocate, and being "disloyal." This "disloyalty" in turn "encourages us to roam through any human mind: it gives to the novelist the extra dimension of sympathy"; "loyalty" confines the writer to accepted opinions (p. 47), and perhaps leads him into clichés.

4. "Mr. Maugham's Pattern," *Spectator,* January 14, 1938. Criticizing the "cardboard symbols" masquerading as characters in the novels of Virginia

As one of the epigraphs for *The Lawless Roads*, Greene selected from Newman a passage describing the human race as "implicated in some terrible aboriginal calamity."[5] Greene explained the nature of this calamity as he reflected on his Mexican journey: "You are not allowed to shelter innocence in your house. If you are lucky, the child may be baptized—if it lives—a few years later when a priest visits the village secretly; but that tardy baptism is not the same, after the world has taken its tarnishing account. The children have no bank of sanctity to draw on—the unstained Christian years—and we cannot tell what human nature may owe to that past fund of holiness. It is not inconceivable that the worst evil possible to natural man may be found years hence in Mexico" (*LR*, p. 202). The epigraph also speaks of a "profound mystery, which is absolutely beyond human solution." Greene's own sense of this mystery, the heart of the matter for a Catholic, was obviously enriched by his discovery of the world of Mexican adolescence.

Often Greene was irritated by the "boyishness, this immaturity, which gets most on the nerves in Mexico": "Grown men cannot meet in the street without sparring like schoolboys. One must be as a little child, we are told, to enter the kingdom of heaven, but they have passed childhood and remain for ever in a cruel anarchic adolescence" (p. 78). Later, Greene conceded that there was a universal Mexican cheerfulness, but this also was "horribly immature," with "no sense of human responsibility; it is all one with the pistol-shot violence" (p. 203). This quality made Mexico particularly appropriate as a symbol of the very soiled world Greene had begun to sketch in his various post-African stories. In Mexico, even more clearly than in Brighton and London, Green could observe: "Le chrétien réside dans un territoire limitrophe, entre le Bien et le Mal, et c'est un pays de brigandage."[6] Greene found a natural and literal boundary between the secular and the religious powers in Mexico,

---

Woolf and E. M. Forster, Greene suggested that men with souls to save or lose are the only ones with "solidity and importance" (*LC*, p. 70).

5. Greene says, "Je me suis toujours nourri de Newman. Je le lisais avant ma conversion. Je le lis encore fréquemment. J'ai une grande admiration pour lui" ("Propos de table," p. 130).

6. "Les paradoxes du christianisme," p. 39. In this discussion, Greene clearly refers primarily to the state of the consciously Roman Catholic Christian.

in contrast to the rather artificial barrier he had placed between Ida's Brighton and Pinkie's or the wavering boundary line between "lawless" Raven and the "lawful" Nottwich citizens.

Naturally, Greene examined very critically the evils of the secular power that was supplanting the old religion. As a reporter, his task was to discover the condition of Mexico in 1938; but he had also to discover the sources of the new power and the way in which Catholicism had been "lost." For the most part, he was a remarkably scientific explorer, leaving final judgment to the reader, and usually content to set the Catholic and the State values or "virtues" in ironic juxtaposition.

Occasionally in *The Lawless Roads* Greene aids the reader's judgment by offering ironical description—of Garrido Canabal's "puritanical" state (p. 129), for instance. The most specific criticism that Greene makes of the secular power is that of the teacher in Chiapas. This village teacher criticized the Spaniards for oppressing the Indians and making them into "mere beasts of burden"; yet even as the teacher spoke, a file of Indians passed his window, "bowed double with enormous crates supported by a leather belt across the forehead." Greene comments on these Indians, who were "cut off from intercourse, speaking no Spanish": "The priests, who had learned the Indian dialects and acted as necessary interpreters between one village and another, who had shown interest in them as human beings, had been driven away. As for the school teacher, his large brown eyes were compassionate, he spoke with pity of their past, and knew no Indian dialect at all" (p. 195). Clearly this schoolteacher, with his sentimental songs and lack of understanding, is a Mexican cousin of the English Ida Arnold. Greene's satiric judgment is further implied by an inscription—"*Wein, Weib, und Gesang*"—upon the wall of a nearby lavatory.

Once again, the secular and sentimental view of life comes off rather badly. Yet Catholic faults do not escape Greene's criticism. He records a mass baptism of several hundred children, a baptism denied to one child whose mother lacked fifty centavos. He comments, "It is a depressing fact that persecution does not necessarily produce Father Pros [the Mexican martyr]" (p. 200). Nevertheless Greene does admit an important qualification: "Who can judge the temptation to such a priest [as the one who refused baptism], living in a Godless state, seeing the world and the flesh grossly triumphant among the swaggering do-nothing pistoleros . . . ?" (p. 200).

Catholicism was most disappointing in the churches of Las Casas during Holy Week. Greene had gone to this "very Catholic" and "moral" town in the heart of Mexico expecting to discover the lost religion. Instead, he found "all the symbols of God's presence and nothing there at all—just flowers and drapery and cardboard angels starting from the wall with trumpets in their hands to blow a trump for nothing" (p. 221). He saw the gross, stuffed figure of "the brother of Judas," and he heard of San Miguelito, the saint in a box, "something astute and amateurish," perhaps a radio receiver designed to gull the ignorant peasants. At Las Casas, Mass was still celebrated, although in a private house, where the priest with a face "hideously disfigured with mauve patches" (p. 222) brought the Body of God out from the altar to a balcony, "handing Christ across the bowed heads." Yet the housewife who had sheltered God in her house showed "a touch of pride, of condescension"; instead of displaying true Catholic piety and humility, she too had been stained by sin.

This "holy" city also made Greene feel like "the one unpopular boy at school" (p. 227), an appropriate sensation in the land of adolescence. Memories of his school had provided Greene with similes for *Journey without Maps,* in which the map of Liberia symbolized the lost childhood. In the Mexican constitution Greene found a symbol for the adolescent population of the land of lost Catholicism. The constitution seemed ". . . a little pathetic, that muddled idealism which speaks of 'an exact and rational conception of the Universe': one thinks of men like Samuel Butler with hideous crippling childhoods; and in the dry Sonora or Michoacán plains . . . childhood *was* no doubt crippled—in the Mexican way of the pistol shot and the crooked judge and the cock-fight and nobody caring for another's life" (p. 84). Childhood's pleasures and terrors had here been replaced by an adolescent "façade of *bonhomie* . . . with which they hide from themselves the cruelty and treachery of their life" (p. 211).

Always very close to the façade of the most beautiful scenes and during the most peaceful moments, Greene was conscious of cruelty and decay. At first he had been "ready to think of Mexico in terms of quiet and gentleness and devotion" (p. 41), as he watched the demure courtships in a city square. He saw lovers "happy together in the dark bound by the rules of a game they both knew; no fear, no exasperated nerves; what was left, sentiment and the demurest sensuality." He admired also the Indians in their "gawky and innocent embrace . . . [with] no sense of passion at all" (p. 78). Greene thought that the people of Mexico at least maintained a finer love of man, although this was an unsatisfactory substitute for the love of God. Before long, however, he found the corrupt and soiled heart of this love. He saw "lovely sexual instruments wearing little gold crosses" (p. 88); he was shown a horrible waxworks booth depicting monks flogging native women whose bodies had been constructed "with tender sensuality" (p. 100).

The heart of Africa had revealed the purer terror and the purer pleasure that enriched the imperfect world of childhood. The heart of Mexico showed corruption instead of purity; the Mexicans' adolescent smiles symbolized this corruption with their display of gold teeth.[7] A scene might be washed clean by distance and air, scarlet tulipans, bright yellow lemons: but this too was deceptive appearance. Perfect beauty was an illusion, a prelude to the world's sordid business; in such a setting the phrase "The country remains quiet" could become a sinister one (p. 111).

Unexpected beauty was much rarer in Mexico than it had been in Africa. Once, at Orizaba, Greene found a scene of "elegant decay," a town in which loudspeakers near the church were "braying sentimental music" and a place where all religious enthusiasm seemed spent. He was surprised to find an evening of happiness and to meet a priest who made him reflect: "What right had an English Catholic to bitterness or horror at human nature when this Mexican priest had none." Coming from Confession, Greene no longer watched the flares and listened critically to the cheap music. Instead, he felt that this "was how a saint's day should be cele-

7. The gold tooth and Greene's symbolic dentist, whose task is the curing of pain, are discussed in more detail below, pp. 127–28 and Ch. 6n10.

brated—joyfully, with fireworks and tortillas, domestically" (p. 115). But the change in Greene's view had been effected through his Faith. Priest, church, and Confession had combined to remind him of the benefits of living "under the shadow of religion."

Next morning he was again disappointed, as he had been whenever he expected too much of Africa. Greene remembered again that happiness never lasts. The Mass was "more like an English Mass, sedate and unenthusiastic and familiar," except for the presence of a black-haired Indian baby. Under the heading of "The Morning After," Greene records the town's appearance in different terms, seeing it through the realistic eyes of an artist instead of with the distorted vision of a falsely romantic tourist. In the writer's account, Indian soldiers wear "grubby" uniforms, a woman trails through a "dingy" yard, the chapel is "decaying," the rubbish dump is "stinking." Politicians lounge on a balcony overlooking the square. Again we are reminded of the discovery Greene made in Africa: conversions (i.e., sentimental responses) don't last.

The extent and nature of Mexico's squalor rarely encouraged the sentimental response. In spite of the *bonhomie,* the adolescent attitudes, the gold-plated beauty, most of the land Greene surveyed was unashamedly dirty. Beggars swarmed along the railroad tracks; a child leaped upon the back of a hideously crippled dwarf in an ugly struggle for a small coin. On the other hand, the shadow of religion usually made such squalor seem less depressing than its European counterpart. In Mexico at least the beggars "had hope and self-respect—they gave something in return for what they got; a prayer in which they believed. . . . They had a place in the world, unlike the poor bitter men playing gramophones in London gutters" (p. 230).

From the civilization of London's beggars, Greene had fled to Africa looking for the point at which we had gone astray; he found a few of the African threads back to the heart of darkness even in Mexico. He encountered "a glimpse of life as it should be," a hint of a world before "the road went irremediably wrong"; unfortunately, the moment "passed almost as quickly as a dream" (pp. 116–17). There was also a scene "not exactly of beauty but of consciousness, consciousness of something simple and strange and uncompli-

cated, a way of life we have hopelessly lost but can never quite forget." Warned that Villahermosa was in "a very evil land," Greene
nevertheless felt himself "drawing near to the centre of something—if it was only of darkness and abandonment" (p. 139). Again
Greene perceives a difference between Mexico's mystery and Africa's.[8]

A few Mexicans shared with the African natives an "unspoiled"
quality. Some even shared the ancient tribal memories of religious
power and magic. Far into the Mexican mountains the world
seemed "like a scene from the past before the human race had bred
its millions—England of the Conquest before the forests had been
cut" (p. 216). Behind this racial memory was an even older world,
represented by the Indian religion, and very different from the lost
Catholicism of Mexico's towns. The Indian religion was ". . . a dark
tormented magic cult. The old ladies might swing back and forth in
the rocking-chairs of Villahermosa, the Catholics might be dying out
'like dogs,' but here, in the mountainous strange world . . . Christianity went on its own frightening way. Magic, yes, but we are too
apt to minimise the magic element in Christianity—the man raised
from the dead, the devils cast out, the water turned into wine" (p.
216). Later Greene saw these Indians coming down into the world
from which Catholicism had been banished, like an "invasion." On
Holy Thursday they brought bunches of lemon twigs and came to
see the crucified Christ, making mysterious symbolic gestures. Their
almost pagan cemetery provided Greene with an appropriate symbol in the whisky priest's Mexico; it became "a short cut to the dark
and magical heart of the faith" (*PG*, p. 201), more meaningful than
the "unknown" dark and magical heart of the African continent.

8. Only once did Greene compare Mexico's scenes with ugly African
memories; he found one place as "squalid" as anything he had seen in the
West African bush (*LR*, p. 44). In this instance, squalor was apparently a reflection of Greene's mood, repeating his weary failure to respond to beauty in
Africa (described in *JM*). It was in Mexico that Greene commented, "Beauty
is only an emotion in the observer" (*LR*, p. 197); broken glasses resulted in
eyestrain that caused Greene's "almost pathological hatred" for Mexico (p.
182). In *The Power and the Glory*, Greene used this observation in explaining
hate: "just a failure of the imagination" (p. 170). Yet whatever the emotional
reasons for his responses, Greene remarked on the rarity of a Mexican hovel
resembling an African hut, containing "what you seldom find in Mexico, the
feel of human goodness" (p. 209).

Greene also looked at the contrasting symbols of corrupt civilization through the eyes of an Indian boy at Chiapas. In *The Lawless Roads* this child's innocent eyes expose the ugliness of a civilized "home": a square room, its chairs arranged in meaningless order around the walls. Its decorations are gaudy, boastful, outsize: wedding favors, family photographs, scarlet silk. A packing case stands beside a sewing machine, a modern gramophone beside two old oil lamps. The room's hanging streamers of mauve, orange, and white inevitably remind the reader of Greene's recurrent pubs with their sad remnants of Christmas gaiety. The room also shows how far Greene himself had traveled since his earliest picture of "home"—Andrews' version of "civilization" in *The Man Within*: "The enjoyment of quiet—gardens and unboisterous meals, music and the singing in Exeter Cathedral" (p. 25).

That was a youthful vision. In Mexico, Greene faced up to "all the cares and irritations and responsibilities of ordinary life" that waited for him in Mexico City. Here indeed was civilization: a libel suit brought by Shirley Temple, bills, a lost overcoat, missing proofs of Greene's latest book. In the night he heard a woman screaming, a love affair breaking up publicly and loudly, and a waiter "nibbling" outside his door. All these aggravations "seemed more than usually in the picture—of a country of disappointment and despair" (p. 266). Yet Greene also admitted the universality of these experiences: "They might happen anywhere" (p. 265).

These are in fact the wounds of civilization, perhaps as necessary to its salvation as the stigmata of Christ. Even the ugly mestizo, the Mexican Judas, is no more than a typical part of this world: "A world of treachery, violence and lust in which his shame was altogether insignificant. How often the priest had heard the same confession—Man was so limited: he hadn't even the ingenuity to invent a new vice: the animals knew as much. It was for this world that Christ had died: the more evil you saw and heard about you, the greater glory lay around the death; it was too easy to die for what was good or beautiful, for home or children or a civilisation—it needed a God to die for the half-hearted and the corrupt" (*PG*, pp. 123–24). Generally lacking kindness, or gentleness, or courtesy, civilization is a world of goodness dying out, its death symbolized in a tiny two-year-old blonde girl asleep in her nurse's arms, with "ears already drilled for rings and a gold bangle around the little bony wrist—handcuffed to sophistication at birth—like goodness dying" (*LR*, p. 119).[9]

Naturally a glimpse of Paradise in Mexico contains always a hidden flaw. Journeying through the country, Greene continually heard tales of a beautiful and peaceful finca to be found at the end of an unknown path. It proved indeed to be a pleasant place. But it also proved to be flawed by a bullet hole and by cattleticks that wedged themselves firmly in Greene's arms and thighs. In *The Lawless Roads*, the "lesson" of the finca is recorded as advice to the novice "not to take things too seriously" (p. 179). In *The Power and the Glory*, however, the scene undergoes artistic transformation. The finca becomes a setting in which to dramatize the whisky priest's coming to terms with his fears (as Greene had faced his own fears in an African hut). No longer a novice, the priest does take things seriously: he walks back into the land of betrayal and lost Faith.

In Puebla, Greene found another relic of the lost religion, a true symbol of lost innocence, although not a symbol that he could use in *The Power and the Glory*. "The Hidden Convent" was a tourist attraction, run by Freemasons offering anti-Catholic propaganda. Greene's guide was unlike his brother masons. He quietly referred to the displaced nuns as "those poor women"; he plucked a rose from the nuns' garden for Greene to remember them by. Later, finding the rose thrust at random between the pages of *Barchester Towers*, Greene commented, "It seems a long way from Barchester to Puebla, to the dark burial place and the pit of skulls where the Masonic guides crawl on hands and knees through the bathroom wall into the deserted chapel, a good deal farther than a few thousand miles, all the immeasurable distance between two human minds" (*LR*, p. 262).

---

9. Greene uses this image in describing Coral Fellowes, whose "gold bangle on the bony wrist was like a padlock on a canvas door" (*PG*, p. 37). Coral belongs with Greene's various dead and dying children, children who often die outside the story (e.g., Scobie's daughter and the child of Querry's "parable"). These children are ironic symbols of the "lost" childhood that is Greene's recurrent theme.

To Greene, the distance between the European and the Mexican minds seemed very short. He therefore set *The Lawless Roads* in a framework of European scenes, helping the reader to measure the distance for himself. At the same time, and much more precisely than in *Journey without Maps*, Greene sets down his own memories of a "lost" boyhood. His own recollections of two separate "countries," the school world of suffering and the home world of faith and romantic belief, provide further symbols of a divided Mexico. Memories of the Berkhamsted childhood and of the English secular world then accompany Greene as he travels.[10] But his narrative abandons the opening memory of English Catholic persecution (expressed in Campion's cry against Elizabethan persecution—a sound that at first struck Greene as a forerunner of Father Pro's defiance). Instead, *The Lawless Roads* examines Mexican Catholicism in its own context. Occasionally, Mexico reminded Greene of England: its "political" art made him think of those "great empty Victorian conceptions that life denies at every turn" (p. 80). But only at the end of the narrative does he record his feelings about England. Returning to a London of Air Raid Precautions posters, of headlines of violent crimes, and "the long waste of the Clapham Road," Greene found nothing to recall the earlier child's cry at Dover. Instead he wrote, "I wondered why I disliked Mexico so much: *this* was home" (p. 288).

"Home" brought Greene a realization that whatever seemed horrifying in the past had already become tinged with regret—even the horrors of his Berkhamsted school and the depressing scenes reported in the opening pages of *The Lawless Roads* as well as in

10. There were two "countries" on either side of the school's green baize door: School's cruelty, cracked bells, and lack of privacy where "Hell lay about them in their infancy" (p. 4); and home's romantic atmosphere of books, fruit, and eau-de-cologne. From the "home" side (his parents' apartment at the school) Greene could walk out into the garden where faith "came to one—shapelessly, without dogma, a presence above a croquet lawn, something associated with violence, cruelty, evil across the way" (p. 5). The European framework of *The Lawless Roads* begins with a Prologue ("The Anarchists") containing Greene's memories of Berkhamsted. "The Faith" compares the Mexican scene with the "dusty rationalist lines [of] nineteenth century materialism reminiscent of Herbert Spencer and the Thinkers' Library" (p. 14). The travels close with a European Epilogue (pp. 276–89) describing Germans and Spaniards on the homebound ship. (Parts of this section appeared separately as "The Escapist" and "The Blind Eye"—see Bibliography.)

"Twenty-four Hours in Metroland." Previously, Kailahun, a place that had impressed Greene at the time with its dirt and disease, had become in his memory "a clean village" (*JM*, p. 63). Now Mexico's ugliness faded too, before the "curiously fictitious" Mass in Chelsea (*LR*, p. 289), the nuns' preparations for wartime evacuation of schoolchildren, the civil defense activities on the common outside a London school. Although Greene felt, "We are in need of violence," the moment of death was delayed (this was the year of the false Munich peace) and the English ugliness resumed: "Poverty and lust called to each other in the early wintertime dark." *The Lawless Roads* concludes with a paragraph that might serve as an additional epigraph for *The Power and the Glory*: "And in Chiapas the white churches fell to ruin staring up at Serrabia's planes flying overhead—like faces the world has corrupted waiting through the dry months and the rains for the footstep, the voice, 'Is it easier to say your sins be forgiven you . . . ?'" Out of such an impression of Mexico did the world of the whisky priest emerge.

The priest himself emerged from specific memories. In particular, there was the hunted priest of Tabasco (p. 129), a man "who existed for ten years in the forests and the swamps, venturing out only at night; his few letters . . . recorded an awful sense of impotence—to live in constant danger and yet be able to do so little, it hardly seemed worth the horror." Almost as soon as he had embarked on the river leading into unknown Mexican country Greene had met the second remarkable character of his novel, Doc Winter, an American dentist with "a mestizo wife and two blond washed-out little boys with transparent eyelids and heavy brown Mexican eyes" (p. 132). Greene also heard of a whisky priest who drunkenly baptized a boy "Brigitta" (p. 150), while later on his journey Greene encountered the Norwegian lady Fru R and the ugly Judas of the novel, "a clerk I grew to loathe, a mestizo with curly sideburns and two yellow fangs at either end of his mouth" (p. 192).

In addition to providing these characters for his novel, Mexico offered a natural atmosphere very appropriate for its action. Tabasco, "the godless state," provided both setting and symbol: it reflected a larger world in which law and order seemed more like "banditry," and it was a place in which honesty was not on the faces of the police but "on the faces of the men and women waiting to be fined or blackguarded" (p. 143). Greene gained "an overwhelming sense of brutality and irresponsibility" from this view of Villahermosa. On the other hand, he learned to recognize the varieties of his Faith: a kind of social Catholicism in Puebla, "different from the faith of San Luis on the edge of violence, the inanition of Orizaba, the patient carrying-on in the capital, the wild beliefs of [Indians in] Chiapas" (p. 258). He observed the easy substitutions of values, where children were encouraged to chop up religious images in return for little presents of candy (p. 181). He also heard of a hardworking Scots Catholic, Dr. Fitzpatrick's father, a man of legendary heroic quality who had endured many hardships in earning the money to bring "my beloved Anna and dear little Tom" to St. Juan Bautista. But this heroic world had vanished: St. Juan Bautista was now Villahermosa. The secular, political power had achieved its corrupting victory.

It is therefore appropriate that Greene gained the necessary artistic distance between the actual world of *The Lawless Roads* (1939) and its fictional re-creation in *The Power and the Glory* (1940) through a story dealing with secular, political corruptions in European civilization. Greene's first literary response to Africa had been an entertainment; his first publication after the Mexican journey was another, *The Confidential Agent* (1939). Greene made use of the Spanish Civil War—the violent events referred to in the closing pages of *The Lawless Roads*—to set in motion the adventures of a man named simply "D." Although D is an agent who perceives the world in terms of a war map—even the deck of the ship carrying him to England seems to him "a map marked with trenches" (p. 4)—he belongs to the world of Greene's whisky priest rather than to that of the lieutenant. For it is not on D's side but the other that civilization has "no religious faith"; his enemies have permitted Gregorian chants and picturesque ceremonies to survive, but only as part of the "interesting" superstition of religion (pp. 21–22). D's preference is for the distrust, the barbarity, the betrayals, even chaos: "The Dark Ages, after all, had been his 'period'" (p. 22)— and the reader is reminded of Greene's own view of European civilization now as the Dark Ages.

Ironic comments on Europe's adolescent civilization include D's first "action of trust": he gives Rose a gun! In this world, "a child had to fix her love on an old foreigner and a prostitute for want of anything better" (p. 42). The foreigner's view of a city "at peace" echoes Greene's belief that we deserved and needed violence. D thinks, "If this was civilization—the crowded prosperous streets, the women trooping in for coffee at Buzzard's, the lady in waiting at King Edward's Court [reference to a book of presumably racy memoirs], and the sinking, drowning child—he preferred barbarity, the bombed streets, and the food queues; a child there had nothing worse to look forward to than death" (p. 40).

Greene was not yet prepared to work out more precisely the ugly implications of this world. D's sense of pity for Rose remains undeveloped; the "infection" of violence that goes everywhere with the agent is a passing reference instead of a theme. Even the various examples of lack of trust are only peripheral, symbolized by the agent's credentials: "Credence no longer meant belief" (p. 4). In this territory, nobody trusts a "confidential" agent; his secret mission becomes a public and even farcical display at a road-house, a pathetic party, and a balcony harangue. Nevertheless, D is Greene's first truly "committed" hero. He says, "You've got to choose some line of action and live by it. Otherwise nothing matters at all" (p. 47). In spite of the generally secular tone of this book, D is also the first character with a truly adult perception of God—of a God who is neither a pious platitude nor an Enemy but a mystery: "God, he thought, could only really be pictured as a joker. It was absurd to have come all this way only to encounter Captain Currie at the end of it" (p. 162).

It is less easy to conceive of the whisky priest's God as a joker, unless we consider carefully the range of the novel's irony, the coincidental encounters, and the episode of the sacramental wine. This last episode especially reveals the dilemma of a Catholic in our Absurd world; in this respect, it foreshadows Querry's parable of absurdity in *A Burnt-Out Case*. The priest of *The Power and the Glory*, like Querry recording the later parable, comes to self-realization through an incident that on the surface is only an amusing anecdote. But beneath the farcical account of the priest's vanishing wine Greene has concealed two more levels of meaning: religious values coming to terms with secular power, and erring steps by which the Catholic may weakly yield spiritual necessity to worldly demands.

Greene shows the whisky priest entering the corrupt secular world in which the government simultaneously sells crime and punishes it. The wine merchant is the cousin of the governor; he plays billiards with the chief of police. Although the police chief clearly remembers his first communion, he can only speak now of the "painful duty" of watching his men shoot the priest who had given him the sacrament. There is no feeling behind the chief's statement "I wept" (p. 145); he has given up his religious values with the ease of a shot.

Yet the Roman Catholic priest does no better. The whisky priest yields readily to the world's demands: he gives up the wine that should have been preserved for the sacrament and in doing so loses all—wine, brandy, and freedom. The steps of his fall are carefully recorded. First, "painful anxiety" as the cork is pulled and the wine level falls; then, "making allowances"; finally, the sacrifice of personal need and public duty. Nothing makes up for his refusal to fight for the spirit in which he believes. Sitting under the shadow of the Governor's cousin instead of under the shadow of God, the priest watches the storm beat around the seedy hotel room and sums up his sense of loss: "This was the atmosphere of a whole state—the storm outside and the talk just going on—words like 'mystery' and 'soul' and 'source of life' came in over and over again, as they sat on the bed talking, with nothing to do and nothing to believe in and nowhere better to go" (p. 147).

In this empty world, there is no communication between the secular power and the people they are supposedly rescuing from an "evil" religion. The beggar is welcomed when he brings customers for illegal liquor, but he is not permitted to join the conversation. He is rejected with such remarks as "Who cares?" and "You talk too much" (pp. 142–43). All of these failures and the weaknesses that the priest faces in himself are summed up in the terrible irony of the episode's conclusion: "The smell of spirit rose all around them— not very strongly: there hadn't been much left" (p. 153).

Nevertheless, the priest at least recognizes both the smell of the spirit and its symbolic value. In the residue of the spirit lies the source of his own spiritual regeneration. His growth is in part a movement from childish irresponsibility through adolescent giggling and sins to the maturity of acceptance. He even prepares for the leap to God. Although the priest's sainthood is only declared by a pious mother, his leap is foreshadowed in his infinite compassion and Christ-like sense of charity and mercy. His compassion encompasses alike his corrupted daughter and the traitor mestizo. Imprisoned for "carrying spirits" the priest enters the darkness of the prison cell, where he finds himself in sympathy with all the world's sinners. In this episode, described in more detail below, the priest faces his tears. From the cell he later wanders "in a kind of limbo" (p. 191), passing into this "region of abandonment" because he was not "good enough" or "bad enough" yet to walk toward God or the Devil.

The "goodness" and "badness" of the priest are, as in all Greene's character studies, a matter of perspective. We see him at one moment permitting a woman to beat down the price of Mass— buying God as Major Grant bought girls. On the other hand, his weariness does not prevent the priest from performing good actions, such as meeting an old man's demands for night confessional. The fact that the women who come to Confession have been badgered into doing so by the old man's insistence does not make the priest's sacrifice any less valuable. Nor does the most obvious sin prevent the priest from serving God: "I can put God into a man's mouth just the same—and I can give him God's pardon. It wouldn't make any difference to that if every priest in the Church was like me" (p. 253).

For the secular power, however, the phrase "It makes no difference" has another meaning. The lieutenant simply judges all priests "bad." In his view, all priests make "immense demands" from the altar steps while themselves remaining unaware of the meaning of sacrifice (p. 22). To a typically pious woman parishioner, the priest is "bad" for different reasons: she thinks that a lack of virtue in the priest's person disqualifies his virtue in God. The priest sometimes admits his personal "badness," accusing himself of pride, for instance, in staying to ransom his child. Later, the priest feels "immense envy" of those who have enjoyed the benefits of Confession. Once again, Greene is using his technique of shifting the fragments of a life-map; he suggests that the picture of the priest cannot be put together correctly if we look at its pieces from one direction only.

Greene, however, discourages judgment. Even in juxtaposing the priest's actions and those of Padre José—"a traitor to God," according to the pious mother who later declares the whisky priest a saint (p. 28)—Greene keeps in mind his observation on the Mexican journey: "Who can judge what terror and hardship and isolation may have excused him in the eyes of God?" (*LR*, p. 150). José has taken a wife, not out of love or need or loneliness, but out of cowardice. José's relation to his wife is made terribly clear by her grotesque appearance, her perpetual nightdress, and her nagging power over this pitiful figure who had once trembled only before the elevation of the Host. At that time, when José's fear was properly reserved for God instead of being given to an ugly wife, the whisky priest had still been imperfect. While the Padre trembled before God, the whisky priest had bowed to social Catholicism, the ladies of the Altar Guild, and the Daughters of Mary; he had told little jokes and enjoyed rich food, admiration, and gifts from the parish ladies. But at that time he was as a child, and now he can face a man's danger. Now the whisky priest can recognize the terrors of a secular trap, and he can subordinate his fear to the power of God. While José has been reduced to a coward trembling before his mountainous wife and denying God, the priest becomes a heroic figure, walking into danger as he grants Absolution, hears Confession, and celebrates Mass.

The whisky priest's words urge us to judge him very harshly. He compares his own actions with those of José; he holds ambition "responsible" for his own failure to follow José's example. If this is "ambition," however, it is surely more properly regarded as a good quality, since it leads the whisky priest ultimately to make his leap to God, while José is held fast in the grip of despair. José no longer loves either man or God. His marriage is loveless and he denies God's love. The little children taunt him. But the whisky priest continues to feel "affection" for the half-caste and love for his betrayers. Even the priest's repeated self-accusation of pride can be discounted if he is compared with the monsignor, a priest who almost forgot to say his final prayers because he was too busy explaining his superior rank (p. 26). Moreover, at the very moment when the priest is accusing himself of pride, he is giving his shirt to the mestizo.

It is true that the whisky priest carries with him the "wound" of sin, but Catholic doctrine offers him the healing power of God's mercy. The priest's sin includes the fathering of his daughter: the result of five minutes following fear, despair, half a bottle of brandy, and a sense of loneliness. He had committed the act with a woman who still calls him only "father"; the act has resulted in alienation from his heavenly Father and his earthly daughter. Yet the priest still carries his own wound toward that "ugly wounded face of God" and the Crucifixion symbolizing His forgiveness. The priest travels through a country controlled by the scarred face of the lieutenant: "Perhaps the scar on [the lieutenant's] jaw was the relic of an escape" (p. 19). It is not clear whether the lieutenant has escaped from the wound of sin or the forgiveness of God.

From his first appearance in *The Power and the Glory*, the lieutenant evolves as the complement of the priest, but in more subtle relationship than that of the complementary "good" of Rose and the "evil" of Pinkie in *Brighton Rock*. There is "something of a priest in his intent observant walk—a theologian going back over the errors of the past to destroy them again" (p. 25). His room looks "as comfortless as a prison or a monastic cell"; but instead of the Crucifix and a picture of the Sacred Heart, he displays a picture of the President and a calendar. He knows that it is the hour of prayer, but this thought only infuriates him, since his own "mysticism" is the experience of vacancy as "a complete certainty in the existence of a dying, cooling world, of human beings who had evolved from animals for no purpose at all" (p. 25). His life had "begun" only five years ago (p. 26), not with baptism or innocence or ordination but with the overthrow of God.

In spite of his rejection of the religious view, the lieutenant seems unable to discard from his own person a response to children,

a love for them, a desire for their welfare. As a secular "pastor,"
however, he knows neither the language nor the gestures of his religious counterpart. The lieutenant finds only an "insecure happiness" in showing his gun to the children. He would eliminate from
the children's world everything which had made him miserable in
his own childhood—all that was poor, superstitious, and corrupt.
His cure is unfortunately not spiritual but violent: he is "quite prepared to make a massacre for their sakes—first the Church and then
the foreigner and then the politician. . . . He wanted to begin the
world again with them in a desert" (p. 71). Again, the spiritual
terms—the fast in the desert and the desert rebirth of early Christianity—have been corrupted by the secular perspective.

The resemblance between the lieutenant and the whisky priest
dramatizes the struggle between political or secular and religious
values. On the one hand is the lieutenant, "a little dapper figure of
hate carrying his secret of love" (p. 71). On the other is the priest:
"He alone carried a wound, as though a whole world had died" (p.
85). But the lieutenant cannot communicate his love as a priest can
communicate love through the sacrament of God's body. The lieutenant's gesture of affection—pinching a boy's ear—only causes the
child to flinch in pain. When the secular power has captured the
religious, the lieutenant finds out just how inadequate his love is,
how small his victory. Seeing the boy again, the lieutenant tries to
smile, "an odd sour grimace, without triumph or hope" (p. 262).
After the priest's death, the boy who had admired the lieutenant's
gun and watched the soldiers respectfully now spits upon the revolver butt. The child's gesture symbolizes man's ultimate rejection
of violence in an evil and sinister world.

But in the novel the gesture is only made by a child; the adult
reader must temper his judgment of the lieutenant. Although the
lieutenant may seem a figure of Evil or a symbol of secular failure,
he is in the religious view of the whisky priest "a good man" (p.
181). Moreover, when the lieutenant is not handicapped by the
cliché of judging all priests "bad," he can see the whisky priest as a
man, one of Mexico's innumerable poor. At this moment the priest
ironically becomes one of the men for whom the lieutenant would
destroy all traces of the old religion. Once again, Greene is reveal-

ing his artistic perception of the "truth" to be found in fiction when convention and cliché are discarded.

The cell in which the priest discovers his truth and himself is a dark place suggesting "the heart of darkness." It forms an appropriate setting for Greene's—and the priest's—critical appraisal of our conventional judgments of action and intention. The cell is a place "very like the world: overcrowded with lust and crime and unhappy love: it stank to heaven; but he realised that after all it was possible to find peace there, when you knew for certain that the time was short" (p. 161). Further, "people snatched at causes of pleasure and pride in cramped and disagreeable surroundings; there was no time to do anything worth doing, and always one dreamed of escape" (p. 171). In this little world, "crime" ranges from murderous assault with a broken bottle to possession of a crucifix. Men demand food, money, and comfort; they make individual choices of piety, passion, and pain; and they laugh and sing and cry and suffer just as men do in the shoddy world outside.

In the cell's narrow world, the priest finds an understanding he had not been able to reach in the blinding light of his earlier and simpler religious life. Greene's own explorations presumably had helped him to recognize the symbolic value of the dark cell as a place for fully revealing to the priest "the convincing mystery—that we were made in God's image—God was the parent, but He was also the policeman, the criminal, the priest, the maniac and the judge" (p. 129). With his clearer vision of this world, a vision paradoxically obtained in total darkness, the priest feels charity, compassion, and a real affection for his companions. No longer is he "afraid" of darkness.

By the darkness of the cell, man is reduced to the sounds of passion, the simplest needs of the body, and the naked voices that are usually hidden by society's pious and hypocritical masks. The priest later reflects: "God might forgive cowardice and passion, but was it possible to forgive the habit of piety?" (p. 218). This habit of piety is in fact one of the greatest sins in Greene's canon, not because it is the defense of the weak or the wicked, but because it is the greatest obstacle between man and God. In contrast, salvation can strike like lightning at the evil heart (p. 218); the truth may occasionally seed in the interstices of a cracked character (*BC*, p. 186).

Cramped in his corner of the cell, the priest analyzes the fault of piety, its illusion that brings men to death "in a state of invincible complacency, full of uncharity" (p. 164). The pious woman in the cell is its least charitable inmate. Her only official crime has been the possession of holy books, but her greater crime is the failure to love her fellow men. She is really no better than the mestizo with his repeated avowal that he is a "very good Christian"; her words have no more meaning than the phrase "Mother of God" has on the lips of the lieutenant and the red shirts. For her there can be none of the priest's compassionate realization: "When you visualized a man or woman carefully, you could always begin to feel pity . . . that was a quality God's image carried with it. . . . When you saw the lines at the corners of the eyes, the shape of the mouth, how the hair grew, it was impossible to hate" (pp. 169–70).

Yet if the priest's story is that of a man coming both to maturity and to God, and if the cell does indeed bring enlightenment, we may well ask why the priest's most characteristic sound is a giggle. Perhaps this symbolic gesture was inspired by a contrast Greene had observed in Mexico between the "real" religion and the "giggling" adolescent Mexican girls (*LR*, p. 38). The priest giggles most often at moments of terrible irony—when a beggar asks him, "Haven't you a heart?" (p. 133); when the pious woman says, "We have a martyr here" (p. 163) or thinks that "they are everywhere" refers to good books instead of to thieves and murderers (p. 166). His giggle is the foreshadowing of Querry's perception of the Absurd in *A Burnt-Out Case*, especially when the will to escape casts "a momentary and appalling humour over the whole situation" and the priest "giggled and panted and giggled again" (p. 150). But it is also the sound accompanying the priest's ridiculous eating of onions to conceal the odor of wine from his pursuers (p. 91). It even carries memories of the Children of Mary eating pastries—an ironic response to the mestizo's comment "If I was a rich man—only a little rich—I should be good" (p. 127). The priest giggles because "he could never take the complications of destiny quite seriously" (pp. 127–28) or because he has retreated into the false childhood of card tricks and games instead of maintaining his priestly role. The priest had once giggled at the mestizo's absurdity, seeing his resemblance to the stuffed effigies that made of Our Lord's betrayer "a figure of fun . . . [instead of] a Prometheus, a noble victim in a hopeless war" (p. 115). He giggles again as he shares a final drink with the mestizo (p. 239) at the frontier of Mexico's darkest province.

The priest's giggle diminishes as his understanding grows and as he draws closer to God. It is a response that "didn't come off" at the Lehrs' (p. 219); a "nervous" response to the lieutenant's conversation as the priest journeys to his death (the priest says, "You'll know all there is to know about me," p. 254); and "unconvincing" when he says to the lieutenant, "I dare say the first time you saw a man raised from the dead you might think so [that it was magic] too" (p. 260). Laughter comes slowly. At first it is only the false response to an illusory happiness as the priest is driven where he most wants to be—to the village that is the home of his daughter. For in this village the priest is no longer welcome; corruption mocks him through the sniggers and knowing laughter of his child. Before long, however, he is reacting with "astonished laughter" to the realization of his own comic ambition (pp. 120–21) and to his recognition of the absurdity of "human dignity disputing with a bitch over a bone" (p. 187). The priest's final giggle, when Padre José will not come to hear his confession, is no more than an "attempt" (p. 266); it precedes his terrible feeling of abandonment and a spiritual darkness very different from the physical darkness of his earlier night in the crowded cell.

This, however, is the essential moment of loneliness, the dark night of the soul rather than the darkness of ignorance. It is specifically to be contrasted with the lieutenant's emptiness after the priest has been shot: the lieutenant "felt without a purpose, as if life had drained out of the world. He said with bitter kindness (he couldn't summon up any hate of this small hollow man), 'Try to sleep'" (p. 268). In spite of the gradual convergence of images of priest and lieutenant toward the recognition scene of the priest's first imprisonment, this final failure of the lieutenant's understanding reveals their essential difference. The priest thinks it "a treachery that he was more afraid of the pain of bullets than of what came after" (p. 251). He and the American fugitive have even "looked [like] two of a kind, dirty and unshaved: the lieutenant seemed to belong to a different class altogether" (pp. 247–48). And they are indeed different. The lieutenant moves from "contempt" (when he asks the priest if he has a child) through grudging communication ("You're a man of education . . . I've had to think things out for myself," pp. 256–57) to the final kindliness of bringing the condemned priest brandy and of reflecting, "You aren't a bad fellow" (p. 261). But the lieutenant here fails to uphold his secular values; in contrast, the priest dies true to his Faith.

The lieutenant's final kindness to the priest is a strange wandering from the familiar paths of his ugly, godless world. He has no map to guide him in the right direction. But the priest has help in charting his path. Once more Greene uses the map metaphor. The priest experiences an ache "like a tiresome voice explaining to him that he had taken the wrong path: he remembered a map he had once seen of the two adjoining states"; and the ache tells him, "You're on that blank paper now" (pp. 202–3). The priest finds, however, that in some ways "it was better over there, across the border. Fear and death were not the worst things" (p. 217). Worse things include a pious merchant bargaining over the blood of Christ (wine for the Mass), as well as the priest's setting of a price on God's blessing (the price of baptism). Finally, the priest dies saying "something that sounded like 'Excuse'" (p. 281). Thus the priest at last travels to the end of the path that leads from the world of man's justice to the world of God's infinite and eternal mercy.

Greene does not presume to know the nature of this Mercy. His priest has said, "I don't know a thing about the mercy of God: I don't know how awful the human heart looks to Him. . . . I just want justice, that's all" (p. 259). The lieutenant's secular judgment is obviously wrong, for he declares: "There were no more priests and no more heroes" (p. 286). But at this very moment young Luis' mother is including the whisky priest in the popular canon of religious heroes. The new priest is already coming up from the river to continue the work that the lieutenant was determined to stop forever. These are hints of God's mercy on earth. In spite of the tears shed by the whisky priest when he saw "all the hope of the world draining away" (p. 145), there is new hope. However inadequate he may have seemed as a man, the priest's life and death have contributed new religious strength to Mexico. In carrying out his religious duties, he has provided one more generation of Mexicans with the fund of baptismal innocence. His death serves as a new symbol—a means of drawing the people back to God's glory and of showing them the way to reject the pain (the lieutenant's false gesture of love) and the power (symbolized by the lieutenant's holster) of an evil, secular world.

Greene has written, "The plot of the novel catches the attention, but the subject lies deeper."[11] Too often, criticism of *The Power and the Glory* focuses on its pursuits by secular and divine "hounds" while missing the novel's deeper subject. *Stamboul Train* offers a clue to the interpretation of this deeper subject, for in that entertainment the fugitive patriot Czinner carried a map whose meaning was not clear until a mysterious sheet of lines and symbols was placed beneath it. Similarly in *The Power and the Glory*, there is the "map" of the plot, an exciting and sometimes terrible narrative. There are also special marks—the allusions to Catholic teaching and the very title of the novel, which is a phrase in the Anglican version of the Lord's Prayer, although it is commonly omitted from the Catholic.[12]

By placing these special marks and symbols together, we discover the appalling irony of man's assumption of the power that should be God's and the resulting chaos of a world without glory. The falsely powerful bodies of the lieutenant and the mayor, like the schoolteacher Greene had described in Mexico, lie between the people and the Body of God. In this world, Catholicism survives only in fragments unrelated to "the complete picture"; only the "heretic" Lehrs (who "hadn't the prying insight of fellow Catholics," p. 225) and the curious child Coral treat the priest as a guest rather than as a criminal or a sinner.

11. "Books in General," *New Statesman*, October 2, 1954.
12. Greene was not converted to Catholicism until 1926. It is fitting that he should use the version of the Lord's Prayer remembered from his own adolescence (see *The Lawless Roads*) in his novel of Mexico's "adolescent" civilization. (The Roman Catholic version ends "Deliver us from evil.")

In spite of the critics' ingenious attempts to interpret this priest-without-honor as a Christ-figure, he remains a man. His very weaknesses remind us of Greene's repeated assertions that his characters live in *this* world. Through his life and death the priest may restore God's power and God's glory, but he does so in man's way rather than in Christ's. The restoration of the power and the glory to God's troubled earthly kingdom is symbolized in the closing paragraphs of the novel, where another man—the new priest—brings God's body to His people.

The boy who had been unimpressed by his mother's reading of Juan's martyrdom, and more concerned with the exciting progress of soldiers outside his window, has now rejected the lieutenant. He wakens in the night to hear a knocking at the door. Feeling himself "the only man in the house," the boy goes to the door, where he finds the stranger, "a tall pale thin man with a rather sour mouth, who carried a small suitcase." The man identifies himself as a priest, "My name is Father ——"; but the boy's recognition is immediate. There is no need for the stranger to say more: "The boy had already swung the door open and put his lips to his hand before the other could give himself a name." This Father remains an unnamed symbol, while the boy—who does not yet understand all that has happened—responds through the priest's body to the Power of God.

Here is Greene's recurrent "optimism," once more contradicting whatever hints of pessimism might lie in his reports of Mexico's deterioration and of the extermination of Catholic life. The bitterly soiled hands of the whisky priest have not profaned the Host or withheld God's blessing. His influence lives on through his successor and through the symbolic importance of his death. When the boy welcomes the new priest, he is not part of a "miracle"—as some critics have asserted—or of some semi-magical or facile Catholic conclusion. He is only revealing Greene's subject, the cycle of man in time. As the boy opens the cottage door to welcome once again the sacraments, he opens the way to the return of God. The context is Roman Catholic, but the Anglican version of the Lord's Prayer states the theme even more clearly than Greene's conclusion in the novel: "For Thine is the Kingdom, the Power and the Glory, for ever and ever."

Chapter 4 FITTING THE PIECES
TOGETHER

IN THE YEARS following his two best-known journeys, Greene
continued to fit together the pieces of his map of civilization. He tried to bring out of the confused fragments of violence
and hate a clearer picture of love. This had been one of the major
perceptions of his Mexican journey, made as Greene looked at a
church mural drawn by Indians: "The last and most difficult lesson
of all—the lesson of love and the mysterious death of the Creator
on the cross" (*LR*, p. 96). In *The Power and the Glory* Greene had
shown that the kinds of love exhibited by the whisky priest and
the lieutenant might appear quite similar to anyone who did not
understand the immense difference in their sense of values. Yet the
"lesson" of love in the Mexican novel was still too restricted to provide an adequate chart for our fragmented civilization. The lines of
the Mexican map and its specifically Roman Catholic symbols could
not be properly imposed on the larger territory.

It was many years before Greene was prepared to fit the pieces
together in a larger map. His next major novel, *The Heart of the
Matter*, was not published until 1948, when the war that had just
begun when *The Power and the Glory* was published had been over
for three years. To the experience of his original journey to Africa,

Greene had added wartime service in Sierra Leone and in Nigeria, the violence of Europe's war, and the terrors of London's burning and bombing. Out of all these experiences, rather than out of a specific journey, Greene constructed the novels and plays of his postwar writing. Each revealed Greene's growing perception of the many varieties of violence and cruelty in a world without love.

The world to which Greene had returned from his Mexican journey seemed a world of hate. It was not a world that Greene cared to use directly in his novels.[1] Even the map metaphor—which had been specifically related to battlefields and warring sectors in *It's a Battlefield, Brighton Rock,* and *The Confidential Agent*—becomes a more subtle symbolic expression. Beginning with the entertainment that bridges the gap between *The Power and the Glory* and *The Heart of the Matter,* Greene's map suggests new ranges of human understanding.

In *The Ministry of Fear* (1943), Greene repeats his earlier literary pattern of placing an entertainment between his own experience and its ultimate fictional expression in a novel. In this entertainment he again works out themes and symbols and sketches the characters who will walk the paths of his newly mapped territory. Written during Greene's wartime duty in Sierra Leone (*SC*, p. xiv), *The Ministry of Fear* is his only full-length story of the violence of world war and the London blitz. (Both *The Heart of the Matter* and *The End of the Affair* depend structurally on World War II; but only the entertainment of 1943 takes structure, theme, and characters from the war.) It is a story that charts the loss of love.

The Heart of the Matter shows the corruption of love by pity. Scobie's pity is one aspect of his faulty judgment, of an overconfidence expressed in Greene's recurrent map metaphor. Scobie's map has been borrowed by younger men; he thinks that he has no more

1. Greene did publish one "Fragment de journal: le grand bombardement du mercredi 16 avril 1941," in Victor de Pange's *Graham Greene.* "Convoy to West Africa," a brief diary of Greene's wartime journey from England to Sierra Leone, appeared in *The Mint* (1946) and *In Search of a Character* (1962). One essay, "At Home" (*LC*), briefly describes the bombed London of 1940. His short stories of these years are relatively weak, although "Men at Work" (1940) describes the Civil Service and foreshadows Bendrix' interest in Henry Miles. (Details of "Alas, Poor Maling" and "When Greek Meets Greek" appear in the Bibliography.)

use for it (*HM*, p. 7). He thinks he understands his world, but he does not. This is a more subtle expression of Arthur Rowe's problem in *The Ministry of Fear*: a sensation of being in a strange country with no maps to help him, or of being "sent on a journey with the wrong map" (pp. 18, 127). Later, Bendrix carries the enlarged map metaphor a stage further: "If this book of mine fails to take a straight course, it is because I am lost in a strange region: I have no map" (*EA*, p. 56). Greene's epigraph for *The End of the Affair* further clarifies his postwar map-making, with Léon Bloy's words: "Man has places in his heart which do not yet exist, and into them enters suffering in order that they may have existence." With this echo of the blank places on the African map, of the continent shaped "like the human heart," Greene shows the chart by which the explorer may find God, as he travels from love of man to love of God.

But there is little even of man's love in *The Ministry of Fear*. At one level, it is simply a forthright commentary on the mess that Western civilization had made out of itself in the 1940s. It describes what Greene has referred to as the "deserved" violence of the war years, a time when the mystery of God's love seemed even less comprehensible than it had seemed in Mexico. Greene commented on such violence in his "Fragment de journal": "Quand je regarde en arrière, je ne retrouve que l'horreur sordide de cette nuit: ces hommes et ces femmes debout dans des ouvertures de porte, avec leurs pyjamas sales et déchirés, éclaboussés d'un peu de sang, véritables foules de Purgatoire. Ces images étaient inquiétantes car elles représentaient ce qui, un jour, pouvait arriver à chacun de nous."[2] But while most Europeans were suffering in this contemporary Purgatory, Arthur Rowe had been living in a private Hell. War's treachery and a bomb's violence, however, take him from his private Hell back to the false innocence of a childhood Heaven. He is psychologically reborn in this ironically rendered paradise, and grows to new maturity. Yet once again the supposedly "happy" ending of Greene's fairy story turns out to be only a prelude to real and presumably harsh existence. For the entertainment concludes with hints that Rowe will be living with his contempo-

2. In de Pange, *Graham Greene*, p. 122.

raries in the earth-bound Purgatory, in a world from which innocence has been lost forever.

By the end of his story, Greene's hero has traveled from his
private suffering and joined the world of Everyman. He is no longer
beyond the reach of the Ministry of Fear (an organization that cannot blackmail either "saints—or outcasts with nothing to lose," p.
94); he has begun to feel love for Anna. And all who love belong to
the Ministry of Fear since "if one loved one feared" (p. 174). The
mature man must face such fears and suffering. He must cross a
frontier that Greene had first observed in Liberia, and that Scobie
was later unable to face. Rowe, however, learns to live with his
fears when he discovers that one can exaggerate happiness, that
"happiness should always be qualified by a knowledge of misery"
(p. 145). In this world an immature enthusiasm for romantic adventure and a primitive idea of justice end only with Rowe's confrontation of Willi Hilfe; the climax is a pistol shot in a lavatory.

On the surface, Greene's *Ministry of Fear* seems no more than
a good spy story, and undoubtedly it is the finest of his tales of violence. Yet there is further significance to Arthur Rowe's adventures
with the Mothers of the Free Nations. The story is an ingenious
parable on the nature of Love; in it Greene picks up the threads
from his earlier views and follows them not into darkness but forward to new interpretations. He weaves together God's love and
man's, and love and hate. Much of Rowe's fairy-tale adventure even
resembles Greene's own career: a return to childhood innocence, a
period of artificial adolescence, and a violent act that propels him
to the threshold of true maturity.[3]

3. Rowe's development parallels Greene's Roman Catholic baptism (a
journey "so far back as innocence," *JM*, p. 116), explorations of African innocence, Mexican adolescence, and wartime adult suffering. At the sanitarium,
Rowe attempts to "catch the hints," a phrase echoing Greene's search for hints
in Africa. The story also includes appropriate references to "the Freudian censor" and to the connection between experience and dream: all these are reminiscent of Greene's accounts of his own psychoanalysis, his "Analysis of a Journey," and his reasons for going to Africa. Rowe even shares many minor
memories with his creator. Details of Rowe's life that might have been drawn
from Greene's autobiographical allusions include references to his favorite books,
an interest in lepers (Greene's use of lepers is discussd below, Ch. 7n12), dancing lessons like those described in "The Innocent," and a donkey who carried
the family laundry (see "The Cinema," *Spectator*, April 14, 1939).

Rowe's confused sense of pity had led him, before the story opens, to murder his suffering wife. His "justification" is left ambiguous—we cannot judge whether Rowe truly wished to spare her pain or whether he could not bear his own. But such confusion of motives and actions is normal in our false concept of "adult" behavior. Greene tells us that "the law had taken a merciful view [of Rowe's crime]; himself he took the merciless one. Perhaps if they had hanged him he would have found excuses for himself between the trapdoor and the ground" (p. 54). With this satirical restatement of Pinkie's lines on mercy ("Between the stirrup and the ground . . ."), Greene repeats an earlier theme: faced with man's perverted "justice," Rowe might still receive God's mercy.

Certainly Rowe's is not a clear case of self-pity, although many critics have incorrectly judged his disease to be the prototype of Scobie's. The reader's view must be qualified by Rowe's memory of a "pitying" judge, jury, and spectators—all of whom looked upon his action as a "mercy" killing. Again, Greene suggests the distance between man's mercy and God's; he is making his usual careful distinction between the Love of God, which passes all understanding, and the love of man, which is often both incomprehensible and deficient. The view of "mercy" killing also foreshadows Sarah's view of God's mercy looking like punishment (*EA*, p. 178), and recalls the priest's comment in *Brighton Rock*: "You can't conceive, my child, nor can I or anyone—the . . . appalling . . . strangeness of the mercy of God" (p. 331).

In addition to his subtleties of feeling, Rowe experiences a literally "dangerous" pity. This emotion traps him into a situation with a bomb-carrying bird fancier, an insane general, and a charming refugee. Although it seems an unavoidable aspect of adult existence (Mr. Prentice comments, "Adolescents don't pity. It's a mature passion," p. 135), pity is actually "the worst passion" of all.

It is worth following Rowe's journey in detail, as we earlier followed Greene's, in order to identify the clues by which we may see Greene's work, his map of life, whole. The bazaar at the opening of *The Ministry of Fear* is "entangled in childhood" and calls Rowe "like innocence"; it is soon revealed as the world of childhood darkness that Greene has so often described. Feeling himself both an intruder and an exile, Rowe pays his shilling admission "joyfully," with a child's excitement; he finds himself in the forgotten world of dreams and romantic distortion. The childhood that Rowe discovers is as terrifying as the childhood of Greene's dreams and memories and as filled with unexplained incidents as the racial childhood of Liberia. Hints of magic are ironically fulfilled: Rowe's "fairy-tale" wish that he could mislay the events of the past twenty years becomes a fear-filled reality. Stumbling through a "magic" door in the fortune-teller's tent, and speaking the magic words that guard the secret to the treasure (the cake containing stolen secret plans), Rowe finds that the world takes "a strange turn, away from innocence."

Through a further series of adventures, the suffering Rowe becomes transformed into "Digby," enjoying the false childhood of lost memory. Before this amnesia, Rowe has already known the sensation of being "in a strange country with no maps," i.e., of being confused in our world of betrayal and death. He has been scarred by a bomb; the scar marks him for salvation while serving as his passport to the artificial childhood of Dr. Forester's sanitarium. Here, Digby-Rowe seeks to discover the "point of failure" as Greene had done in Africa. (Rowe-Digby uses the phrase in discussing a news story that describes the theft of secret plans; he does not realize that this is the "mystery" at the heart of his own self-knowledge, as it is also the mystery at the heart of this spy story.) He finds himself surrounded by a garden in which there is a lavatory "like a potting shed" (p. 95). But this garden is not Eden. The shed lacks the theological implications of the one in Greene's play.

Since *The Ministry of Fear* is an entertainment, Greene does no more than hint at religious meaning in the innocent garden, the apple trees, the magic island, the flowers. The sick bay over the garden wall has "no more reality than the conception of Hell presented by sympathetic theologians—a place without inhabitants which existed simply as a warning" (p. 97). But Greene artfully suggests larger meanings. Rowe's paradise is flawed, in terms reminiscent of the finca on Greene's Mexican journey. Entitling the section "The Happy Man: Conversations in Arcady," Greene shows that no one can maintain such happiness in today's world. Hitler

and Mussolini and the betrayals of Willi Hilfe's spy ring gradually
intrude on romantic innocence, eventually forcing "Digby" back into
Rowe's life of action and participation. Greene uses Rowe's reawakening in the insane asylum as another "double" map: it simultaneously comments on the larger insanities of the 1940s and plots
an individual path to maturity.

Even the "blind passionate innocence" of an adolescent in love
does not save Rowe from being "driven relentlessly towards inevitable suffering, loss, and despair" (p. 101). Yet as he approaches
this maturity by way of the adolescent's awakening sense of cruelty,
Rowe gets a new perspective on the fragments of life. Instead of
seeing through the eyes of a youthful adventurer, or a boy reading
The Book of Golden Deeds or *The Little Duke* (a world in which
there are no unhappy endings and no one is "disturbed by a sense
of pity for the beaten side"), Rowe drives back toward the asylum
along a road that is bordered "like the coloured fringe along the unexplored spaces of a map." He awakens to the "real" world, much
as Greene had reawakened to it in Africa:

> Over there among the unknown tribes a woman was giving
> birth, rats were nosing among sacks of meal, an old man was
> dying, two people were seeing each other for the first time by
> the light of a lamp: everything in that darkness was of such
> deep importance that their errand could not equal it—this
> violent superficial chase, this cardboard adventure hurtling at
> forty-five miles an hour along the edge of the profound natural
> common experiences of men. Rowe felt a longing to get back
> into that world . . . the longing was like the first stirring of
> maturity (p. 140).

Without the religious orientation of the previous novel or the specifically religious choice demanded of Scobie in the next, Greene
here succeeds in pointing the way toward adult "wholeness."

Rowe's longing had included a desire for the world of "homes
and children and quiet love and the ordinary unspecified fears and
anxieties the neighbour shared" (p. 140). Greene's next novel
examines the inevitable problems of such a world. *The Ministry of
Fear* ends on a characteristic note; its closing words might well
serve as epigraph for its successor, *The Heart of the Matter*: "Like

a piece of a jigsaw puzzle which clicks into place and makes sense of a whole confusing block, that stolid figure took up its place in his memory" (p. 132). In the entertainment, the stolid figure is Rowe, so many of whose failings and problems specifically foreshadow Scobie's even as they make sense of "the whole confusing block" of Greene's previous artistic experience.

Scobie's failing trust in Ali recalls the effect of the Ministry of Fear: the Ministry makes "you feel you can't depend on a soul" (p. 93). Arthur's primitive sense of justice is at the heart of Scobie's error. Scobie shares the terrible poignancy and sense of loss suggested in Rowe's feeling: "like a man in mortal sin [watching] other people receive the sacrament . . . [he was] abandoned" (p. 120). But whereas Rowe had echoed Rose's position in *Brighton Rock,* believing that it was right to "suffer damnation with [people you loved] rather than be saved alone" (p. 103), Scobie reverses the terms. For Scobie, it is right to suffer damnation alone for the people you love rather than to suffer with them. Scobie loses his Paradise because he commits the sins of the rebellious angels: Pride and Disobedience.

At the opening of *The Heart of the Matter,* Scobie is revealed as an honest and just man, but one ignorant of love. As Greene delineates the love Scobie feels for the natives (based on a "desire" for their "trust and affection," p. 13), for Louise, for Helen, for every vulnerable person he meets, we see Scobie exposed as a man who has confused his own sense of pity with God's love and mercy: "The word 'pity' is used as loosely as the word 'love': the terrible promiscuous passion which so few experience" (p. 189). In his wish to ensure the "happiness" of those he pities or loves, Scobie is even forgetting the admonition contained in his Missal: the happiness must be given not in terms of the five senses but through gifts to "satisfy the immortal soul."

Clearly Scobie's judgment is at fault. Trying always to do what is "right," as befits the just man, Scobie continually chooses wrong routes because he suffers from a false pride in his own intellect, because his love of God is as distorted as his pity for men. Scobie's false pride is in part symbolized by the map he has given to younger men, wrongly assuming that he "carried the whole coastline of the colony in his mind's eye" and that he had "no more use" for the map (p. 7). The broken rosary in his drawer is a subsidiary symbol, a hint of the direction in which Scobie should be turning for help and understanding. This rosary literally marks Scobie's broken "love" for his servant; it is a symbol of his broken faith with Ali. It is also a symbolic suggestion of the breach in Scobie's love for God.

Greene himself has asserted that Scobie's final cry ("Dear God, I love . . .") is purposely ambiguous because Scobie himself is uncertain. He has also suggested, "At the moment of death even an expression of sexual love comes within the borders of charity. . . . It is love pure and simple."[4] This very uncertainty is surely the real tragedy of Scobie's existence: at the moment of death he is still unable to distinguish between Divine and human love. Earlier, he had written to Helen, "I love you . . . more than God I think" (p. 215). He had been unable to yield his own theories to the discipline of his Church. Instead of turning to God for love and mercy, he continually tried to assume that role for himself, feeling the responsibility of a Father and mistaking his own puny sense of pity for the Mercy of God's Love.

Scobie fails to learn the lesson suggested by Rowe's analysis: "One can't love humanity. One can only love people" (p. 145). Scobie responds to people as though he were the Divine parent, indiscriminately identifying as children Pemberton, with his "spots of puberty"; Helen, with her memories of school and her child's body; Wilson, with his apparently "defenceless" and "plump boyish" face; and Louise, whom Scobie would like to warn "as a mother might teach a daughter" (p. 29). Wrongly, Scobie assumes that he is responsible for maintaining happiness in those he loves (p. 20); he believes himself unique, the only one who recognizes the "weight" of misery at the temporary hospital, for instance. Repeatedly he is overwhelmed by a terrible impotent feeling of "pity and responsibility"; but his pity is an automatic response to the supposed immaturity of those he encounters. He does not really see "people"—

4. In "Lettre de Graham Greene." Pointing out the fault of the way the words had appeared in the French translation of *The Heart of the Matter,* Greene said, "My own intention was to make it completely vague as to whether [Scobie] was expressing his love for the two women or his love for God. My own feeling about this character is that he was uncertain himself."

individual human beings—but "humanity." Scobie almost seems to betray false and sentimental responses; his automatic pity is lacking in discrimination.

"Corrupted by sentiment" (p. 60), Scobie is bound to Louise by the "pathos" of her unattractiveness (p. 23). Louise may appear romantic in her choice of reading, and Scobie may seem a realist who rejects poetry in favor of life. Nevertheless, Scobie is often trapped by sentimentality, i.e., by the Hollywood version of life that bears no relation to life as it really is.[5] Scobie's first error, according to Greene,[6] is his behavior during the episode of the captain's letter. Scobie fails to confiscate and report the captain's concealed letter to his daughter (his "little money spider"). This breach of duty results from Scobie's distorted view of the Portuguese captain as "an unattractive child, the fat boy of the school" (p. 53). The pity that "smouldered like decay" at Scobie's heart (p. 211) is a terrible corruption, much worse than the petty bribery of "corrupt" minor policemen. Again Scobie's error comes from his original fault, the substitution of man's flawed compassion for God's divine mercy.

Scobie further presumes to know God's will, to evaluate in terms of his world the application of God's justice. He is convinced that "there must be mercy for someone so unformed" as Pemberton (p. 98), or that "against all the teachings of the Church, one has the conviction that love—any kind of love—does deserve a bit of mercy" (p. 252). In this substitution of his own false reasons for true faith, Scobie is not sharing the views of the priests in *Brighton Rock, The Heart of the Matter,* or even *The End of the Affair* concerning the ultimate mystery of God's will. He is merely forcing God's infinite goodness into the confining mold of his own desire to

5. This is Greene's continual complaint against Hollywood films and "popular" fiction. In "Fiction," *Spectator,* June 1, 1934, Greene referred to "the Baser Passions—I mean sentimentality and self-pity." Similarly, "Self-pity is one of the chief pleasures in sentimentality"—"Fiction," *Spectator,* October 20, 1933. Scobie's universal "pity" is suspect.

6. Greene said, "La première faille dans l'intégrité de Scobie, c'est à mon avis, la faute professionelle qu'il commet comme officier de police à propos de la lettre du capitain portugais" ("Propos de table," p. 129). Throughout Greene's fiction there are many characters variously "snared" and endangered by pity.

do good. He makes similar errors in claiming "even God is a failure" (p. 309), and in confusing the images of Ali and God as he looks down and sees his murdered servant as part of the broken rosary: "I've killed you" (p. 302).

A Catholic seeing God as a "failure" or identifying the beloved servant Ali with God is hopelessly ensnared by his own dialectic of pride. Perverting the Catholic view of Christ as Victim, Scobie forgets the reasons for Christ's sacrifice. He tries to express the "Mystery of God's love upon the Cross" in hopelessly literal terms. The Mystery that Greene had perceived in Mexico has become for Scobie a very muddled attempt to solve the insoluble equation.[7] Finding it impossible to "love God at the expense of one of his creatures" (p. 223), daring to assert that he "loved" God but never trusted Him (pp. 316–17), Scobie continually dwells on the injury that he does to God. In his false pride, Scobie turns away from the mercy of Christ's restitution.

"The hint of an explanation" of this mystery is "too faint to be grasped," although a clue lies in the officer's account of the little girl's forty-day ordeal in an open boat: "Of course they looked after her on the boat. They gave up their own share of the water often. It was foolish, of course, but one cannot always be logical. And it gave them something to think about" (p. 137). This account is as close as we can approach to answering the question Scobie ponders —"the mystery, to reconcile that [ordeal] with the love of God."

7. Later, Bendrix was to demand a God "simple as an equation," but Scobie is quite sure that he has "known the answers all the time" (p. 315). Scobie's self-confidence is a form of spiritual pride: he falsely convicts himself of being "the only guilty one," instead of submitting himself to God's judgment. Holding a dialogue with God, Scobie dismisses the consolation of God's words ("If you live you will come back to me sooner or later," p. 316); he can only answer, "I love you, but I've never trusted you. If you made me, you made this feeling of responsibility that I've always carried about like a sack of bricks. I'm not a policeman for nothing. . . . I can't shift my responsibility to you" (pp. 316–17). As a Catholic convert, Scobie should have been more correctly instructed. He has forgotten the text stating that God is "The Father of the Just" (Prov. 23); he appears to read only literally the Mass prayers of thanks for "the pure Victim, the holy Victim, the all-perfect Victim." He has forgotten the Sinners' Remembrance—a prayer for sinners "trusting in the greatness of Thy mercy." And in placing his role as policeman ahead of his role as Catholic, Scobie has most certainly forgotten his Catechism: "I believe that the chief purpose of my life is to give *glory to God* and to *save my immortal soul.*"

Scobie reveals his faulty reasoning in concluding that "if one reached what they called the heart of the matter," one might have to feel pity even for the planets (p. 141). This rather quaint anthropomorphism scarcely accords with Catholic tradition and is a flat contradiction of all Greene's own writing.[8]

Nevertheless, according to Greene's own statement, Scobie retains at least a hope of Purgatory. He "watch[es] God bleed" (p. 289) and enjoys the hope implicit in Pascal's words, later quoted by the Superior of A Burnt-Out Case: "A man who starts looking for God has already found him" (BC, p. 255). In contrast, Wilson only "pretends" to look at the map; he is the entirely self-absorbed man, feeling his own veins open instead of meditating on Christ's. He had not expected "a country so strange" (p. 90) as the one in which he finds himself. His responses to the actuality of a country he had only conceived romantically are always those of an adolescent. His love is little more than a literary pretense in which his feelings for Louise are an extension of his enthusiasm for poetry,[9] and bear no relation to a larger Love.

Scobie's kind of love is not necessarily "better" than Wilson's; the difference is one of values, comparable to the difference be-

---

8. In "The Hint of an Explanation" (1948), Greene tells of Blacker's attempt to steal the consecrated wafer and desecrate it. This short story might well serve as a footnote to The Heart of the Matter: to Scobie's description of the Black Mass ("striking God when he's down—in my power," p. 253) and his sensations at Mass with Louise, when "the words of the Mass were like an indictment" and he visualized ruined priests presiding at a Black Mass, "performing the act of damnation with an emotion larger than human love." On that occasion, Scobie felt that he was desecrating God because he loved a woman (pp. 269–70). The truth at the heart of the matter is God's; the only true pity is God's pity for sinful man. Man cannot presume to feel pity either for God's creatures or his creation (e.g., the planets).

9. In his adolescent romanticism, Wilson resembles Arthur Rowe and Alden Pyle. He is also one of Greene's many victims of lost childhood; he had been "condemned in childhood to complexity" (p. 199). When Wilson feels melancholy lust for a young native girl and hatred for those who have brought him to the brothel, when he recalls schooldays during which he had felt that he was on the outside of doors, Wilson is clearly another example of Greene's civilized man, one who is perpetually poised on the border between childhood and adolescence, unable to move along the dusty way to adulthood. He is moreover quite unaware of that further step, the leap from maturity to God. The only time that Wilson ever really feels "inside" he does so in a tragically ironic sense—the brothel seems like a vault in which "his dead veins would bleed again" (p. 209).

tween Rose's sense of good and evil and Ida's sense of right and wrong. Scobie's world gains importance from the Divine context. Unfortunately, Scobie's assertions—"I am going to damn myself" (p. 315) and the earlier "I am the responsible man" (p. 270)—are not evidence of his good judgment or of his moral strength but of his false logic. Powerless to convey the importance of any entry in his diary (p. 129), so also he is powerless to judge the relative values of the events recorded. Whether he is judging God as too "accessible" (p. 181) or the happy man as an example of "egotism, selfishness, evil—or else an absolute ignorance" (p. 141), Scobie is caught up in logical and semantic errors. He is unaware that in his own case God is proving remarkably inaccessible. He is forgetting that happiness can be a positive and unselfish state rather than the sort of "ultimate border . . . [of] happiness" he experienced once in his own life—a total vacancy more like Purgatory, "in darkness, alone, with the rain falling, without love or pity" (p. 156). Scobie's conviction that "only the man of goodwill carries always in his heart [this] capacity for damnation" (p. 67) is no more to be regarded as the heart of the matter than his conviction that he himself is "unpitiable" (p. 211).

Scobie's alleged entrance to Purgatory is presumably God's merciful response to his dying desire for Love. Suicide is more commonly regarded as a sure doorway to Hell. In his examination of suicide, however, Scobie reveals that his action is the result of error rather than of the sins against hope (despair and presumption).[10] He has falsely identified his own name Ticki with that of young Dickie Pemberton, the pimply faced adolescent suicide. Scobie's question "Was it more impossible for [God] to put out a hand of forgiveness into the suicidal darkness and chaos than to have woken himself in the tomb, behind the stone" (p. 227) is scarcely acceptable Catholic argument. When he asserts that Christ had hung himself on the Cross as surely as Pemberton had hung himself from the picture rail, Scobie is speaking on the ignorant level of Raven,

10. Here, interpretation depends on an understanding of Catholic doctrine. Sins against hope are related to loss of faith and are thus more serious than they might appear to a layman or non-Catholic. Presumption ("expecting to attain eternal happiness by one's own unaided efforts") is closely allied to Scobie's particular sin of pride.

whose "Christian" training at his "home" had resulted in similarly false logic.

In final analysis of the action of *The Heart of the Matter,* we must bear in mind the assumptions underlying Greene's remark about Scobie's Purgatorial destiny. In Scobie's final gesture Greene is exposing the self-deceptions inherent in the clichés of thought that so often masquerade behind the term "love." At one point, Scobie identifies love as "the wish to understand" (p. 308); here he is on the correct path, expressing through Greene's map metaphor every man's as well as the artist's quest for truth. He also speaks of "the intense interest . . . in a stranger's life . . . that the young mistake for love" (p. 160); here he shows an adult's proper perception. But when Scobie thinks, "Here you could love human beings nearly as God loved them, knowing the worst" (p. 34), he reveals in the clearest possible terms that he is a lost traveler. In neither God's way nor man's does he "know the way about."

Greene's description of Arthur Rowe suggests one way of knowing Scobie's difficulty: Rowe "hadn't the hard strength of mind to walk away and leave the little man to drag his own burden" (p. 73). Scobie failed to avoid such error, although experience had supposedly taught him "that no human being can really understand another, and no one can arrange another's happiness" (p. 93). We might be tempted to go back to the novel preceding *The Ministry of Fear* and falsely identify Scobie with the whisky priest. Each does his duty; each is uncertain in his relation to God; each is moved by pity (although the priest is more properly compassionate, as a part of his religious duty); each makes small gestures of charity while apparently committing larger sins. Scobie even offers his hat to the betrayer Wilson, as the priest had offered his shirt to the mestizo; and Wilson's look of hatred for the man who has seen his weakness and whom he plans to betray bears a superficial resemblance to the resentment that lies behind the Judas-mestizo's assertion that he is "a good Christian."

There is, however, an important difference between Scobie's all-encompassing pity and the priest's often reluctant affection. The priest exaggerates his spiritual limitations; Scobie underestimates his. The priest in his humility is already on the road to Heaven;

Scobie in his pride must inevitably suffer in Purgatory. Moreover, the priest at his consecration had been spiritually chained to God and to His people, while Scobie had only been "handcuffed" by false pity and an exaggerated view of man's ability to judge independently of God. The priest could extend the strength of God to the man dragging his burden; Scobie supposed his own strength equal and even superior to God's.

Even at the end Scobie believes himself damned for all eternity "unless a miracle happens," quite forgetting the power of God's mercy. His salvation requires not a miracle but a word of repentance. Greene offers a hint of that word in Scobie's "Dear God, I love . . ."—the words by which Scobie may escape eternal damnation. In his next novel, Greene was to offer several miracles and to suggest a variety of paths to salvation. *The End of the Affair* rejects the adolescent and father-child confusions of *The Heart of the Matter*. Its subject is the true "heart of things": the Mystery of God's love turning man's footsteps away from human lust and toward the Divine Passion.

The End of the Affair (1951) includes the polarities of physical lust and metaphysical Love, but it begins as a story of human hate. The terrible resemblance between love and hate has been a continuing theme in Greene's work.[11] It is stated most explicitly by Bendrix: "Hatred seems to operate the same glands as love: it even produces the same actions." Strangely, for a man who is so deliberately refusing to acknowledge the Person of God, Bendrix adds: "If we had not been taught how to interpret the story of the Passion, would we have been able to say from their actions alone whether it was the jealous Judas or the cowardly Peter who loved Christ?" (p. 27). Bendrix finds in hatred a resemblance to physical

---

11. In *It's a Battlefield*, for instance, Milly had told Conrad, "Hating doesn't get you anywhere, any more than loving does. A bed in a hospital, that's about where both get you" (p. 134). She had not been close enough to life to see "the confusing details . . . [showing] that one loved and hated for the same reasons" (p. 116). In "The Lottery Ticket" (1938), Greene wrote: "The action dictated by hate was like an action of love" (*19S*, p. 138). Similarly in *The Power and the Glory*: "We wouldn't recognize *that* love. It might even look like hate" (p. 259). Even in *A Burnt-Out Case*, Dr. Colin asserts: "Love is planted in man now, even uselessly in some cases, like an appendix. Sometimes of course people call it hate" (p. 160).

love ("its crisis and then its periods of calm," p. 70); he wonders whether his hatred is really as deficient as his love (p. 64). Gradually he comes to recognize that his "hatred" for Sarah is really fear —fear of the leap to God. He sees that if Sarah loves God and God exists, then by hating Sarah he is admitting the existence of the object of her love, and that God indeed exists. Bendrix cries to God, "I hate You as though You existed" (p. 236); finally he acknowledges the existence of God with the direct plea "I'm too tired and old to learn to love, leave me alone forever" (p. 237).

Sarah had been aware of the problem. In her diary she asked, "Would I have hated [Maurice] if I hadn't loved him too?" (p. 133). She was sure that Maurice thought he hated, but, "He thinks he hates, and loves, loves all the time. Even his enemies" (p. 120). This love may be imperfect. Yet it is never the pitying love experienced by Scobie; it is closer to true Christian compassion because it is more often founded on understanding, a compassionate awareness of Parkis, or an ability to comprehend the nature of the relationship between Sarah and Henry. Only rarely is there a trace of the earlier novel's "pity" in Bendrix' story. For instance, in responding to Sarah's last request ("Just go away. . . . Have a bit of mercy"), Bendrix concludes, "One gets to the end of badgering and contriving: I couldn't go on, with that appeal in my ears. I kissed her on the tough and knotty hair and, coming away, I found her lips, smudgy and salt, on the corner of my mouth" (p. 158). This deep and real perception is very different from the sentimental responses of Scobie's pitying regard for Louise.

When Bendrix responds gently to Sarah's coughing as to "a small animal cornered" (p. 35), he recognizes love itself as being like "a small creature caught in a trap and bleeding to death" (p. 37); but his response is a recognition that he must shut his eyes and "wring its neck"—there is none of the romantic coloring found in Arthur Rowe's destruction of the rat or of his wife. Bendrix also perceives Henry as "one of misery's graduates," a "fellow stranger" (p. 10). More often, however, Bendrix feels openly angry instead of indulging in adolescent dream-deception.

It is this quality of anger that marks Bendrix' advance over the previous confused lovers in Greene's work. The end of his feeling of anger marks his recognition of God's love. Bendrix of course has been walking toward God throughout his narrative, although apparently unaware of his direction, or else deliberately resisting. At first, he reflects: "They say a God made us; but I find it hard to conceive of any God who is not as simple as a perfect equation, as clear as air" (p. 6). Later, after he reads Sarah's diary, Bendrix behaves toward God as toward a rival, yet he refuses to express the hatred he feels for this rival, recognizing that such hatred would constitute belief. Eventually, Bendrix does acknowledge the "person" of God: God is "as underhand as a lover . . . like a hero seducing us with his improbabilities and his legends" (p. 213). He is reluctant to accept the evidence of Sarah's intervention after her death, however; if he starts believing that she has answered his prayer to save the girl at the crematorium from him, then Bendrix has to believe in her God and even love Him, but "I'd rather love the men you slept with" (p. 224).

Such comparisons between the lusts of the flesh and the love of the spirit are typical of Bendrix' attitude. Through these comparisons Greene extends his theme of the narrow boundary between hate and love and between man's everyday life and eternity. Bendrix, however, reverses the usual terminology. He writes: "The words of human love have been used by the saints to describe their vision of God; and so, I suppose, we might use the terms of prayer, meditation, contemplation to explain the intensity of the love we feel for a woman" (p. 52). Reflecting that anyone who loves must be jealous, Bendrix also finds that love and fear act like conscience, and "If we had believed in sin, our behaviour would hardly have differed" (p. 63).

But *The End of the Affair* is not a tract on sin. It is Greene's finest treatment of human love, an emotion that can "happen" over a dish of onions, that can be "caught" like a disease, that includes both Henry's winning cards of "gentleness, humility, and trust" (p. 26) and Bendrix' losing passion. There is no trace of Scobie's false identification of Helen or Louise as his "child" for whom he must be responsible. Instead, we have on the one hand Henry's "possession" of Sarah's "presence at the table, the sound of her feet on the stairs, the opening and closing of doors, the kiss on the cheek" (p. 46);

and on the other, Sarah and Bendrix making love on the floor, while Henry is sick in bed upstairs, or snatching a kiss in the street, or quarreling with a hopeless anticipation of inevitable loss. Earlier, Greene had described as "the hardest thing in the world" the task that he sets himself in *The End of the Affair*: "To describe understanding, to express without sentimentality the degree of tenderness possible in human relationships."[12] A reader unconvinced that this is a "tender" story would do well to reconsider the passages on Henry's affection, on Sarah's love, and on that terrible sense of loss experienced in Bendrix' "hatred."

Comparison with his earlier heroes will make the advance in Greene's ability to characterize more clear. In *The Man Within*, Andrews made an oversimplified choice between candle-lit "saint" and a lusty wench whom he imagined in "disgusting poses." For the immature Anthony Farrant of *England Made Me*, love was "a good time, love was Annette, was Mabel," and he was surprised that love could include the "inconvenience" of shared pain (p. 98). His concept of love was no better than Hall's "pained possessive love" for Krogh (p. 218)—a love that he expressed by giving Krogh gaudy cuff links or by using knuckle-dusters to "protect" him. Phil in "The Basement Room" discovered as a child that when you loved "you got involved" and for the rest of his life deliberately "extricated" himself from love. To D, willingness to love seemed like "treachery." Pinkie's passion consisted of an affection for vitriol and razor blades; his faint stirrings of tenderness could not overcome his rigid hostility. Even the whisky priest's love strayed from the charity proper to his priesthood and into his "sinful" love for a daughter he should not have fathered. At their least tender moments, Bendrix and Sarah are clearly an improvement over such earlier lovers as these and the oddly gymnastic Jules and Kay in *It's a Battlefield*.

Much more significant is the inseparability of flesh and spirit in *The End of the Affair*. The fine taste of Sarah upon Bendrix' tongue is as much a part of the love of God as the taste of God's body at Communion. Greene is not at any time using Bendrix and Sarah as examples of "profane" love leading to "finer" or to "greater" love. He is only following the labyrinthine ways of *The Power and the Glory*:

12. "Fiction," *Spectator,* June 16, 1933.

"[Love] is only wrong when it is secret, unhappy. . . . It can be more unhappy than anything but the loss of God. It *is* the loss of God. . . . 'Lust is not the worst thing. It is because any day, any time lust may turn into love that we have to avoid it. And when we love our sin then we are damned indeed' " (*PG*, pp. 221–22). But Sarah and Bendrix do not love their sin; Sarah finds herself loving God, and Bendrix acknowledges His existence.

Sarah's diary helps us reach this interpretation of the end of the affair by revealing some of the inadequacies and inaccuracies of Bendrix' view. Seeing Sarah through his own prejudices, Bendrix had assumed that she cared only for the moment, that "her abandonment touched that strange mathematical point of endlessness" (p. 57). He was sure that she was "unhaunted by guilt," that she had no doubts, that she shared with him in excluding God from their world. Yet Sarah's diary reveals that even at this time she too was afraid of the "desert" of love's ending (p. 107), and that she was already speculating about God's love. At the level of everyday experience she knew that she was doing to Bendrix "exactly what he is doing to me" (p. 108), and she wondered if she was "a bitch and a fake" (p. 112). But she was also a woman who could keep to the promise in her prayer, "I'll give him up for ever, only let him be alive with a chance . . ." (p. 113), who could pray for the cessation of human love, and who could foresee even in her own distress that Bendrix was on God's side all the time without knowing it (p. 147).

Bendrix believed that he knew "the whole absurd story" of Sarah's vow after he had seen her diary, and that he was now assured of her because "if two people loved, they slept together; it was a mathematical formula, tested and proved by human experience" (p. 154). Ultimately he had to admit uncertainty, in his last view of Sarah in the Church, where he could imagine God blessing her or God loving her, and concluded, "When I began to write our story down, I thought I was writing a record of hate, but somehow the hate has got mislaid and all I know is that in spite of her mistakes and her unreliability, she was better than most" (p. 158).

Actually, neither Bendrix nor Sarah could know the "whole" story, which is reserved for Divine knowledge. At the most literal level, both are ignorant of vital acts, such as Sarah's Catholic baptism, and of the range of God's power. Each makes errors of evaluation, assuming that they are "back in the territory of trust." Yet they are unable to demonstrate this trust; each continually demands an understanding beyond the other's range of knowledge.

Neither of them can escape from the most important of the missing parts of their puzzle: that Sarah *is* a Catholic. Mrs. Bertram's wish that Sarah's baptism would "take" like vaccination is reminiscent of Pinkie's thought ("perhaps the holy water didn't take"). But Sarah's "lost" childhood has brought her to love of God, through conscious lust for men and unconscious love for Man. Mother Bertram is clearly not a "good" Catholic; she has more in common with Ida Arnold and the Ouija board. There is, however, a redeeming and appropriate irony: in using Sarah's baptism as "revenge" on her husband, she has given her daughter to God.

There is no weakness, artistic or theological, in making Sarah a saint. Her special gift is reflected in some of Bendrix' comments. He observes Sarah's "way of touching people with her hands, as though she loved them" (p. 25); later, her touch brings relief to Parkis' boy and to the unfortunate Smythe. Bendrix ironically calls Sarah a "born Catholic" because he believes that she is unhaunted by guilt and that her "remorse died with the act"; he compares her attitude with the Roman Catholic confessional—freeing the sinner from the mortmain of the past (p. 56). In reality, she has been as permanently marked with the sign of God as Smythe had seemed to be marked by Christ's pain.

The specifically Catholic aspects of the affair, especially the disappearance of Smythe's mark,[13] often make the novel unnecessarily disappointing for the Protestant reader, who might declare the miracle ("that foolish newspaper word that was the alternative to 'coincidence,'" p. 233) a minor flaw that should be quickly forgotten in favor of the rest of the story. But Greene is not making

13. The "cure" of Smythe should not be oversimplified into a statement on the defeat of rationalism by Catholicism. Certainly Smythe's definition of love is an example of the inadequacy of rationalism; he regards love as "the desire to possess in some, like avarice: in others the desire to surrender, to lose the sense of responsibility, the wish to be admired. Sometimes just the wish to be able to talk, to unburden yourself to someone who won't be bored. The desire to find again a father or a mother. And of course under it all the biological motive" (p. 127).

his reader's task "difficult"; the ending is appropriate to his whole view of Love. We might put it in oversimplified terms: God must give Bendrix his proofs. If the proofs verge on the sensational, they are still appropriate to the context. We might even say that God has selected his proofs with the hand of a truly creative artist, the very literary quality of the miracles making them particularly appropriate for the writer Bendrix. Bendrix has demanded a God as simple as an equation, and the miracle is remarkably close to serving as a mathematical sign.[14]

The miracles of *The End of the Affair* serve as appropriate proof for the literal and literary man Bendrix, who has rejected any God who is not as simple as an equation. In contrast, the miracle of *The Potting Shed* (1957) is only a very tenuous sign—perhaps not a miracle at all. Perhaps the boy has been restored to life by God's will and his uncle's desperate prayer; perhaps the gardener had misread the signs of death. But whatever the answer to this particular mystery, it cannot be determined without considering Greene's first dramatic "map"—*The Living Room* (1953)—in which the very limited territory is confusingly labeled with contradictory signs.

In *The Living Room* the signs of life and death are deliberately juxtaposed, and the signs of love are even more misleading than in *The End of the Affair*. Specific echoes of the novel's descriptions of love include Rose's discovery that "love isn't all making love" and her declaration that she would be willing to give that up in order to be together at meals, to come into a house where Michael is, to "sit silent with a book in the same room" (p. 101). Her discovery, however, lacks the significance of Bendrix' "envy" of Henry. Her relationship with Michael is too neatly formulated as a problem in the simultaneous failure of pious Catholicism and pat psychology.

Rose's two Catholic aunts, new versions of Greene's omnipresent pious women, offer fear instead of love. Their brother points out that offering Rose love instead of fear might have prevented her turning to Michael (p. 91); perhaps they would also have prevented Rose's death in the last uncontaminated living room. Even

14. According to George D. Smith, ed., *The Teachings of the Catholic Church,* the miracle is a sign of Divine Power and an appeal to man's intelligence. The Vatican Council has described miracles as "most certain signs of divine revelation, and suitable to the intelligence of all" (p. 13).

in this world of failing love, however, some good emerges. Rose's death restores the weak Teresa to a newly active and independent life, it allays Teresa's fears of death, and it removes from power that busybody Helen, a presumptuous woman sure that she could "[take] care of things."

The key to *The Living Room* lies in brother James, for it is in the recurrent figure of the "spoiled" or crippled priest that Greene often symbolizes the task of the writer.[15] James is tainted with piety; his tongue is "heavy with the Penny Catechism" (p. 112). But he resembles the imperfect novelist in his tendency to be restricted by convention and in the hampering effect of his lack of imaginative insight. Nevertheless he presents the problem to Rose in its correct Catholic context, much as Greene himself poses questions in unfamiliar terms, using words and symbols that are often distasteful either to pious Catholics or to ignorant Protestants. Brother James regrets his own failure to provide Rose with spiritual consolation; but he has provided her with a kind of direction to follow through the confusing territory of religious and secular conflict.

Unfortunately, the play seems overburdened with the recurrent landmarks of Greene's maps. The theme of Faith appears as a simple tag: "The more our senses are revolted, uncertain, and in despair, the more surely Faith says: 'This is God: all goes well'" (p. 122). Aunt Teresa's recognition of the living room as "the room where Rose died" (p. 126) is too heavily ironical. Michael's child who died, his conversation about a "just God,"[16] and his rather pompous adultery are imperfect echoes of Scobie's suffering. Out of this unsatisfactory dramatization of his recurrent themes, however, Greene apparently selected a passage that opened upon the stage of *The Potting Shed*: in *The Living Room* he writes, "Death is our child, we have to go through pain to bear our death" (p. 123).

15. See Ch. 7n20. This does not mean that Greene has set up a simple equation in which crippled priest and imperfect writer are identical. But the spoiled priest and the popular novelist are alike in their failure to follow Truth, in their unfaithfulness to a vocation.

16. Michael speaks of "a just God . . . all-wise Judge"; James retorts, "God's exact . . . He's not a judge. An absolute knowledge of every factor. . . . That's why He's merciful" (p. 51), further echoing the priest's consolation of Scobie's widow as well as recalling Bendrix' demands for Divine precision.

Greene's second play was not performed until 1957, two years after publication of *The Quiet American.* Structurally and thematically, however, it belongs with the earlier maps of love and hate, life and death, rather than with the humorous works that followed Greene's novel of Indo-China.[17] Its setting is almost as limited as that of the first play, but Greene's dramatization of the struggle between spiritual and secular values is more convincing, the crippled priest a better representative of pastoral care, the characters less typed. This play opens in a living room also, but instead of being the symbol of dead Catholicism it is the center of a home in which "God was taboo" (p. 61). Instead of ending Rose's life in the living room, Greene restores James' in a nearby potting shed. The name James belongs not to the spiritually and physically crippled priest but to the psychologically crippled man.

This crippled man is also a spoiled writer. He had been working as a reporter on the *Globe* in Nottingham (p. 55); his landlady has a penchant for tinned salmon, which makes his dog sick (an echo of one of Greene's personal memories of reporting in Nottingham, recorded in *Journey without Maps*). James has quite literally lost his childhood, since the moment when Uncle Callifer prayed, "Take away my faith but let him live" (p. 94). With those words the priest brought God into the home where He was taboo and banished young James from his father's care; at the same time, the priest banished himself from the care of his spiritual Father. James follows threads back to the darkness of his past, to discover this mystery that has been hidden from him both by parents and by priest, repeating Greene's first journey to the heart of darkness and the psychological journey of Arthur Rowe. James too tries to gain understanding by exploring and recording the territory of love.

As *The Potting Shed* opens, James Callifer is about to return to his father's house. He wishes he could see "just love"—a condition in which there is "no claim, no hope, no want. Whisky taken neat" (p. 32). His words are reminiscent of Greene's comment on Scobie's death, quoted above, suggesting that any expression of love

17. One of Greene's earliest themes had been that of resurrection, or of the life after death. For instance, it was the theme of "The Second Death" (1929), "The End of the Party" (1929), "Proof Positive" (1930), as well as of "A Little Place Off the Edgware Road" (1939).

at the moment of death is "love pure and simple." James thinks
that he would see this pure love in his father, a man who is dying
and whose creed gives him "nothing to hope for any more, forever"
(p. 32). But the route to love is not so simple; James is denied his
wish. Nor does he find love from his former wife, Sara, who tells him
that he is not alive and that he has never felt pain. Although Sara's
judgment is related to James' peculiar condition, the odd sort of
limbo that has followed upon his uncle's extraordinary prayer, the
reader is not quite convinced. In dramatic terms, the priest's prayer
for the restoration of his nephew's life seems rather forced ("Take
away my faith but let him live"). James' years of vacancy seem un-
justified; the priest's disintegration is not as convincing as the
whisky priest's.

Both James and Sara, unlike their predecessors Bendrix and
Sarah, seem very lightly attached to reality. Paradoxically, the miracles in the story of that convincing couple Sarah and Bendrix are
much easier to accept than the possible "miracle" of *The Potting
Shed*'s unreal world. The play's dubious miracle provides motiva-
tion, theme, and meaning. But it fails to provide any real clues for
reconstruction of the larger picture of love.

Nevertheless, this is the best of Greene's dramatic maps, a true
expression of the world in which "our footsteps make such a pattern
over the world in forty years, they'd have to tread the same path
again sooner or later" (p. 61). Greene's repetition of familiar characters and symbols may even be justified by the existence of this
"pattern." For the path runs directly from the potting shed of *The
Man Within* (a shed in which Greene set the first of his fictional
dreams) to the room in which Anne Callifer dreams of a lion that
"only" licked her hand. Yet the stage is too limited for Greene's picture of our uncivilized civilization. In a play, Greene's world of
imagination is falsely localized in a specific setting where symbolic
values often seem forced or intrusive.

Only as a setting for the mocking treatment of his serious
themes has the stage proved a really adequate medium for Greene.
His third play, *The Complaisant Lover*,[18] like the later *Carving a*

18. Greene's comical terrain is discussed in detail in Chapter 6. *The
Complaisant Lover* (1959) bridges the gap between Greene's amusing Alice-

Statue, is largely comic vision, and perhaps seemed an inadequate expression of Greene's continual concern with moral vision and artistic truth. Before following the thread of Greene's comic and absurd explorations, we must return to the journey on which he discovered new paths between man and God. That journey was a series of four visits to warring Indo-China. Its fictional version was *The Quiet American,* a view of corruption in terms of American "innocence."

---

in-Wonderland charts and the essentially serious map of Absurd existence, *A Burnt-Out Case. Carving a Statue* (1964) is another farcical drama, and one that Greene himself in "Epitaph for a Play" linked to *The Complaisant Lover* (describing it as "a game played with the same extremes of mood"). The play *Carving a Statue,* like Greene's short stories of the 1960s, must be read as part of his (farcical) vision of the human condition, leading to his ultimate jokes, *The Comedians* (1966) and *Travels with My Aunt* (1970)—works discussed in Chapter 8.

Chapter **5** THE PATTERN OF
INNOCENCE

G REENE MADE four journeys to Indo-China in order to assemble material for *The Quiet American*,[1] but most of
his reports from these trips are so scattered in various periodicals
that their importance to Greene's aesthetic exploration is not at first
glance very obvious. Many of the reports appear to be only routine
despatches from a practicing journalist, although two are subtitled
"Extract from an Indo-China Journal," and one other is labeled "An
Indo-China Journal," clearly to be classified with Greene's other
travel diaries. Political appraisals, social comment, religious insights,
and personal observations all find a place within the framework of
The Quiet American and reveal some of the stages by which
Greene reached the lighter touch that is evident in his subsequent
work.

1. Greene says that he made four visits of three months each between
March 1952 and June 1955 and that he could only "afford" these visits by acting as a correspondent (*SC*, pp. xiv, 55n1). Articles referred to in this chapter
include: "Before the Attack"; "A Few Pipes: Extract from an Indo-China Journal"; "The General and the Spy: Extract from an Indo-China Journal"; "Indo-
China"; "An Indo-China Journal"; "Last Act in Indo-China"; "To Hope Till
Hope Creates." Full information on these articles for the *Spectator, The London Magazine, The New Republic*, and *Commonweal* appear in the Bibliography. Greene also wrote for *Life*, the London *Times*, and *Figaro*.

Although the complete picture of *The Quiet American* is built out of fragments Greene discovered on his travels in Indo-China, it also represents his personal map of innocence. It is a commentary not on the old dark innocence of Africa but on the new bright innocence of American "civilization." Fowler says, "I never knew a man who had better motives for all the trouble he caused" (p. 72). These words might serve as epigraph for *The Quiet American* and epitaph for such American "aid" as Greene described in his despatches from Indo-China. Yet it seems clear from Fowler's commentary on Pyle that the apparent indictment of America might with equal justice be applied to Europe's failures.

It was inevitable that Greene should choose as sequel to his journeys in search of creative innocence and religious adolescence a search for today's representative adult. It was also inevitable that Greene should select the innocent American, Pyle. Alden Pyle is the quintessential American innocent abroad; he is also the quintessential European, bearing the whole burden of Anglo-Saxon failure, "its muddled morality and irrational sentiment."[2]

This is the fault Greene criticizes when he speaks of "idealism in the American manner" (*JM*, p. 7), although it is also the weakness of anyone who thinks in clichés. Once again, Greene's criticism is largely aesthetic, his comment on the deadening effects of complacency. In describing the "idealism" of the Firestone rubber plantation of Liberia, Greene had identified the fault: a condition that permits men to live in comfort themselves, assured of their own virtue, while exploiting others under the mistaken guise of kindness. Greene has never ignored British commercialism, or "the ugly smear the British middle class leave on their conquered lands,"[3] but he has always distinguished between colonialists "frankly out for money" and those cloaking their exploitation under the phrase "doing good."

Pyle belongs with the innocent exploiters, the harmful innocents, the complacent, and the pious. Like the conscience of a good-natured heathen (Ida Arnold, for instance) or the soul of a pious

---

2. "The Cinema," *Spectator*, June 10, 1938.

3. "Fiction," *Spectator*, June 1, 1934. Greene also wrote of the British Empire retiring from competition "with a full purse," in "The Cinema," *Spectator*, November 11, 1938.

Catholic, Pyle's heart is closed to the seed of knowledge. Instead of exploring conditions in Indo-China for himself, Pyle subscribes to a textbook ideology; his chromium-plated idealism armors him against the realities of Vietnamese existence. In his devotion to the volumes of York Harding (an "authority" on Indo-China who had been in the country "once for a week on his way from Bangkok to Tokyo," p. 218), Pyle is perhaps not as guilty as a pious Catholic blindly reading the Penny Catechism or Ida consulting the Ouija board. If Pyle is "too innocent to live," it is not entirely his fault; for "his writers and his lecturers made a fool of him" (p. 32).

Yet where does Pyle's innocence lead? According to the American attaché, Alden Pyle dies "a soldier's death" in the Cause of Democracy (p. 31). In reality, Pyle's "war service" has led only to the deaths of civilian women and children. As early as 1936 Greene had commented on "earnest American abstractions about Youth and Alma Mater and the Future . . . the vulgarity of the completely unreligious, of sentimental idealism, of pitch-pine ethics with the hollow optimism about human nature of a salesman who has never failed to sell his canned beans." Greene further declared, "Innocence in the American nature upsets the cart every time."[4]

These remarks might well have come from Fowler, but Greene and the narrator of *The Quiet American* are not identical.[5] Fowler's criticism of American culture, like Greene's, reflects a personal distaste for the glossy and falsely comfortable world in which "even their lavatories were air-conditioned" (p. 192). To Fowler, Pyle belongs "to the sky-scraper and the express lift, the ice-cream and the dry Martinis, milk at lunch, and chicken sandwiches on the Merchants Limited" (p. 16). A few years later, Greene's man in Havana was to be offered poison at just such a lunch. Even Fowler's de-

---

4. "The Cinema," *Spectator*, March 20, 1936; "Short Stories," *Spectator*, May 22, 1936.

5. Many reviewers made this false identification. Greene responded by pointing out: "Those who have read my war articles on Indochina will know that I am myself by no means a neutralist. I share certain of Fowler's views, but obviously not all of them—for instance, I don't happen to be an atheist. But even those views I share with Fowler I don't hold with Fowler's passion because I don't happen to have lost a girl to an American!" (quoted by Robert Clurman, "In and Out of Books," *New York Times Book Review*, August 26, 1956).

scription of American marriage might well have been drawn from Greene's criticism: "A dollar love, of course, would include marriage and Junior and Mother's Day, even though later it might include Reno. . . . A dollar love had good intentions, a clear conscience, and to Hell with everybody" (p. 76).

Nevertheless, in Fowler's eyes the representative American is not the quiet Alden Pyle but Granger, who seemed "like an emblematic statue of all I thought I hated in America" (p. 240).[6] Granger fits more precisely into the American pattern that Greene had criticized on his Mexican journey; he would enjoy the dancing partner Sally, whose "infinitely plain pasty face with all the vacancy of drug-stores and cheap movies" had been formed by "the sinless empty graceless chromium world" of America (*LR*, pp. 89, 234). Greene had contrasted this world with Mexico where, in spite of "idolatry and oppression, starvation and casual violence," people lived "under the shadow of religion" (p. 234). To Greene, this was infinitely better than reading "Rating for Dating" (p. 234) or being satisfied with Pulitzer Prize winning novels about "America as America would like to appear."[7]

Greene's own criticism may seem as ill-informed or as prejudiced as Fowler's first impressions, but it always goes beyond the familiar European clichés about American culture. Greene is continually aware of an appalling irony: the New World has not developed its full potential of fresh and vigorous artistic exploration, but it has developed an industry dedicated to falsifying life. Repeatedly in his film reviews, even while he was praising the vigor of many American films, Greene regretted this artificial world of the Anglo-Saxon film industry. In 1936, he summarized the experience of reviewing 124 films: only 13 had conveyed any kind of aesthetic experience.[8]

6. The "emblematic" Granger is reminiscent of the first fictional American in Greene's writing, another newspaperman (on the staff of the *Chicago Tribune*). This earlier American, Crane, wore a mustard-colored suit and sounded like a stock character from the cliché-ridden novels Greene has since derided; yet in *The Name of Action* he is "representative of the New World" (p. 343). Fowler's kinship with Greene is further reflected in this progression from seeing only the stock figure to perceiving a common involvement.

7. "Fiction," *Spectator*, July 27, 1934.

8. "What is an English Film?" *Spectator*, June 5, 1936. Greene's article

America emerges from Greene's writing as a symbol of civilization's "peril of extinction," its chromium-plated and airconditioned comforts representing the loss of awareness, the extinction of Africa's "purer" emotions and "keener" pleasures. Even the Catholic Church in America has lost the old "mystique" (*SC*, p. 17); it shares with the "dull bourgeois Masses" of Europe a separation from the religious Power at the dark heart of the Faith.

On his journeys through Indo-China, Greene found confirmation of his symbolic choice. He observed a bar "loud with innocent American voices"—innocents abroad in order to "protect an investment" and clearly related to the "idealists" of the African Firestone plantation. American aid for the Vietnamese was stamped with the name of the donor, symbolizing their demand for "a kind of payment—cooperation in the Cold War," a demand that irritated the Vietnamese more than the maladroitness of such American gifts as "razors for hairless chins," useless cheese, and unlabeled dried milk that the villagers were certain must be poison.

These comments, recorded in "Indo-China" and in "Last Act in Indo-China," do not, however, tell the whole story. Travelers along the Vietnamese roads were often related to African and Mexican wayfarers. Sometimes they recalled Greene's English childhood, his recurrent school metaphors. During his stay in Hanoi, for instance, Greene compared Ho Chi Minh to Mr. Chips, and in "Last Act in Indo-China" he regretted that he was "too old to accept the rules" or to believe what the "school" of Ho Chi Minh taught. In "An Indo-China Journal," Greene compared native and European behavior with unflattering conclusions similar to those reached on his earlier journeys. He contrasted the joyful Vietnamese Mass with "the dull bourgeois Masses of France and England, the best clothes and the beadle and the joyless faces and the Gregorian chants," as he had earlier contrasted Mexican worship with the "curiously fic-

---

dealt with both English and American films. In two articles on "The Cinema," he similarly criticized "cellophaned" sex and "moral pretentiousness, a kind of cellophaned intellectuality"—*Spectator*, May 5, 1939, and April 21, 1939. Such artificial wrapping of the essential artistic "truth" leads to an "inability to see life in any shape at all, whether religious or political"; Greene blamed the absence of a "Great American Novel" on this inability (in "Boy Loses Girl," *Spectator*, January 27, 1939).

titious" Mass in Chelsea (*LR*, p. 289). Or he found in Vietnamese views of European culture a commentary on Western folly. Watching and listening to a French play, the Vietnamese were wildly amused at the spectacle of a man kneeling at a woman's feet. To them, the action was as ridiculous as native customs had seemed to some of Greene's African colonialists.

At a more serious level, Greene addressed himself to Europeans who regret the Communist influence on Indo-China; he reminded them that the anonymous peasant had never been treated so like an individual before—except by a priest—and that "endless compulsory lectures and political meetings, the hours of physical training, are better entertainment than [the peasant] has ever known."[9] Greene further reminded the civilized men of the West that the atrocities he described might happen anywhere—wherever there is hate, for hate is never confined to one side. Greene's reluctance to judge others and his recognition of our universal guilt are reflected in the novel in Fowler's reluctance to become "engagé" or involved and in his gradual acceptance of responsibility.

At first Fowler says, " 'I'm not involved. . . .' The human condition being what it was, let them fight, let them love, let them murder, I would not be involved. . . . I took no action—even an opinion is a kind of action" (p. 27). Gradually, like Greene himself, Fowler realizes that there are areas in which a responsible man must become involved. Fowler's growing involvement is subtly revealed in his shift to the use of "we"—differentiating between "your" politicians and "ours" and counting himself one of the "old colonialists." Fowler is forced into holding opinions by his perception of the platitudes of the visiting Idealists. He is eventually forced into action by the shock of civilian casualties, the death of those who have become "engagé" without volition.

Fowler's position grows naturally out of Greene's observations

9. "Last Act in Indo-China," May 16, 1955, p. 12. In the novel, Fowler answers Pyle's facile anti-communism with an echo of Greene. He says that the Vietnamese "want enough rice. . . . They don't want our white skins around telling them what they want" (p. 119). Accusing York Harding of having "a return ticket" Fowler is further echoing Greene's comment in an essay of 1940: Writers traveling in search of violence invariably "bought two-way tickets" (*LC*, p. 190).

of Vietnamese behavior. Greene wrote of trishaw drivers who refused to help the wounded; but they were "indifferent" rather than cruel. Often enough the Vietnamese did not get the aid they wanted; yet one Red Cross representative sat for six months with supplies that no one would accept. General Bay Vien established his "respectability" by closing the gambling centers of Cholon; but he had himself been controller of the gambling, and he proceeded to make up for his lost revenue by opening a neon-lighted 400-girl brothel. In his despatches "Indo-China" and "Last Act in Indo-China," Greene wrote that the politicians, nominally Catholic, often used the name of God to get votes. A political priest told his ignorant parishioners: "God and the Virgin have gone South, only the devil remains in the North." Another politician, Mr. Diem, went everywhere accompanied by his own priest—usually an American.

The religious life recorded in *The Quiet American* is a further reflection of Greene's own continuing preoccupation with "eternal values." Greene's despatches ranged from reports on the "Walt Disney" Caodaist Cathedral to a sensitive appreciation of a Buddhist temple. Founded by a Cochin civil servant, the religion of the Caodaists seemed to exploit the religious devices and pious clichés of older religions. But of the Buddhist temple Greene wrote in "A Few Pipes": "There is more atmosphere of prayer in a pagoda than in most churches. The features of Buddha cannot be sentimentalized like the features of Christ, there are no hideous pictures on the wall, no Stations of the Cross, no straining after unfelt agonies. . . . I found myself praying to Buddha as always when I enter a pagoda, for now surely he is among our saints and his intercession will be as powerful as the Little Flower's—perhaps more powerful here among a race akin to his own." Presumably Greene was not claiming Buddha for the Roman Catholic Church; but he was admitting the universality of religious experience, as he had earlier recognized the resemblance between African "Power" and the "old" religion that had been lost from the clichés of European worship.

In the novel, counterparts of Greene's observations appear in Fowler's accounts of the Caodaists' "cunning and corrupt" representative who speaks so often of "love." The theme of distrust and betrayal is also accurately drawn from the actual events: "Strangers found them picturesque, but there is nothing picturesque in treachery and distrust" (p. 23). Fowler even seems to speak with the voice of Greene's earlier narrators: he wonders if men have invented "a being capable of understanding" (p. 72), and he sees the bombed square's resemblance to a church during Mass (p. 212). These are strange observations from Fowler, who is supposedly as far from religious as from political "engagement."

But Greene is trying to emphasize the ethical aspect of religious experience. In doing so, he repeats his earlier comparison of religious and political principles. Fowler tells Vigot, the French police officer, that he should have been a priest, that he operates his own kind of confessional (p. 220). These terms are reminiscent of *The Power and the Glory*, although the law in Indo-China is nominally Catholic instead of being actively anti-Catholic as it had been in Mexico. But in *The Quiet American* points of Catholic doctrine no longer stand as obstacles in the path of a non-Catholic reader's comprehension.

Greene's earlier novels dramatized Catholic problems, especially the difficulties of a Catholic in a non-Catholic environment, or in conflict with such clearly hostile forces as the Mexican police state. *The Quiet American* extends the religious perspective into one more readily understood by Everyman. Greene's view of the human comedy is more tolerant, his personal religious affiliation less apparent. Fowler's spiritual progress, however, does end with a universal act of contrition that is consistent with the Catholic view. He says, "I wished there existed someone to whom I could say that I was sorry" (p. 247). Without coming to the spiritual crisis characteristic of Greene's Catholic heroes, Fowler shows one way in which modern man may begin to approach God.

Fowler does not suffer through such intense experiences as Scobie's conflict, Bendrix' hatred of God, or the agonized prayers of the whisky priest or of Sarah. He never asks that pain be taken away from a loved child or a sick wife, or bargains with God by offering his Faith in exchange for the restored life of someone he loves. Instead, Fowler at first merely asserts that death is the only absolute value in his world. He feels envy and distrust for those who believe in God. His eventual prayer to "the God he didn't believe in" is simply, "Let me die or faint" (p. 145). Nevertheless, Fowler's apparent plea for relief from his own physical distress is eventually revealed as a response to universal suffering. The sound of a wounded soldier gathers symbolic value, and Fowler speaks of innocence itself as "some voice crying from a tower" (p. 153).

Fowler here unwittingly reveals the deep symbolic significance of an episode that he had reported in quite different terms. Speaking of the cries of that injured soldier, Fowler had claimed that his own actions resulted only from his inability to be "at ease" if someone else was "in pain visibly, or audibly, or tactually" (p. 146). This explanation is inadequate. When Fowler denies that his action resulted from unselfishness, however, he is at least not deceiving himself with complacency. In this respect his response is preferable to the false heroics of Alden Pyle.

In such juxtaposing of Pyle's innocence and Fowler's "guilt" Greene reveals the heart of *The Quiet American,* a book that he has described as a "morality,"[10] thus encouraging the reader to look for symbolic and allegorical clues and to identify Everyman, Vice, and Virtue. Fowler's coming to awareness may identify him as Everyman facing his sins; the "innocent" Pyle, who certainly seems virtuous to Fowler at first, perhaps embodies a Vice.

Fowler's reliability as a narrator is uncertain. But it is clear that his loss of the "comfort" of Phuong is an irritation that helps make Fowler aware of Pyle's "danger." Fowler also attempts to become aware of his own faults. He describes himself as "the cuckold who mustn't show his pain" (p. 17); he suspects that he is "inventing" the character of Pyle. At first glance, Fowler may resemble a Judas, betraying Pyle, although Greene has commented that only a friend can "betray." Moreover, Fowler's action is reminiscent of a minor detail in *The Confidential Agent,* where D "discovered" that the true hero of the Song of Roland was Oliver, who deliberately struck down his friend in order to revenge the lives wasted through Roland's false heroics.

10. "A kind of morality about religion," according to an interview with Harvey Breit, "In and Out of Books," *New York Times Book Review,* January 20, 1957. In an earlier report Greene was quoted as saying that the novel's theme is "religious as well as political" (Robert Clurman, "In and Out of Books," *New York Times Book Review,* August 26, 1956).

Pyle is guilty of false heroism. He rescues Fowler only because he could not have taken Phuong without first "clearing" the situation with his unwilling "friend." Pyle's apparently heroic voyage to the battle zone is no more than a schoolboy adventure. He can accept a combatant's helmet without realizing that he is depriving its rightful owner of protection. In similar circumstances, Fowler declines a soldier's helmet. Yet Fowler never sets himself up as "better" than Pyle. On the contrary, he asks, "Was I so different from Pyle . . . ? Must I too have my foot thrust in the mess of life before I saw pain?" (p. 243). The twentieth-century Everyman recognizes his sin.

Fowler's critical commentary, like Greene's, is invariably qualified by a sense of his own failings. Although he says of Pyle's approval of a good soda fountain that it was an "odd choice of what to observe in a scene so unfamiliar," he also recalls his own response to Guerlain perfume as a reminder that Europe was "only distant thirty hours" (p. 21). Fowler ironically comments on his own complicity in Pyle's actions when he had urged the American to "Go away and play with plastics" (p. 174). Unlike Scobie, who betrayed a faithful servant and then dramatized his action in terms of the Crucifix and God's suffering, Fowler knows what he has done and makes it quite clear at the outset of the narrative. Looking at Pyle's body, he writes: "I told myself again I was innocent" (p. 16). The rest of the novel is Fowler's exposure of his own guilt.

The "innocent" and quiet Pyle, however, had been "impregnably armoured by his good intentions and his ignorance" (p. 214), quite blind to the world behind the surface scenes of Indo-China, viewing the Vietnamese only through the clichés of York Harding. He never discovered "the real background that held you as a smell does," a background to which Fowler is clearly sensitive: " . . . the gold of the rice-fields under a flat late sun: the fishers' fragile cranes hovering over the fields like mosquitoes: the cups of tea on an old abbot's platform, with his bed and his commercial calendars, his buckets and broken cups and the junk of a lifetime washed up around his chair: the mollusc hats of the girls repairing the road where the mine had burst: the gold and the young green and the bright dresses of the south, and in the north the deep browns and the black clothes and the circle of enemy mountains and the drone of planes" (p. 23). This passage reveals Fowler as an exploring writer of Greene's own fraternity, not one of the cynical cliché-peddlers of the press.

Such distinctions help the reader to determine where Greene wishes his allegiance to be given: Fowler, in spite of his faults, is a man in quest of meaning and the reader is urged to follow Fowler's journey sympathetically. Not only does Fowler express many of Greene's own views; he is also a more honest and likeable reporter than any of Greene's other newswriters: Mabel Warren in *Stamboul Train*, whose ambition was to crucify Dr. Czinner; Conder in *It's a Battlefield*, walking along a passage that flashed with distorting mirrors; Fred Hale in *Brighton Rock*, who had been involved in a petty gang murder; Minty, the pathetic Anglo-Catholic of *England Made Me*; or the weary James Callifer living in Nottingham's dim lodgings.

Fowler's emphasis on the term "reporter" (e.g., p. 27) to describe his function suggests that he is at least trying to provide an objective account of events in which he knows he has been quite thoroughly involved. The painful honesty of his attempt is revealed in such scenes as the episode at the monastery's gates. Here, Fowler questions the priest who appears to remain comfortable within the gates while cold refugees huddle outside. But Greene guides the reader to a sympathetic sharing of Fowler's growing realization of his false first impression. The priest observes, "Some of us must keep well." As he speaks, Fowler grows aware of the extenuating circumstances. The monastery is the only hospital available, its nuns the staff. The priest who had seemed to be shutting out the suffering Vietnamese and who even seemed to be remote from action, sitting with his breviary and beads in a tower, is wearing a blood-spattered soutane that reveals him as the only available surgeon (p. 57). Like a true explorer, by mapping what he sees as accurately as he can, Fowler begins to make "a properly connected whole."

Similarly, Fowler learns to look behind the chromium-plated façade of the emblematic American Granger and to perceive the genuine and simple feelings of a man grieving for a sick child. In contrast, the quiet and innocent façade of Pyle conceals corruption: his innocence is as dangerous as "a dumb leper who has lost his bell" (p. 40). Yet Fowler's first instinct had been to protect Pyle; he had felt his "first affection" for Pyle in contrasting the shy newcomer with the crude and loud Granger. Pyle's loyalty to Harding had even seemed "a change from the denigrations of the Pressmen and their immature cynicism" (p. 22). The very adjective "quiet" serves to distinguish Pyle from his compatriots, those drinking, wenching, and adventuring Americans whom Greene had observed on his journeys.[11] Nevertheless, his innocent and "unmistakably young and unused face [is] flung at us like a dart" (p. 12). He enjoys neither the "serenity" of innocence (*EA*, p. 11) nor the romantic innocence that must "die young if it isn't to kill the souls of men" (*HM*, p. 271). He suffers from an excess of that peculiar variety of American innocence recorded in *The Third Man*: a carefully canalized chivalry that does not include the kissing of a leper's sores (p. 111).

Looking at Indo-China with his wide and innocent "campus gaze" (p. 12), Pyle is quite blind to all the real values and needs of the country. Ironically, he manages to "put General Thé on the map" (p. 213) not by providing a helpful explorer's chart but by providing the materials to kill the civilian population in the town square. Pyle blandly assumes that the natives have died "for Democracy" (p. 234), quite unaware of his complicity. The appalling irresponsibility of his "aid" and his adolescent romanticizing of the event are symbolically represented by Pyle's reactions to his blood-spattered shoes. Instead of seeing the blood of innocent victims, the blood-guilt staining his feet, Pyle observes only a material blemish. He looks at his shoes and says, "I must get them cleaned before I see the Minister" (p. 212). And the importance of his action is emphasized by Fowler's triple repetition of the quotation (pp. 75, 212, 226), as well as by Fowler's recognition, already mentioned, that he too must have his foot "thrust in the mess of life."

11. In the novel, "My American colleagues of the Press, big, noisy, boyish and middle-aged, full of sour cracks against the French, who were, when all was said, fighting this war" (p. 20). Pyle does share an American weakness that Greene has often commented on: overemphasis on material values (symbolized in the novel by his arrival at the front armed with "the standard travelling kit of our medical aid teams"—wool-lined sleeping bag, Thermos, spirit stove, hairbrush, shaving set, and tin of rations).

Perhaps Pyle's fault is largely a lack of imagination. The writers and lecturers who have "made a fool of him" have so thoroughly indoctrinated him in American idealism that Pyle is incapable of probing beneath surfaces. Fowler knows that "the war was very tidy and clean at . . . [a] distance" (p. 52), as Greene had earlier observed in looking at a distant Mexican town. Close up, however, Fowler discovers the realities of a river filled with bloated bodies, civilians dead in the path of war, and scared boys forced to play the role of military heroes. Admittedly Fowler at one point turns his head away from the actualities of war; but he looks away from the body because he perceives its resemblance to his own (p. 58). Fowler is finally moved to action by his imaginative perception of the dangers of nonengagement, when he finds that his theories do not fit the struggle in which we are all involved.

In contrast, Pyle wears a look of pain and disappointment whenever "reality didn't match the romantic ideas he cherished, or when someone he loved or admired dropped below the impossible standard he had set" (p. 92). He is as "incapable of imagining pain or danger to himself as he was incapable of conceiving the pain he might cause others" (p. 74). In this failure of imagination, this lack of the true and creative innocence, Pyle's deficiency is exposed. Instead of feeling the charity and love he professes, Pyle is closer to hatred, the quality defined in *The Power and the Glory* as "just a failure of imagination" (p. 170).

Fowler even exposes Pyle's innocence as "a kind of insanity" (p. 213), the terrible folly of a pseudo-child playing schoolboy games or behaving as though he were in "a boy's adventure story" (p. 144). The key to the dangers of this false innocence—and even Fowler had at first responded to Pyle's innocence with trust—may be Querry's remarks in *A Burnt-Out Case*: "God preserve us from all innocence. At least the guilty know what they are about" (p. 238). For the "innocent" earnest Pyle attempts to impose his preconceived false pattern of innocence and idealism on the ancient map of Indo-China. He makes no attempt to appreciate the work of his predecessors. He cannot understand that the map has already been colored by French colonials, smudged by native corruption and apathy. The visiting American newsmen read the map only as a tourist's chart of excursions and entertainments; but at least they do not attempt to reconstruct the old world on the basis of their own ignorance. If Pyle's innocence at first seems superior to the adolescent joking and jostling of his fellow countrymen, it is soon revealed as a shocking ignorance of the actual world that he is so determined to remake according to the faulty blueprint of York Harding.

Admittedly, it is difficult to evaluate accurately the appearances of warring Indo-China. For instance, Fowler is impressed by the "odd comradeliness" of men who appear to be a group of French soldiers. He sees them as "equals engaged on a task they had performed together times out of mind" (pp. 60–61). Later, he discovers that they are a group of Germans. Nor are the words of this world accurate guides to the underlying truths. Pyle's solemn comment "A man becomes trustworthy when you trust him" (p. 107) sounds to Fowler "like a Caodaist maxim." There is clearly a resemblance between Pyle's preposterous clichés and the civil servant's "technicolor" religious invention. The faults of the Caodaists extend beyond their stealing of Pyle's gasoline, and Fowler recognizes the falsity of their "Walt Disney" façade (a false front that Greene himself had described). He comments: "I began to feel the air of Tanyin was too ethical for me to breathe" (p. 107).

Fowler may perceive absurdity in the Caodaist pretensions, but he does not make the mistake of laughing at Pyle's follies. He is angered by Pyle's innocence, although "some judge within myself had summed up in his favour, had compared his idealism with my cynicism" (pp. 204–5). But he also recognizes its dangers. Always Fowler's rueful self-awareness, his sad affection for Phuong, his perception of his wife's pain, save him from the "guilt" that must finally be assigned to the innocent Pyle. Fowler might almost be a cousin of Querry, for he too is aware of his own absurdity; he also anticipates Querry's parable in his thought: "It's a strange poor population God has in his kingdom, frightened, cold, starving . . . : you'd think a great King would do better than that" (p. 56).

Already, in *The Quiet American*, Greene is anticipating the tone of *A Burnt-Out Case*. His tone is lighter and his use of Catholicism more implicit. Fowler may claim, "In any vision somewhere you could find the planchette" (p. 110) and "even a Roman Catholic believes in quite a different God when he's scared or happy or hungry" (p. 118). Yet no one in the novel mocks or parodies the religious beliefs of others, as Greene himself had encouraged mockery of Minty's Anglo-Catholicism, the piety of Catholic ladies, the Ouija board of Ida, or the strangely secular religion of crematoria.[12] Even the Unitarian Pyle—religiously a cousin of these ill-assorted moralists—is generally left free of exclusively religious criticism. The "technicolor" Caodaists are admittedly treated rather ironically, but Fowler's criticism is as much directed at the hypocritical nonbelieving observers and hangers-on.

As a result of his Indo-China journeys, Greene had apparently learned more about the relation between the parts of the puzzle of existence. In the American "innocent" Pyle he was able to symbolize the loss of innocence from the Anglo-Saxon world, the loss that had taken him to Africa so many years before. Like Fowler, Greene had gone "far back in time and . . . [looked] with the old geographer's eyes" (QA, p. 193). He too had made some discoveries about relative values. As Fowler puts it: " . . . What has been a menace for the Etat Major in Hanoi, a worry for the full colonel in Nam Dinh, to the lieutenant in the field is a joke, a distraction, a mark of interest from the outer world, so that for a few blessed hours he can dramatise himself a little and see in a false heroic light even his own wounded and dead" (p. 55). Nevertheless, for the soldiers in the tower, war is real enough. It is terror and hunger and discomfort and pain, without satisfaction, without meaning, without end.

Instead of the "thrill" associated with the metaphors of exploration and crossing frontiers that had been so characteristic of Greene's earlier writing, Fowler is given the frightening perception that strange territory is only "thirty feet off across the plank" (p.

12. Greene's earlier novels were particularly marred by his mockery of Anglo-Catholics, especially Minty's "dry-mouthed excitement of a secret debauchee" when he entered a Lutheran Church, or his telephone box doodles of crosses and biretta-clad head and crown of thorns (all erased too literally to symbolize his growing distrust of Anthony). However convincing such gestures may be in terms of characterization, they are not always properly related to other elements in the story. Passing allusions to Fowler's "High Church" wife are more meaningful and less offensive than Greene's accounts of Minty, or of the shifty Acky in *This Gun for Hire*.

60). When he accompanies a patrol, Fowler's journey is not the exciting one of many earlier stories; he witnesses only the killing of a woman and child. On this excursion, when Fowler sees the oleograph of the Sacred Heart so familiar in Greene's work, the symbol gains new meaning. No longer is the oleograph mocked as an emblem of false piety; it is a sign that the room had been the home of "human beings, not just grey drained cadavers" (p. 61).

Some of Greene's artistic advance in this novel is presumably the direct result of his observation of warfare in Indo-China. In "Before the Attack," admitting to being an old "*voyeur* of violence," Greene reminds us of the part that violence played in releasing him from his own aesthetic "boredom." He is echoing his appreciation of the purer terrors of African childhood and his accounts of the adolescent cruelty in Mexico. Adding his observations of the violence of World War II to the strange war in Indo-China, Greene became aware of the essentially absurd nature of war's cruelty. Greene's comments on this quality appear in the "theatrical" shadows in the partially bombed officers' quarters; a billowing curtain that reminds Fowler of Polonius behind the arras, although it actually hides the flames of war; heroic deeds that seem more appropriate to "a company of barnstormers" (p. 65); and an invitation to "sleep well" that is "like a bad comedy cue" ushering in the sounds of war (p. 70).

The drama of *The Quiet American* is scarcely comic entertainment, of course. Yet in moving from remarks about painful truth to his amused comments on the American "occidental" passion for the truth (p. 101), Greene seems to be suggesting new ways of dealing with his familiar spiritual anguish. Fowler expresses the sad realization of our time: "Wouldn't we all do better not trying to understand, accepting the fact that no human being will ever understand another, not a wife a husband, a lover a mistress, nor a parent a child? Perhaps that's why men have invented God—a being capable of understanding" (p. 72). *The Quiet American* is a "morality" designed to show Everyman how to become conscious of today's distressing and Absurd condition.

Using the observation of his "An Indo-China Journal," his realization that "Under the enormous shadow of the Cross it is better to be gay," Greene turned from the serious political and ethical questions he had raised in *The Quiet American* to a series of frankly entertaining studies in gay absurdity: *Loser Takes All, Our Man in Havana,* and *The Complaisant Lover.* Appropriately for an author trying to construct a helpful map of the Catholic's progress through the territory of the Absurd, Greene in these three amusing charts parodies his own country, his own map-makers, his recurrent symbols, and his own bewildered wayfarers.

Chapter **6** A PLACE FOR LAUGHTER

G REENE's casual comment "Under the enormous shadow of
the Cross it is better to be gay" apparently suggested to
him a new development in his humorous writing. Few critics had
commented on Greene's longstanding delight in practical jokes and
puns until Philip Stratford in "Unlocking the Potting Shed" (1962)
reported several examples of Greene's literary jokes and a number
of escapades in which Greene had participated.[1] Yet even before
his many explorations of comical terrain in the mid-1950s, Greene
was in the habit of seasoning his novels and entertainments with
often quite outrageous jokes.

1. Philip Stratford, "Unlocking the Potting Shed." Much of this account
is concerned with Greene's "obsession" with his own name (Henry Graham
Greene) and with the color green. Stratford describes such practical jokes as
Greene's Oxford lecture on Mongolia, using "irrelevant" slides, and his introduction of an imposter as Rudyard Kipling to lecture at his father's school.
Stratford also lists some of Greene's literary jokes, including the use of the
water closet in *The Living Room*, "to test an abstruse clause in the Lord Chamberlain's Censorship Regulations which formally banishes the sound of flushing
toilets from the London Stage." But Stratford does not discuss Greene's wordplay, perhaps because so often (as in the examples given below) the jokes depend on turns of English rather than American speech. Greene says (in a personal communication) that his use of puns should not be overemphasized and
denies such schoolboyish puns as Anne's thinking the detective should not go
out without "coppers" (slang for policemen as well as for coins).

In one novel Greene ironically juxtaposed cabinet pudding, a tasteless dessert, and cabinet meeting, a meaningless event. In another, he spoke of the immature Anthony as being "as good as in Coventry already"—a statement of fact, referring to the city where Anthony's girl lived, and an appropriate use of the schoolboy colloquialism describing the ostracism and isolation characteristic of Anthony's life. In a third, Greene indulged in an extended bawdy pun involving the "cocksure" Jules' French letter (actually a letter about an inheritance from Jules' French father). These oddities are typical of Greene's early humor, although even in much later stories such familiar phrases as "heads or tails" take on new comic possibilities, as interpretation of the two homosexual seducers of the young honeymooning bridegroom in "May We Borrow Your Husband?"

At first, Greene's sense of humor might seem irrelevant in a serious discussion of his literary map-making. His three excursions in self-mockery—*Loser Takes All* (1955), *Our Man in Havana* (1958), and *The Complaisant Lover* (1959)—appear to be off the path of his literary development. Nevertheless, when Greene permits his sense of humor full play, he takes us into a looking-glass wonderland peopled with mad heroes who lead us to fuller understanding of the recurrent symbols of his fictions.

Understanding the depth of Greene's humorous perceptions is essential if we wish to avoid one commentator's judgment that *Our Man in Havana* is a "farce," a work that "in the age of absurdity . . . is just petty." For Greene, farce is by no means "petty." He wrote in "Epitaph for a Play," his note on *Carving a Statue*: "Farce and tragedy are far more closely allied than comedy and tragedy." And it should be clear from all of Greene's work that his humor is founded on serious concern with today's confusion. Greene may describe *Loser Takes All* as a "frivolity"; but he does not let us forget the epigraph of *Our Man in Havana*: "The sad man is cock of all his jests."

The Narrator of *The Comedians* comments, "Now that I approached the end of life it was only my sense of humour that enabled me sometimes to believe in Him. Life was a comedy, not the tragedy for which I had been prepared, and it seemed to me that we were all . . . driven by an authoritative practical joker towards the extreme point of comedy" (p. 34). To understand Greene's continuing Comedy, we should also remember that as early as 1936 he had written: "The truth is seldom tragic, for human beings are not made in that grand way. . . . Truth is nearly always grotesque as well."[2] Novels and entertainments alike are rich in such grotesques—landlords, newspapermen, do-gooders, self-satisfied petty officials, terribly pious women. Even the "happy" endings of Greene's entertainments are rich in ironic implication, the narratives filled with satirical commentary, tragic and grotesque finely intermingled.

Obviously, none of Greene's entertainments should be read as "simply" amusing. In the preface to *The Third Man* and *The Fallen Idol*, Greene spoke of an entertainment as "too light an affair to carry the weight of an unhappy ending"; he claimed that he used reality only as "background to a fairy tale" (pp. 5, 6). But he was describing a specific story—*The Third Man*—one intended simply as "raw material for a picture" (p. 4). Greene's film criticisms in the *Spectator* make quite clear his opinion of the generally shallow nature of film audiences, however, and this comment on his own film story may be merely a form of self-mockery.

Greene also declared that he and Carol Reed had "no desire to move people's political emotions; we wanted to entertain them, to frighten them a little, to make them laugh" (p. 6). Nevertheless, the film was eventually made with an unhappy ending. Most audiences were not exactly amused; they generally left the theater carrying a haunting picture of sad Vienna, with memories of Harry Lime's "racket." As in other contexts, Greene's disclaimers about his craft provide mocking footnotes for would-be critics, and echoes of the zither's mournful chords give the lie to his statement.

Our Man in Havana, Loser Takes All, and *The Complaisant Lover* are, like *The Third Man*, enriched by hidden, deeper meanings. They appear primarily as light comedy, quite free from the serious implications of the age of Absurdity and more in tune with the innocent age of Noel Coward—an association intensified by the film of *Our Man in Havana*, in which Noel Coward himself offered

2. "The Cinema," *Spectator*, January 10, 1936.

a wickedly light portrayal of Hawthorne, Wormold's secret service superior. The Catholic world seems to be far removed from these tales; secular scenes have an atmosphere lighter and more gay than in any of Greene's previous entertainments. In *Loser Takes All*, for instance, "All the roads of our life had led us to this square" (p. 46): to a gambling casino instead of to God. In *Our Man in Havana*, Wormold's Beatrice is a shocking descent from Dante's, and Milly's Catholicism is little more than a joke. Finally, *The Complaisant Lover* suggests a very un-Catholic marital compromise.

Short stories of this period are as playful as the comedy and the entertainments. "Special Duties" (1954) is a wryly amusing tale of "piety," in which a Miss Saunders is secretary to Ferrara, a man who walks "rather as God walked in his garden"; her duty involves earning indulgences for her employer, who ultimately discovers that she has been enjoying her own indulgences not in church but in Canon Wood, in a man's bedroom. Details of this story include Ferrara's wife, who relies on a whisky priest for her entry into the hereafter; the secretary resembles a holy statue and her "virtues" include service as head girl at the convent of St. Latitudinaria, where she won a special prize for piety.

The hero of "The Blue Film" (1954), Carter, resembles Bendrix in having a birthmark on his shoulder; but instead of suggesting one marked for God, it is the mark that arouses "lust" in his wife, a hag "dry and hot and implacable in her desire." The third story of this period, "The Destructors," is a nasty tale of children who are not innocent; they pull down the shell of an old man's house to a chorus of mocking laughter. Greene's short stories return to this vein of rather macabre humor in 1962.[3] In "Dear Dr. Falkenheim," children see Father Christmas (Santa Claus) beheaded by a helicopter. In "Dream of a Strange Land" a leper commits suicide outside the window of a house transformed into a temporary casino. Scenes of seduction feature Lesbian ladies ("Chagrin in Three Parts") and the pair of homosexual interior decorators who capture the young honeymooning bridegroom in "May We Borrow Your Husband?"

Such scenes and characters are by no means evidence that

3. See Bibliography and Ch. 8.

Greene has grown bored with Catholic heroes, however. Arthur Rowe had observed in *The Ministry of Fear* that God and the Devil had used "comic people, futile people, little suburban natures and the maimed and warped to serve His purposes" (p. 22). Greene himself is not a Devil's advocate in his works of the 1950s; he seems to be using such comic people to clarify his own views of God's purposes. Moreover, the three major works are in one sense a return to "the heart of darkness," to the unmapped world of the unconscious. Under the cover of actual scenes in Monte Carlo, Havana, and a London suburb, Greene presents man's three recurrent dreams: infinite wealth, infinite knowledge, and infinite sexual gratification. Apparently Greene had discovered that Freud's threads could lead in directions rather different from those of his first journey.

Loser Takes All scarcely seems to lie in the "shadow of the Cross." The scene is mockingly set in the shadow of the GOM, "that egotistical bastard on the eighth floor who . . . makes the world and . . . goes and rests on the seventh day" (p. 63). Action begins in a building decorated with "modern carving in alcoves and niches like statues in a Catholic church" (p. 7). Bertram is a forty-year-old hero whose second marriage would not be possible in the Catholic context. Leaving his unheroic office job at the GOM's whim, willingly exchanging a church marriage for a civil one, Bertram substitutes for the discovery of Truth a vision of gamblers "like theologians, patiently trying to rationalize a mystery" (p. 51).

Once again Greene mockingly plays on the conventional phrases of Christian piety. Outside a church, the lovers watch a wedding party and read the text displayed: "Come to Me all ye who are heavy laden, as much as to say, 'Abandon Hope'" (p. 25). In contrast, Greene had used this text in *Journey without Maps* as part of his bitter commentary on commercial colonialism: "Come to me all ye who are heavy laden and I will give you commercial privileges and will whisper for you in the ear of a Minister of State" (*JM*, p. 95).

When the GOM's yacht fails to arrive, the lovers of *Loser Takes All* "don't believe in the Seagull any more" (p. 53)—not a blasphemous allusion to true Belief, but ironic commentary on the sort of easy piety that assumes all prayers will be answered automatically. The lovers even wonder if they might borrow from the Other. Mr. Bowles, alias A. N. Other, is a "devil" whose temptation the gambling Bertram finally rejects. Faces in this story "remind one of Original Sin" rather than Original Innocence (p. 48), while the promise of "I carry with me good tidings" gives Cary "a touch of shivers, of *diablerie*—the devil at his old game of quoting Scripture" (p. 54).

Yet behind all these jokes, behind apparent parody of his religious symbols, there lies Greene's familiar territory. Bertram's choice is reminiscent of the recurrent references to Good and Evil. Admittedly his final reward is promotion rather than the Kingdom of Heaven, but at least Bertram rejects "the great system." The entertainment ends with Bertram tossing the scraps of his gambling scheme out of a porthole. Since this is ostensibly a gay tale, however, he is urged to "come back" not from the heart of darkness but to bed with Cary.

Our Man in Havana is the most outrageous of all Greene's "fairy stories." Every phrase, every symbol, every character brings mocking echoes of his earlier work. The story opens with the theme most often discussed by Greene's critics: pursuit. But the Hound of Heaven is absent. Wormold looks quickly over his shoulder "as though somebody were hunting him" (p. 4). He is not, however, hunted by God but by the Red Vulture, secret agent Hawthorne, and the good Dr. Hasselbacher. Wormold's adventures end in a "seedy hotel," where he finds Beatrice waiting in a "wilderness of sage-green chairs" (p. 241).[4]

Catholicism comes off rather badly. Milly is a Catholic who takes her faith lightly (unless she is praying for the gift of a horse); her Catholic mother has run away with another man, leaving Wormold with "a Catholic on his hands." Only one memorable cross appears in the story: it is on a picture postcard and marks Wormold's hotel bedroom, a sign preposterously linked to a nonexistent love

4. Greene's vultures are usually ugly symbolic birds, flapping through *The Power and the Glory* and *The Heart of the Matter*, for instance. Greene's use of the "seedy" is discussed in Ch. 1n19; he stayed at a "seedy" hotel before sailing to Liberia. In *The Heart of the Matter*, Wilson stood in a "wilderness" of chairs pretending to look at a map.

affair, and leading to Hasselbacher's death. Milly's baptismal name is Seraphina ("a double of the second class," p. 13); her horse, also named Seraphina, is out of Santa Teresa by Ferdinand of Castile—surely an improper union. The other Teresa of the story is not a saint but a stripper. For the terrible bargaining prayers of Father Callifer or Sarah or Scobie, Greene substitutes Milly's prayers for a horse. Beatrice tells Milly: "If there's a God, he's not a God of formulas" (p. 211); but the God here is scarcely the One of Bendrix' equation.

Africa's "lost childhood" is now only a joke: "Who knows whether there may not be a moment in childhood when the world changes forever, like making a face when the clock strikes?" (p. 20). The important border of *Journey without Maps* has become in Wormold's world only "the frontier of violence, a strange land he had never visited before" (p. 208). And in the movie Greene added a visual joke in which the secret service agents could not identify the correct map. An ambassador appears to possess souvenirs appropriate to Greene's own journeys—an odd-shaped pipe, a tile, an African mask, an ikon or two (p. 232). Greene's mockery of American values is reduced to the caricature of a Pan American meal of champagne, sweet salad, tomato soup, Chicken Maryland, ice cream, and a "decadent" orchid (p. 85), and to the macabre account of tourists more impressed by the cost of a lens ("five hundred dollars gone just like that") than by the death of a photographer (p. 24).[5]

Occasionally, Greene even parodies his own style, especially the inflated metaphors of his early novels. In *Our Man in Havana* a blind Negro beggar's ribs show through his torn shirt like a ship's under demolition, and he is ironically compared to an energetic passenger on a transatlantic liner (p. 3). Wormold feels "guilt nibbling around him like a mouse in a prison cell. . . . Soon the two of them would grow accustomed to each other and guilt would come to eat out of his hand" (pp. 80–81). This image echoes one in *The Man Within,* where disturbing facts "nibbled like a brood of

5. The name "Atomic Pile Cleaner" would "go down" in the States but not in Havana, "where the clergy are preaching all the time against the misuse of science" (p. 6). Bearing in mind Greene's picture of Havana, however, we can scarcely read this as a criticism of American values.

mice. . . . Yet the mice must have continued their nibbling" (p. 93). Greene also uses the Conradian rhetoric that he claims to have rejected back in the 1930s.

Even the characters in *Our Man in Havana* are amusing mirror-images of the figures in Greene's more straightforward writing. The blind husband of Emma suggests the blind cuckold in *Brighton Rock*. Hawthorne's pajamas initialed "H.R.H. gave him a royal air"; they have been copied from Sarah's view of Henry Miles' initialed pajamas, "His Majesty and His Majesty's consort" (*EA*, p. 122). Carter of course is a recurrent figure, the bully of "The Revenge"—one of Greene's personal school memories.[6] Carter is also the name of such petty troublemakers as the woman who sent news of Scobie's adultery to Louise; the man who committed adultery while Farrell's plane was crashing in *The Bear Fell Free*; Calloway's junior officer in *The Third Man*; one of Molly's employers (Carter and Galloway) in *Brighton Rock*; the unfortunate hero of "The Blue Film"; and the beleaguered bridegroom of "Mortmain" (1963). Marie, the girl at Milly's convent who tells of Sister Agnes having an unhappy *coup de foudre*, is an echo of two earlier figures —Maria, the mother of the whisky priest's child, and Marie, the murdering manageress of the hotel in *The Confidential Agent*—as well as being a forerunner of the novel-reading Marie in *A Burnt-Out Case*.

It is not surprising that *Our Man in Havana* is so very rich in allusions to Greene's earlier plots and characters, for it is a story that he had apparently had in mind in 1936. At that time, he wrote in a review: "What an amusing film of the secret service could be made if the intention was satiric and not romantic, the treatment realistic and not violent."[7] Certainly Greene makes gentle mockery of the Secret Service. One of the funniest moments for a devoted Greene-watcher is the scene depicting the Secret Service chief in a basement room (reminiscent of scenes in *The Fallen Idol*, of Bendrix' spying landlady, of Conrad's dim affection for Milly in *It's a Battlefield*); the chief sips milk, a deliberate reminiscence of villains in *This Gun for Hire*, of the GOM, and of Myatt skimming

6. See Ch. 1n16.
7. "The Cinema," *Spectator*, January 17, 1936.

milk for his father Jacob in *Stamboul Train*. The whole scene has "the effect of a grave," again echoing earlier stories of the point beyond death, the graveyard humor of "A Little Place Off the Edgware Road" or of "Proof Positive," and the serious implications of Wilson's sensation that he was in a vault.

As an agent, Wormold's ability is limited. He can detect the approach of Milly "like a police car" from a long way off; but the sound he hears is only the enthusiastic whistle of Cuban watchers. He learns to make secret ink from "bird shit" (tactfully changed to "bird droppings" in the movie, but expanded to an elaborate scene in which Wormold scrapes up the raw materials of his trade). His confidential encounters frequently occur in lavatories; he is less worried about his danger than interested in "what enormous bladders Cubans had" (p. 30). And the only secret weapon he sketches is a vacuum cleaner.[8]

When this apparent foolery is compared with the earlier adventures of Greene's agent in *The Third Man*, a shift in point of view becomes clear. Instead of carrying a serious burden of political and social commentary, the story is a gay account of human folly. Familiar symbols of corruption, pain, and broken faith here appear in strange guises; the pursuit is a joke; death is encountered only at an incredible banquet, in the squeals of a poisoned dog.[9]

8. Perhaps an echo of Greene's dream in Mexico: He was buying "The Trojan Women" for his wife—a "painting" that turned out to be "a surrealist object of black rubber, rather like a vacuum cleaner, which moved across the floor on wheels and said, 'Alas, for Troy!' " (*LR*, p. 196).

9. The dog's death is another version of Greene's running attack on the Englishman's best friend. The dog who dies in *Our Man in Havana* is a dachshund, reminding us of Greene's essay on the dachshund of "Great Dog of Weimar" (*LC*). Pyle's companion is an obnoxious black dog whose paws lead the police to Fowler. Apparently Greene identifies dogs with the sentimental attitudes he is continually attacking: ". . . national characteristics . . . in terms of dog, something large, sentimental and moulting, something which confirms one's preference for cats"—"The Cinema," *Spectator*, April 10, 1936. *Our Man in Havana* also provides a mocking allusion to teeth: Hasselbacher's suits hanging in his wardrobe "like the last teeth in an old mouth" (p. 157); and there are literary jokes, including the American from Miami named Harry Morgan. But while such touches are indeed entertaining in these works of 1958 and 1959, Greene's continued use of prankish "in" jokes becomes rather tiresome as he keeps up the banter in the short stories of the next decade, in *Carving a Statue*, and in *The Comedians* (where the Ambassador's dog, Don Juan, is a miniature dog "all gray hair like a centipede"). Such jokes, however, are nicely

Both *Loser Takes All* and *Our Man in Havana* appeared also as films—*Loser Takes All* before and *Our Man in Havana* after the book version. The third work in this odd trilogy is a play, *The Complaisant Lover*, first performed in June 1959. This play continually urges us to laughter, from the opening speech in which Victor thanks God for a sense of humor until the curtain falls on the lover Clive—a heroic figure who will "maybe" get used to dining regularly with his partner and her husband, and who has said: "Perhaps I don't care for innocence." Yet in this comic triangle Greene simultaneously parodies *The End of the Affair* and makes witty use of his recurrent symbols, the dentist and gold teeth.[10]

This play is a true puzzle map, for in its picture of a topsy-turvy domestic world Greene conceals clues to the pain afflicting travelers along his dusty Catholic path. Victor Rhodes tells us that his wife has referred to his profession poetically as "curing pain." His name (Rhodes) is one of Greene's earliest African associations, reported in "Analysis of a Journey," while Victor suggests man's coming to terms with our confusing and absurd world. This new hero, however, is a "victor" whose triumph includes the partial loss of his wife and the acceptance of her lover.

Dentistry symbolizes the inevitable failure of man's attempts to cure pain; he can only cover decay and corruption, as the dentist covers it with a gold-capped tooth. In *Journey without Maps*, Greene even identified "the man with gold teeth" as a symbol of Evil (p. 220). In his second travel book, Greene described the dentist as looming "big as a symbol," although he was not quite sure what this dentist symbolized. Greene concluded that the dentist

---

laid to rest in *Travels with My Aunt*, with its account of a "doggie church" and the last sacrament offered in the form of a ritual bone.

10. A unique character with "strong and perfect teeth" appears in Greene's "Dream of a Strange Land" (1963). More often teeth are painful and decayed: Fred Hall's, or Billings' in "The Other Side of the Border." Mr. Tench of *The Power and the Glory* had been making gold teeth for soldiers and false teeth for the Customs officer; he noted the yellow teeth of the whisky priest, in whose mouth death was already present. On his travels Greene similarly noted gold and decayed teeth, especially the gold fillings of Mexican teeth, which he associated with false *bonhomie*, and the general's one gold tooth like "a flaw in character" (*LR*, pp. 132, 58). Greene's symbolic linking of leprosy and dentistry is discussed in Ch. 7n12, and he continues to use the gold tooth, as in *The Comedians*: "A gold tooth always attracts greed" (p. 186).

symbolized "the aboriginal calamity, 'having no hope and without God in the world'" (*LR*, p. 156). In *The Ministry of Fear*, Arthur Rowe is puzzled because he has been brought up to think it is "wrong" to inflict pain, while inefficient Mr. Griggs the dentist can inflict pain quite freely (p. 68). Journeying on his "Convoy to West Africa," Greene discovered a Catholic presbytery parlor "hung with pious pictures, as unlived in as a dentist's waiting-room" (*SC*, p. 77); in *The Potting Shed*, this room becomes a symbolically appropriate setting for the spoiled priest.

As in other strange maps of this period, *The Complaisant Lover's* symbols have been removed from their familiar contexts. Greene's dentist Rhodes enjoys the profession of "curing pain," in contrast to Rowe's memory of Mr. Griggs and to Mr. Tench's "profession" of pain (*PG*, p. 55). At the same time, Rhodes suggests the difficulties of the ordinary man attempting to deal with his corrupt world; such a man must mature through the stages of childhood and adolescence so familiar in Greene's work. Like the traveling Greene and like his fictional heroes, Victor Rhodes progresses from childhood (the practical jokes enjoyed only by his twelve-year-old son), through adolescence (a sad awareness that something is happening beyond his understanding and that the "grownups" do not find him funny), to an adult perception of life's oddities. Victor further suggests the changing direction of Greene's writing: he comments that gold fillings have gone "out of fashion" (p. 52). Like Greene, he works with new material.

Mary Rhodes' conduct also suggests Greene's development. Her "poetic" view of the dentist as one who cures pain changes under the stress of reality to continual irritation at his dental jokes, his punning use of such clichés as "I'd give my eye-teeth," and his pathetic trickery with dribble glasses and musical cushions. Nevertheless, she refuses to renounce the responsibilities of her everyday domestic world. In spite of her love for Clive Root, Mary is willing to face the demands of "this world": half-term holidays, school clothes, and fretful children.

None of these serious implications, however, interferes with the play's essentially comic qualities. The triangle of dentist, wife, and lover Root ("the root of all evil," p. 8) turns around a dental prac-

titioner who is a lover of practical jokes and a lover who is a prac-
titioner in affairs with married women. Characters and situations
that provided tragedy in earlier stories are here only comic. Carbon
monoxide poisoning (a tragic possibility in *Brighton Rock* and an
actuality in "A Drive in the Country") becomes "not exactly a
Roman death"; "Roman" here is no more than a punning allusion
to lost Faith and false heroics. Mary's love is "like a sickness," but
she does not "catch her death" as Sarah had done in *The End of
the Affair*. Victor defines marriage as "living in the same house with
someone you love" and finds it "a damned boring condition even
with a lover"; his need for Mary is expressed as "sixteen years of
habit" (pp. 56–58). But the dentist's acceptance of his wife's lover
is far from Henry's pathetic acceptance of Bendrix; the echoes of
the earlier affair are hollow.

Even Ann, Greene's recurrent heroine,[11] in this play lacks the
virtues of most of her predecessors. She too is primarily a source of
humor. She offers to go away with Root, she reads Zane Grey, and
she rejects the affectionate, faintly Freudian gifts of the dentist's
twelve-year-old son Robin. Robin's mouse, "not stuffed very well,"
and his electronic eye serve the same purpose as other farcical elements in the play. They have a cumulative effect, along with such
incidents as the husband entering on the lover's cue, the jokes borrowed from variety show bawdry, and the crudely mocked foreign
speech of the Dutch dentist.

Victor points out this is no tragedy: "We're only dressed for a
domestic comedy" (p. 69). Tragic, poignant, serious moments—all
are disrupted by musical cushions, dribble glasses, phallic cigars,
and bad puns. Humor is identified as "compensation" for sex. As
Clive says, "We aren't allowed a tragedy nowadays without a
banana-skin to slip on and make it funny" (p. 42). So that Victor's

11. In *The Name of Action*, Anne-Marie Demassener was a Catholic
whose marriage had not been consummated. In many stories, Anne or Anna is
a minor character: the Viennese servant in *Stamboul Train*, the picture of Annette in *England Made Me*, the news item about Annie Collins in *Brighton
Rock*. Anne is also the name of Arthur Rowe's girl in *The Ministry of Fear*
(Anna Hilfe); of Mather's girl in *This Gun for Hire* (Anne Crowder); and of
the dramatically important twelve-year-old girl in *The Potting Shed*. Anna
Schmidt was Harry's mistress in *The Third Man*. The only girl Fowler had
really loved, the one left in England, was also named Anne.

discovery of his wife's affair is mockingly accompanied by "Auld Lang Syne," as the stunned dentist absentmindedly sits down on his favorite musical cushion.

Greene's own comments linking farce and tragedy point up the difficulty here: the laughter tends to linger after the serious implication is lost. Greene sometimes gives the impression in his comic exercises of only poking around the edges of human experience, in the seedy fringe of suburban London. The metaphor is reduced to "a scarf with a map of Amsterdam"; the only traveler here is "a stranger to marriage." Yet Greene's comic play with his own symbols serves a useful function.

Dentist, lovers, familiar names—these force us to remember their solemn predecessors. Sometimes Greene seems to be playing a psychoanalyst's game, not with the "X" of his earlier essay ("Analysis of a Journey") but with the reader. Greene attacks the reader's unconscious with associations and allusions; meaning emerges from the unconscious depths. Thus Greene prepares us for *A Burnt-Out Case*, in which he interprets the symbols of his literary equation.

As preparation, Greene went "in search of a [representative] character." Having found this man by returning once more to Africa, Greene could write: "The sharp sour smell of chlorophyll from rotting vegetation and swamp-water fell like a dentist's mask over Querry's face" (*BC*, p. 63). At last the dentist *will* cure pain, the protagonist will return to the heart of darkness and beyond, and a hollow man will discover that life is not necessarily Absurd.

Chapter 7 "THIS IS ABSURD OR ELSE..."

GREENE HAS CONFESSED to an "odd African fixation" (*LC*, p. 14). It is therefore appropriate that he returned to Africa, although to the Congo instead of to Liberia and Sierra Leone. Traveling up the Congo in search of a character, Greene came back with material for *A Burnt-Out Case,* his case-history of Querry, a man who has burned himself out in pursuit of today's Absurd existence.[1] The novel also uses themes and symbols that have appeared throughout Greene's work; and it carries deliberate echoes of his earliest travel book, *Journey without Maps.*

In spite of these echoes, Greene's novel of an African leper colony is primarily based on his later travel experiences, the journey he made in 1959 and published as "Congo Journal" and "In Search of a Character."[2] This journal opens with a statement that helps us understand the sources and growth of *A Burnt-Out Case,* a novel of which Greene has written, "It seemed to me when I

1. Greene's allusions to "Un raisonnement absurde" of Camus are discussed in more detail on p. 142.
2. Excerpts from "Congo Journal" were published as "In Search of a Character"; the complete journal was printed with "Convoy to West Africa" (1946) in *In Search of a Character* (1962).

wrote the last words that I had reached an age when another full-length novel was probably beyond my powers" (*SC*, p. xiii).[3]

The first entry in Greene's Journal reads:

> . . . [Greene's ellipsis] All I know about the story I am planning
> is that a man "turns up," and for that reason alone I find
> myself on a plane between Brussels and Leopoldville. The
> search for the character cannot end there—X must have known
> Leopoldville, come that way, but the place where he emerges
> into my consciousness is a leper station, many hundred miles up
> the Congo. . . . I cannot even picture the scene, or why should
> I be here? . . . The novel is an unknown man and I have to
> find him: a situation that I cannot yet even vaguely imagine:
> a background as strange to me as it was to him at his first
> entrance (*SC*, p. 3).

Already, a major difference between this journey and the first is apparent. Instead of seeking a broad understanding of man's lost childhood through examination of his racial sources, or a life "farther back" in the region where dream and reality merge in a primitive analogue of the contemporary imagination, Greene looks for one man, X, and finds Querry—a single complex personality through whose individual problem Greene can express his recurrent preoccupations.[4] In this character, Greene finds not only the character

3. Later, in an interview with Tanneguy de Quénétain, Greene said: "Mon dernier roman, *La Saison des Pluies* [*A Burnt-Out Case*], m'a complètement épuisé. Et puis je vieillis, il est peut-être temps de me retirer de la scène." As a source of inspiration for his novel, Greene cited Teilhard de Chardin's *Le Phénomène humain*: "Ce livre a produit sur moi une impression énorme, je le tiens pour l'un des ouvrages capitaux de notre siècle. C'est après avoir lu ce livre que j'ai écrit *La Saison des Pluies*."

4. Greene comments that he does not know how "X" of the journal became "C"; nor does he explain "Querry," although commentators usually note the suggestions of *query* and *quarry*. Perhaps Greene combined "C"—the only initial that seemed possible (*SC*, p. 52n3)—with Wery, a man he met on the journey who praised the character of Scobie (*SC*, p. 57). "X" is the conventional symbol for an unknown quantity; but it also recalls Greene's first "Analysis of a Journey," referred to above. Greene repeats the terms of his own imaginative and artistic exploration in *A Burnt-Out Case*, using them to describe Querry's "journey": "It surprised him to think that he had been so misled as to believe that the boat had reached the furthest point of its journey into the interior when it reached the leproserie. Now he was in motion again, going deeper" (*BC*, p. 168). In his dedication to Dr. Lechat, Greene describes his novel as "an attempt to give dramatic expression to various types of belief, half-belief, and non-belief."

who "is" the novel but one who represents all today's Absurd men. Querry is a burnt-out case psychologically and morally; he has lost his belief and he has never known simple faith. Through Querry's reawakening sensibilities, however, Greene sketches a map suggestive of Pascal's view: The man who starts looking for God has already found him (*BC*, p. 255).

Instead of vaguely "wanting to know" and seeking answers in the African unconscious, Greene wants to know the unknown man. He shares his quest with the reader: "I know no more about him yet than do his involuntary hosts" (*SC*, p. 3). Here as elsewhere in the journal, Greene consciously echoes Conrad's Congo Diary and *The Heart of Darkness*. But at the end of his voyage Greene finds enlightenment instead of the Horror. Even as he "discovers" details about his character, however, Greene decides that the man must retain a certain ambiguity. Since Greene does not want to offer a neat solution, the equation of man and message, the death of his burnt-out case is a means of preserving this essential uncertainty, of leaving unanswered the questions that he has said the novelist may ask but never answer.[5] If we can solve the riddle of Querry, however, and his parable of the Jeweller and the King, we shall discover behind Greene's own repeated question the heart of the matter, which is not simply man's recognition of God's love but is also the awareness of his own absurdity.

Throughout his journey in search of the man Querry, Greene continually echoes the observations, techniques, and similes of his earlier journey in search of our lost childhood. The parallels are of more than casual significance, for Greene has written that he set his novel in Africa because he was "already fairly familiar with the west . . . [and] Negro Africa whether west or central has much in common" (*SC*, p. 55n1).[6] His attitude, however, is rather different.

5. "Fiction," *Spectator*, September 22, 1933. Greene was quoting Chekhov: " 'You confuse two conceptions: *the solution of a question and the correct setting of a question*. The latter alone is obligatory for the artist.' " Of his novel, Greene writes, "I feel that X must die because an element of insoluble mystery in his character has to remain" (*SC*, p. 38).

6. Greene contemplated setting the novel back at Mosambolahun (*SC*, p. 24), especially when he discovered that the Liberian and Congo forests seemed to "mingle" (*SC*, p. 42). In contrast, Greene drew sharp distinctions between the atmosphere of Liberia and Sierra Leone in *Journey without Maps*.

Instead of expressing surprise at the parallels between African and European corruption, this most recent traveler is already wise in the ways of Africa and of himself. No longer does he write of the unexpected discovery of his own passionate interest in living, as he had done in *Journey without Maps*. He now savors every absurd moment of his own responses.

This charming self-mockery is perhaps most noticeable in Greene's sexual commentary. "A girl with beautiful heavy breasts made me aware of how sex was returning after satiety," he writes, and we anticipate one of his Liberian remarks on aesthetic re-awakening. Instead, the next sentence records simply, "Another girl with nipples like billiard balls" (*SC*, p. 34). When Greene speaks of the beautiful backs of black women, he may sound momentarily like the repressed Wilson, an immature Englishman, although on his earlier African journey Greene had also appreciated such lines. But neither Greene on the journey nor Querry in the novel is limited by moral or artistic inhibition. Greene even records apparently serious remarks on the relative cleanliness of African women and the infrequency of venereal infection, only to express his gentle amusement at the prostitutes' line: "There is lots of gonorrhoea and syphilis. We are safe" (SC, p. 56).

Only a writer with Greene's more recent and delightful sense of humor could record the wife-buying incident, an episode quite different in tone from his account of the "kittenish" daughter of a chief in *Journey without Maps* (p. 197). Greene admired a beautiful young black woman (dressed in green) and asked the Father aboard his river boat about the possibility of buying her as a wife for his trip. Those critics who insist on praising the Catholic and "philosophical" Greene must have been rather taken aback by the good Father's response—a practical rather than a moral objection to the purchase.[7] Greene also comments on such irrelevant topics as the healthy-mindedness of the young that "has now robbed men of their periodic rest: where we used to have four or five days in a month, we cannot now expect more than two" (*SC*, p. 40). These

---

7. The Father pointed out that the girl would return to her family when she became pregnant; if Greene still wanted her afterwards, he would have to pay the purchase price a second time (*SC*, p. 35n1).

anecdotes and comments are particularly noteworthy because they do not appear in the novel, in spite of the novel's concern with such topics as Querry's sexual prowess and Rycker's extraordinary "Christian marriage."

The journal is allegedly the result of notes taken only to "establish an authentic medical background" (SC, p. xiii) for the novel, yet Greene repeatedly makes such digressions. He ranges as far from the Congo as a Brazilian brothel, with its elaborate ceremonial (very different from the businesslike meat-buying of Major Grant in *Journey without Maps*). At another time, Greene speculates about the plastic rings worn as "bustles" by the native women and wonders whether they continue to wear these bustles during intercourse (SC, p. 59); in the novel, however, Greene mentions the women without recalling his perplexing question. Furthermore, Greene's journal, beginning as a journey *In Search of a Character*, ends with a visit to the Frégate, a scene of black prostitutes on the tiny dance floor at Douala. Greene's concluding sentence speaks not of the burnt-out Querry or the horrors of leprosy but of "one girl of great beauty with sad and humane eyes" (SC, p. 67).

The many fragments of Greene's journal that do appear in the completed novel are more often drawn from his observations on the beauty of scenes along the Congo, the vagaries of colonial protocol, and the forms of suffering experienced by the leper. As on his first journey to Africa, Greene responds to the flash of bright flowers and fabrics, to coffee-colored cattle and egrets "like patches of arctic snow," to water the color of polished pewter, to an African's smile like an open piano (SC, pp. 7, 31, 8). Similar observations appear in the novel, mirroring Querry's growing awareness, his return to feeling, as Greene's own observations in 1935 had reflected his increased understanding. Greene is alert on this journey as he had been before to the "character" and the lively anecdote. For instance, he hears of a Greek shopkeeper who bought a car for the sole purpose of destroying the seducer of his Congolese wife and who told the police, "It is not a case of what I have done, but of what I am going to do" as he shot himself. This story "bridges a gap" (SC, p. 7n3) in his novel. On the other hand, Greene does not use in the novel the madman in a red fez and yellow-green robe who sounds like a typical Greene man—giving valueless instructions, sitting with "parliamentary" air, wearing sunglasses with only one lens, clutching the symbols of his authority, and "like ourselves . . . in control under God" (pp. 43–44).

Perhaps the omission is related to Greene's determination to write *A Burnt-Out Case* in a tone far different from much of his earlier work. The most noteworthy difference between the earliest and the most recent journal is Greene's intense awareness of the absurdity of existence, whether in a rabbit named Brigitte Bardot, or in Father Pierre's belief that a bidet was "an ideal footbath for ulcers" (p. 55), or in the posture of a native washerwoman that reminded him of an anecdote in *The Golden Ass* (p. 35). Greene does not entirely abandon the sort of social observations that were characteristic of his *Journey without Maps,* but he enjoys the irony when he discovers that "discrimination has taken a turn the other way" (p. 58). On the earlier journey, Greene would have made the observation a means of criticizing Europeans' behavior or their corruption of native innocence.

On his second African exploration, Greene's eyes are apparently on the egrets rather than on the vultures. He prefers to focus on beauty and to follow the flight of comedy instead of the dark flappings of doom. The contrast is clear in such incidents as the shooting of a bird. In *Journey without Maps* the captain shot a hawk that plunged down "like a reminder of darkness" (p. 29). But when a priest enjoys the "sport" of shooting beautiful birds along the Congo, Greene's comment is phrased humorously. Remarking on the Cardinal's justification for the killing, Greene says: "And if that is a correct view in moral theology, to hell I would say with moral theology" (*SC,* p. 41n2). When he does compare African and white in situations that are to the African's disadvantage, Greene forsakes the earlier satirical note for a joking allusion. For instance, athletic dancers "would have been put to shame by any second class music-hall troupe in Europe" (*SC,* p. 23). But in *Journey without Maps,* Greene associated dancers and witchdoctors with childhood terrors and ancient religion; they served as intensely serious symbols.

Another difference appears in Greene's explicit rejection of the last traces of Africa's Conradian romanticism. Paradoxically, Greene is now actually in Conrad's Africa, the Congo, to which he had so often referred both in *Journey without Maps* and in his novels and essays. He chooses this region as a fitting one in which to reject formally the writer who had influenced his original choice of African exploration. Greene comments, "How strange it is that for more than a hundred years Africa has been recommended as a cure for the sick heart" (*SC*, p. 17). Although he still looks at parts of Africa through Conrad's eyes, he does so only to re-interpret the dark continent through his new understanding. Looking at Leopoldville, Greene "hears" Marlow's words: "And this also has been one of the dark places of the earth" (*SC*, p. 5). Seeing the Congo for the first time, he comments that it has not changed since Conrad's day: "'An empty stream, a great silence, an impenetrable forest'" (*SC*, p. 8). For the first time since he had "abandoned" Conrad,[8] Greene read *The Heart of Darkness*. But now he was quite critical of Conrad's language, "too inflated for the situation."

Allusions to Conrad had of course colored all of Greene's earlier fiction, as well as his reviews. Not only did Greene allude to "the heart of darkness," but also to phrases and characters from the Prefaces, the Diary, *Victory*, and *Nostromo*; he referred to the "romantic and false" *Lord Jim* (*LC*, p. 72) and to the evil in *The Secret Agent* ("cruder" than Jamesian evil—*LC*, p. 22). In *A Burnt-Out Case* the shadow of Conrad is reduced to one detail in Greene's mocking characterization of the cynical and "corrupt" newspaperman Montagu Parkinson, Querry's "helpless" betrayer. In the novel, furthermore, Greene's use of "heart of darkness" changes to "what geographers might have called the centre of Africa" (*BC*, p. 11).[9]

When Greene discovered the "burnt-out case" among the lepers

8. See Ch. 1n5. Greene now added: "The heavy hypnotic style falls around me again, and I am aware of the poverty of my own. Perhaps now I have lived long enough to be safe from corruption [by Conrad's style]" (*SC*, p. 31).

9. In "Convoy to West Africa," Greene says, "Africa will always be the Africa of the Victorian atlas" (SC, p. 93). He acknowledges that the human heart he had discovered in the "shape" of Africa must retain its mystery, blankness reminiscent of the unmapped territory of the Victorians. The blank unexplored continent is a fitting symbol of the fact that no man can fully "know" another and that only God is Omniscient. Each writer explores the territory as imaginatively and as honestly as he can.

on his Congo journey, he also discovered the ultimate expression of his theme of pain. A burnt-out case is a leper whose disease is arrested; but he carries with him the mutilations of his disease. The burnt-out leper is afraid to reach out and touch his surroundings lest he discover the absence of pain. And so as the novel opens, Querry —exhausted both as man and as artist—can record only vague feeling: "I feel discomfort, therefore I am alive" (p. 3).[10] The feelings of others are so remote that he is "vexed" by their pleasure and "irritated" by laughter (p. 9); he lives in "his own region where laughter was like the unknown syllables of an enemy tongue" (p. 11).

The reader is faced with the mystery of this man, as Greene had once been faced with the mystery of Africa; the goal is not the heart of a continent, but the heart of the mysterious figure Querry. Soon the reader who knows Greene's country begins to "construct the familiar" (p. 25); he will recognize the alienation of a man "across the border" in the passenger's inability to communicate. Clearly the passenger is only an observer, even of the captain's religious duties; yet obviously he once knew this religious experience himself, for he is reminded of the Benedictions of his youth. Significantly, the memory does not come at the moment when the passenger hears the sanctus bell, or when he watches the captain reading his breviary or constructing cheap rosaries; nor does it come from the picture of a church under its "soutane" of snow. Instead, the religious memory is stirred by a flickering candle, the obtrusive emotional symbol of Greene's first novel, *The Man Within*.

Querry, like Andrews, is a man on an enforced journey in unfamiliar country; pursued beyond the end of the river, where he is "a man who had turned at bay" (*SC*, p. 14n5), Querry finally reaches self-awareness.[11] We are reminded of such other journeying

10. In one of his earliest novels, Greene had similarly played with Descartes' words. In *Rumour at Nightfall* Chase says, "It was Descartes' philosophy with a difference. 'I suffer, therefore I am'. . . . My body suffers, therefore it exists." (Dr. Czinner of *Stamboul Train* had said, "I am alive again . . . because I am conscious of death as a future possibility.")

11. Andrews was lost in unfamiliar country, his feet rather than his mind feeling from grass to path. (Cf. the Auden epigraph of *Journey without Maps*: "'Oh do you imagine,' said fearer to farer. . . .") Action in *The Man Within* also took place on a "borderland." Other resemblances between the two novels in-

"strangers" as Rose of *Brighton Rock*, "a stranger in the country of mortal sin" (p. 253); Bendrix in *The End of the Affair*, "lost in a strange region" without a map (p. 56); and even Wormold in *Our Man in Havana*, feeling "as if he had come with [his daughter] a little way on a journey that she would finish alone" (p. 32). Querry, however, eventually finds himself "on the verge of acceptance into a new country" (p. 207).

The map by which we interpret Querry's journey is "the atlas of leprosy,"[12] a fitting symbol with which to complete Greene's pic-

---

clude timely dreams, the prayer shared by the two men (Querry's only remaining prayer is for a "brown teddy bear," p. 45, while Andrews had prayed for a bear rather than a live puppy that would need looking after, p. 4). Andrews knew that sooner or later he must face his fears; he could not tell whether the twisted feeling at his heart was love or hate; he was more afraid of pain than of anything else in the world—and in these aspects of his character he anticipates the characters of other novels that lie between Greene's first novel of betrayal and his most recent one.

12. In view of Greene's recurrent references to lepers, his final identification of the burnt-out case with diseased modern man is especially appropriate. In such earlier novels as *England Made Me*, leprosy provided a simile: Anthony carried his smile always with him as a leper carried his bell—"It was a perpetual warning that he was not to be trusted" (p. 11). In *The Heart of the Matter*, Father Rank's laugh rang out like a "great empty-sounding bell . . . like a leper proclaiming his misery" (p. 80). In *The End of the Affair*, Sarah wrote, "If I could love a leper's sores, couldn't I love the boringness of Henry? But I'd turn from the leper if he were here, I suppose" (p. 144). Greene also used the image in his entertainments. D thought, "I ought to wear a bell like the old lepers" (*The Confidential Agent*, p. 12); Calloway appeared to express Greene's own criticism of American values, remarking, "American chivalry is always, it seems to me, carefully canalised—one still awaits the American saint who will kiss a leper's sores" (*The Third Man*, p. 111). Greene referred to Father Damien's work with lepers in *Journey without Maps* and in "Les paradoxes du christianisme." Greene's symbolic use of the leper is richer than the conventional Christian equation of leper and sinner, although he may be playing with the linking of Simon the leper and Judas in Matthew 26. Dr. Colin says that people "learn their strange ideas . . . about leprosy from the Bible. Like sex" (*BC*, p. 19). Greene also links leprosy with pride, which is "like a skin-disease" (*QA*, p. 157); and with fear, for the leper of the epigraph to *A Burnt-Out Case* is "suspicious of society," and Greene faced his own fears (p. 21, above) after he had been "enclosed like lepers with a dead rat" (*JM*, p. 185). *The Complaisant Lover* gives a further meaning, linking the dentist (the man who tries to cover corruption, pp. 127–28, above) with lepers: recalling his wife's description of dentistry as "curing pain," Victor compares the difficulty of loving a dentist with the problem he remembers from "a poem by Swinburne about a woman who loved a leper and washed his sores with her hair" (pp. 55–56), an allusion echoing Sarah's reflections on Henry. More recently, in "Dream of a Strange Land," the suffering leper watches gamblers (who are compared to "theologians, patiently trying to rationalise a mystery"

ture of today's "dissected" life. In charting Querry's travels toward discovery of himself, Greene also mirrors in *A Burnt-Out Case* the organization, the religious life, the social problems, the petty jealousies, and the larger lies that he had found mutilating both travelers and maps in Sierra Leone, Indo-China, Mexico, London, Sweden, Havana, and Monte Carlo. Dr. Colin feels "some of the shame of a deserter as he walked away from his tiny segment of the world's battlefield" (p. 132), a clear reminiscence of the isolated travelers of *It's a Battlefield*. Querry's feet become familiar with the long laterite road that glows in shades of rose and red (p. 154); this is the path that Greene himself had walked in *Journey without Maps* and had used in *The Heart of the Matter*. Parkinson even reaches "what he calls the heart of the matter"—he claims to have learned from Rycker "the meaning of the mystery," Querry's secret of love (p. 172).

After twenty pages of *A Burnt-Out Case* we have already encountered all Greene's recurrent themes and metaphors and major symbols. He refers to home and to a strange country, to the cockroach ("the badge of an unconquered virginity," *JM*, p. 174), and to the whisky bottle. He has shown us the priest and the child as well as the bewildered stranger in unfamiliar country. The territory is unknown to Querry; but the reader recognizes Greene's familiar world of school and religion. Greene also writes of pain and of a wound, although now the wound is "secret." Once again he connects Christianity and magic. And the religious life of the Congo echoes the secular life of Greene's first overtly Catholic story, *Brighton Rock*. This routine religious life out of touch with reality is equated with the "suburban embrace on a Saturday night"—an odd and disconcerting echo of Pinkie's horror of sex, of the "game" played every Saturday night by his parents in their Brighton slum home.

Later in the novel, Greene works out more thoroughly his

in *Loser Takes All*, p. 51); ignored by the Herr Professor who would not break the law for a suffering man but does break it for a gambling general, the leper watches through a window—and a shot scarcely heard by the gamblers reminds us of Greene's words on suicide and perhaps of "The Revolver in the Corner Cupboard" as well as providing the one piece missing from the illusory picture (characters had commented that the gambling scene needed only a suicide for completion).

themes of the confusion between love and hate, suffering and innocence, false piety and true love of God, combining all his symbols
in a novel that reveals a truly philosophical perception of man's
frailty. The tone is generally ironic, the narrative is continually
jolted by flashes of wry humor, yet Greene's perspective is more
charitable than in any of his earlier writing.[13] Middle-aged man and
child-wife, pompous husband and pathetic newsman, priest and
colon—all take their turns as the butt of Greene's jokes, and all are
in the final analysis no more than charmingly absurd.[14]

Laughter in fact becomes a major symbol, a mature man's response and a sign of the reawakening self, in contrast to the adolescent giggles of the whisky priest or the empty laughter of Father
Rank. Dr. Colin's final diagnosis of Querry's case suggests the symbolic value of laughter: "He'd learned to serve other people . . .
and to laugh" (p. 255)—that is, Querry has regained love (for
others) and acquired understanding (of himself). Beginning with
a vaguely irritated response to laughter, a sense of its foreignness,
Querry finally dies laughing. He makes "an odd awkward sound
which the doctor by now had learned to interpret as a laugh" (p.
251); Rycker's belief that Querry is laughing at him is, however,
incorrect. Querry gasps, "laughing at myself." As he dies, he adds:
"Absurd, this is absurd or else. . . ." But what alternative, "philosophical or psychological," he had in mind they never knew (p. 252).

Querry's dying remark clearly has some connection with

13. Social and political comment is softened, except perhaps in passing
references to the "vices" and stupidity of *colons* (*SC*, pp. 16, 23) in Greene's
Journal, and in the novel: "Hola Camp, Sharpeville, and Algiers had justified
all possible belief in European cruelty" (p. 49).

14. Rycker receives the harshest treatment, yet still provokes both laughter and pity (see pp. 145–47, below). Most remarkable in Greene's changed
view of the territory he maps is his picture of the religious life. The journal
tells of fathers "different" from those in Europe and resembling such secular
figures as legionnaires (*SC*, p. 9). In the novel, Greene speaks of the "hum-
drum" marriage of those who marry God and of the barrenness of life at the
"red brick" seminary where tragic grandeur is replaced by the commonplace:
life is characterized not by "imitation of an action" but by "imitation of an act
performed long ago" (p. 9). In Querry's growing acceptance even of the irri-
tating *bonhomie* and "innocent" laughter of the fathers, Greene suggests some
of the adjustments and charity necessitated by Absurd existence. Only the
proud Father Thomas is fittingly humbled (like Scobie, he presumes to know
too much); other priests, "too busy to worry about motives" (*SC*, p. 24), are
treated with gentle affection.

Camus' "Un raisonnement absurde." Camus writes of the absurd man as traveler, a mutilated creature, the contrary of the reconciled man; he describes weariness coming at the end of the acts of a mechanical life but at the same time inaugurating the impulse of consciousness. In Camus' view, the consequence is suicide or recovery, the Existential attitude is "philosophical suicide."[15] Querry's remarks on suicide and his nausea of success ("disgust of praise," p. 248) are further echoes of the comments in Camus' essays. Nevertheless, it is not fair to assert that Greene is engaged in an "implicit debate" with Camus,[16] as though Greene were taking part in a philosophical quarrel. Greene never loses sight of the fact that he is a writer, one whose concern is "the correct setting of a question," rather than its answers.

An additional example of this question-posing is Greene's recent mocking reference to the Prometheus myth. In "Dream of a Strange Land," the doctor who breaks the law because of "failure of nerve" (he had declined to break the law for the suffering leper), Herr Professor, salvages "the massive bronze paperweight more than a foot high"; the doctor carries this figure of Prometheus to his bedroom "for safety, though it was the least fragile thing in all the house." But neither the Prometheus-loving Herr Professor nor the suffering leper is given a clear symbolic value. In showing the doctor's concern for a symbolic paperweight, Greene is not necessarily alluding to Camus' Rebel, to *Le Mythe de Prométhée*. Similarly, Querry's "or else" is not necessarily the same as Kierkegaard's "God!"[17]

15. Albert Camus, *Le Mythe de Sisyphe.*
16. R. W. B. Lewis, *The Picaresque Saint*, p. 224, identifies this alleged debate. François Mauriac had written of *The Power and the Glory*: "C'est dire que ce livre s'adresse providentiellement à la génération que l'absurdité d'un monde fou prend à la gorge. Aux jeunes contemporains de Camus et de Sartre, proies désespérées d'une liberté dérisoire, Graham Greene révélera, peut-être, que cette absurdité n'est au vrai que celle d'un amour sans mesure" ("La Puissance et la Gloire"). Querry's dying words might appear to support the views of Lewis and Mauriac, for as Lewis points out (p. 271), Camus claims that such thinkers as Kierkegaard react to absurdity not with the cry "Absurd!" but with the cry "God!" Querry's "or else . . ." at least suggests God; moreover, Greene himself has referred to being "impressed" by Kierkegaard (see the English version of the *Réalités* interview already cited—Guy Martin includes this comment, but Tanneguy de Quénétain does not).
17. The range of possibilities in "or else" does distinguish Querry from

Greene is of course continually aware of "supernatural values"; but such awareness does not reduce the humorous implications of *A Burnt-Out Case*. One of the fathers, ironically echoing St. Thomas Aquinas, says: "Sometimes I think God was not entirely serious when he gave man the sexual instinct. . . . Nor when he invented moral theology" (p. 245). Other references to absurdity are sprinkled through the novel as they were through the journal: "A man who cares for nothing finds it difficult—or absurd—to be angry" (p. 61); Deo Gratias is an "absurd" name (p. 64); even the terrible problem of total vacancy, of its cause, and of its effects in "breaking the rules" is complicated "to the point of absurdity" (p. 204). The relation between this sort of absurdity and the closely linked classical comic and tragic spirits is suggested by Querry seeing himself as "the innocent adulterer . . . not a bad title for a comedy" (p. 249). One of the fathers compares Rycker's vengeful pursuit of Querry with a "Palais Royal farce" (p. 245). But moments later, Querry is dead—"a terrible waste," and one that is characteristic of Absurd civilization.

Querry's function as commentator on this civilization is demonstrated in his "dim nostalgia for the past" (p. 221), reminiscent of the nostalgia (for "the seedy" and for "the stage farther back") that had taken Greene on his own African journey. Greene reveals the "waste" of Querry's life through the fragments of Querry's unconscious remarks, through Dr. Colin's observations, and even through Querry's diary, which is a more subtle journal than Sarah's

---

the picaresque saints and the empty heroes of much current fiction, as well as linking him to his various burnt-out predecessors in Greene's work. The whisky priest had found his feet "lifeless: all feeling gone" and discovered that his "dead" feet were "like leprosy under his haunches" (*PG*, pp. 164, 166–67). Scobie felt "empty"; he was not sure that he even believed (*HM*, p. 181). Bendrix seems to foreshadow Querry in thinking "as long as one suffers one lives" and "I have come to an end of my interest in work now" (*EA*, pp. 168, 180); also Bendrix' progress resembles Querry's as he becomes "nearly human enough to think of another person's trouble" (*EA*, p. 45). Various commentators have attempted to make Greene's characters into "existential" heroes. Robert O. Evans asserts that Fowler adheres to "French existentialist political philosophy" (see "Existentialism in Greene's *The Quiet American*"). Francis L. Kunkel proceeds to relate Querry to this Fowler, claiming that both are "drained of emotion, seeking refuge in nihilism" (see "The Hollow Man"). The rueful self-mockery displayed by both Fowler and Querry, however, is typical of Greene's humor; it is not typical of existentialist philosophy.

in *The End of the Affair*. At first, there seems nothing left of Querry's life to lose. He writes in his journal, "I haven't enough feeling left for human beings to do anything for them out of pity. . . . A vocation is an act of love. . . . I've come to the end of desire and to the end of a vocation" (pp. 57–58). His earliest response to another person is the sense of "unimportant disappointment" (p. 62) when Deo Gratias fails to report for work. Slowly, however, "interest [begins] to move painfully in him like a nerve that has been frozen" (p. 65). Then in response to Dr. Colin's speculations about Deo Gratias' Pendélé, Querry takes another step. To the amazement of Dr. Colin, he attempts his first joke (p. 69).

From this moment on Querry's self returns to wholeness. He discovers that "one could still feel the reflection of another's pain when one had ceased to feel one's own" (p. 92). He surprises himself by saying, "You know I am happy here" (p. 119), although he immediately seems to regret having spoken at all. Dr. Colin soon discovers that Querry is again showing curiosity about another human being, but as feeling returns to Querry, so does his susceptibility to pain. When for "the first time for a long while . . . he had voluntarily made a move towards companionship" (p. 206), Querry discovers only an unfamiliar ship's captain. At this moment, Querry is no longer the stranger on the boat. Facing this newly arrived stranger, "It was as though [Querry] were on the verge of acceptance into a new country" (p. 207).

Greene himself had similarly used journeys into new country in developing his artistic perceptions; Querry often seems to echo the particular terms of these travels. He quotes "something about having to be as little children if we are to inherit . . . [Greene's ellipsis]. We've grown up rather badly" (p. 93). This is Greene's own opinion, the reason for his journey through Liberia in 1935. Once again Greene is alluding to his recurrent theme of betrayal in the lost childhood of Judas. For Querry is betrayed by two Judas figures, Rycker and the "corrupt" newspaperman Parkinson. He is also betrayed by the "innocence" of Marie, Rycker's child-wife. Although Marie is "a very pretty child" in the eyes of the Superior (p. 88), she is different from Greene's earlier immature women. She is reminiscent of Helen Rolt in her reluctance to abandon childhood—"she was happy at school"—but has little of her predecessor's naïveté.[18] Furthermore, Greene never lets the reader forget that Querry is the truly responsible man (unlike Scobie, who erroneously declared his own "responsibility"). Such a man must come to realize that he has not been betrayed by Judas. He has betrayed himself.

Querry's is not another story of man betrayed by innocence, although he does remark, "God preserve us from all innocence." Admittedly Marie sometimes appears in the guise of a child whose development has been cut off at the stage where lying is the natural response. She sees no harm in saying, "If I hadn't thought all the time of you, I'd have been all dried up. . . . So in a way it is your child" (p. 236). On the other hand, Querry had remarked to Parkinson, expressing annoyance with Rycker, "He almost tempts me to seduce his wife" (p. 144). If this seems like "guilt," however, Greene invites us to see Querry's death as one consequence of his good intentions.[19] Querry had asked Dr. Colin to permit him to help; in helping Dr. Colin, Querry drives to Luc, a journey leading to his meeting with the *colon* Rycker and his little "companion" Marie.

Marie's husband is in some ways the most unpleasant of the traitors in Greene's novels; he is a man whom even the fathers treat cautiously. Rycker asserts, "I shall respect your incognito. I will say nothing. You can trust me not to betray a guest" (p. 37). The ensuing betrayal is not a straightforward example of treachery but is made up of Rycker's misplaced "enthusiasm" for the hero he has constructed out of rumors and misinformation, including a confused account of Querry's journey into the bush to "rescue" Deo Gratias. It is also made up of Rycker's false Catholicism, his wounded pride, and a preposterous parody of Catholic marriage.

Rycker's treatise on marriage completes the picture of modern

18. Marie's false innocence appears in her enthusiasm for *Manon Lescaut* and *Marie-Chantal* and her ready shift from *orange pressée* to whisky. From her convent she had learned rather odd lessons: devices for evading the truth, the exclamation point in her diary that convinces Rycker of her adultery with Querry.

19. Unlike Scobie, Querry is not betrayed by pity. He sees Marie as "a child forced to entertain a caller until her mother returns" (p. 41), and he thinks of her "rashly" as "a poor frightened beast" (p. 192). But Querry's pity is grudging and later, when he imagines Marie is crying, "he felt no pity, only irritation" (p. 193). Ironically, the result is almost as bad: Querry goes into her room to investigate and thus sets in motion the events leading to his death.

love (and its complement, hate) that Greene had been constructing in the 1940s. Rycker says, "At the bottom of my heart I believe very profoundly in love," but he makes the claim "as some men might claim to believe in fairies" (p. 40). Nevertheless, he claims to be both a student of love ("Agape not Eros," p. 44) and an authority on "the true meaning of Christian love." In fact he is neither. "The heart of what really troubles me" (p. 44) is for Rycker only that his wife does not understand "the true nature of Christian marriage." There is no correlation between his success at the Jesuit seminary, as a student of moral theology, and his present values. Unlike the true spoiled priests, ranging from the whisky priest to Querry,[20] Rycker has never had a real vocation. He can only remark petulantly, "Have I given up the priesthood for nothing at all?" (p. 46) when his wife fails in her "duties." His hollow phrases—"grace: sacrament: duty: love, love, love"—echo like the croaking of frogs (p. 47).

As a self-appointed "good Catholic" (p. 43), Rycker stands for the falsely religious characters who corrupt the world in all Greene's fiction. He belongs with the pious and condemning women of *The Power and the Glory* and *The Living Room*. Unlike Parkinson, in whom "virtue had died long ago" (p. 138), Rycker has sealed himself off from God with a display of false virtue. For "there were interstices in that cracked character [Parkinson] where the truth might occasionally seed. But Rycker was like a wall so plastered over with church-announcements that you couldn't even see the brickwork behind" (p. 186). Rycker's continual allusions to Christian marriage are exposed as hypocrisy. His long and emotional lec-

20. Querry again echoes Greene's own words. He tells Parkinson, "Men with vocations are different from the others. . . . Behind all of us in various ways lies a spoilt priest" (p. 138). Greene's essays and literary criticism have included such figures as Rolfe, "the spoiled priest" whose choice of Hell demonstrates the thesis that "the greatest saints have been men with more than a normal capacity for evil . . ." (*LC*, p. 93). The priggish Rycker, however, lacks the accomplishment of an earlier spoiled priest, Acky, that man in *This Gun for Hire* with "crazy, sunken, flawed saint's eyes" (p. 155). The connection between writer and priestly vocation is appropriately drawn: in Greene's view the writer's task is to present truth—although his is artistic (a matter of style), while the priest's is religious (a matter of belief). Pious priests and sanctimonious parish ladies together symbolize the cliché-ridden world of poorly written novels.

tures invariably have "ended on the bed" (p. 83), and Marie knows that news of her pregnancy will not be Rycker's idea of a Divine blessing. Like an earlier "good Christian"—the yellow-fanged mestizo—Rycker shows little sign of comprehending himself. He spends most of his time insisting that others adhere to Catholicism. His own "imitation of Christ" is limited to petty reproaches of Marie, grandly phrased as "Could you not watch by me one hour?" (p. 177).

In contrast, Querry the "retired" Catholic is an active participant in the Mystery. Querry and even the apparently atheistic Dr. Colin have remained in touch with the "Christian myth." As Dr. Colin says, "Sometimes I think that the search for suffering and the remembrance of suffering are the only means we have to put ourselves in touch with the whole human condition. With suffering we become part of the Christian myth" (p. 157).

Greene presents an "alternative" to suffering. At times in *A Burnt-Out Case*, pain is only a "mirage" (p. 91), when we enjoy a reality that helps us hide from the truth. But the mature man has to discover that pain is an essential quality of existence; its only alternative is specifically "mutilation," a loss of parts that can never be replaced. Such a view of pain is very different from Greene's early and crude conception of pain. His immature characters shared the view of Andrews in *The Man Within*: "I'm more afraid of pain than of anything else in the world" and "[fresh love] is too close to pain" (pp. 202, 214). Or they followed the false conception of happiness in *Stamboul Train*, where Coral felt pleasure because "pain was behind her" (p. 166). None of these characters could bear the pain of journeying from granite to grass, of standing on the frontier between Good and Evil, or of choosing the laterite road to God instead of the macadam road to civilization.

By the time he wrote *This Gun for Hire*, Greene had developed his perception of pain into a metaphor that suggested all such difficulties of travel and exploration. Recalling his own aesthetic return to life in *Journey without Maps*, Greene was able to write of the painful awakening of Raven's imagination, symbolized by the Snow Queen "ice chip." In direct contrast to Raven, Greene created an unimaginative and cliché-trained policeman, Saunders, who could only quote a line of poetry expressing the common opinion that a man must be "wicked" to deserve such pain (p. 89).

Another discovery that Greene had brought back from Liberia was the recollection of his adolescent belief that the way to enjoy life was to appreciate pain. The immature Pinkie was convinced that "the finest of all sensations" was the inflicting of pain. The whisky priest became accustomed to the expectation of pain coming between him and his faith (p. 87), although he had preached, "Pain is part of joy . . . pain is a part of pleasure" (pp. 85, 86); the lieutenant, on the other hand, simply regarded suffering as "wrong," although he had never been troubled by the pain he inflicted on priests. The fear of causing pain became a serious moral flaw in *The Ministry of Fear* and in *The Heart of the Matter*. But it was not until *The End of the Affair* that Greene gave full expression to the adult awareness of pain as "bearable because it was inescapable" (*JM*, p. 151).[21]

The extraordinary complexity of Greene's concept of pain has not received adequate critical interpretation, yet it is the clue to the complete picture of his work. Through the facing of pain and the understanding of suffering, the men of Greene's fictional world look at life and reconstruct the lost childhood; their struggle makes up the fragmented map of civilization that has been Greene's concern for thirty-five years. The first of Greene's characters to link correctly the pain of this world with the meaning of the next was Sarah, in *The End of the Affair*. As she kissed Smythe's birthmark she thought, "I am kissing pain and pain belongs to You as happiness never does. I love You in Your pain. . . . You might have killed us with happiness, but You let us be with You in pain" (p. 147).

Other characters expressed in different terms their recognition that pain is essential to mature existence. Father Browne in *The Living Room* told Rose that pain was inescapable. He suggested that we must all choose between suffering our own pain or suffering other people's, and "Death is our child, we have to go through

21. Greene had always kept in mind an idea he expressed in a very early review: "An artist's parallel to the Catholic ideal of the acceptance of pain for a spiritual benefit" in "A Note on Hans Andersen," *Spectator,* December 8, 1933. But he did not always succeed in subordinating the Catholic ideal to his artistic purpose.

pain to bear our death" (p. 123). In *The Potting Shed*, Father Callifer literally gave his nephew back to life by bearing the pain of the
boy's death. Pain also restored Fowler, when his own injury and
the suffering of the young soldier in the tower awakened him to the
suffering of his wife and the true horrors of war, and when the mutilated Vietnamese in the bombed square showed him the danger of
Pyle's "innocence." His own physical pain and that of the sentry
further merged in the pain symbolic of Fowler's becoming "engagé."

The "mutilation" of the natural man, the success that has
burned out Querry, is in life—as in the disease of leprosy—an alternative to pain. Instead of learning to "know the way about"
through self-examination, the mutilated civilized man has practiced self-worship; he has forgotten the way to God. Mutilation is
the "stigma of leprosy" (p. 159). Querry's mutilation is less easy to
detect; his "secret" wound lies much deeper than the scars of his
visibly mutilated counterpart, Deo Gratias.[22]

The mutilation of Querry as it is recounted in his parable of
the Jeweller and the King shows the mutilation of modern man by
the chromium-plated "blessings" of civilization. His cure is more
difficult than that of Deo Gratias, but Deo Gratias' condition is our
clue to Querry's. No longer does Deo Gratias feel pain; no longer
must he live in isolation with others of his kind. Yet what is his condition now? He has neither fingers nor toes; he has learned to do
slowly and with infinite difficulty a few simple chores—fetching
water, carrying messages, cooking food. Unwilling to return to the
rigors of the familiar world, in which his "stigma" will forever mark
him off from other men, Deo Gratias gratefully continues to work
at the leproserie. Such protection from the world, such retreat, cannot provide satisfying answers. Thus even the simple African grows
restless under the care of the fathers' routine, the habit of their
Mass, the daily tasks of his own service. Deo Gratias must go off

22. Greene describes success (Querry's original "ailment") as "mutilation of the natural man" (*BC*, p. 253). Deo Gratias' role as "natural man" is
emphasized by the description of his knuckles, like a rock that had been
eroded for years by the weather, warm and wet like a hummock of soil; he also
resembles part of the tree-trunk "bridge." Significantly, Querry sees Deo Gratias in these terms as he pursues his servant into the heart of the jungle, toward
the dark mystery of Pendélé. In "A Discovery in the Woods" (1963), the only
men still surviving are "*mutilés*."

into the bush, seeking his Pendélé—a dimly remembered past where *"nous étions heureux"* (p. 95). No one can understand his quest. Even the experienced Doctor Colin can only speculate on the meaning of Pendélé: "Pride, arrogance, perhaps a kind of dignity and independence if you look at the good side of the word" (p. 67). Deo Gratias himself cannot find words to describe his objective; he is too mutilated to fulfill his longing.

Seeking Pendélé, Deo Gratias slips from the path and lies in the mud, fear-filled, until Querry guides him back to the fathers' world, away from the primitive. Like Deo Gratias, Querry has been sick and bears the marks of his disease. Like Deo Gratias, he has a vague feeling, perhaps dissatisfaction, as he travels in search of his scarcely formulated image of peace. Going back to the more simple existence of the leper colony does not, however, remove Querry's difficulties. Again like Deo Gratias, he stumbles from the path and has to be pulled back by others. Querry's adventure is clearly linked to Deo Gratias'; it also offers a larger meaning, a parable for modern man.

In Querry's exploration of the self, Greene suggests the "civilized" man's need to look back over his life, to put the pieces together, and to see it whole. The difficulty of interpreting Querry's motives warns us against too readily fitting the parts of this jumbled puzzle into the picture *we* think Greene has designed. By questioning Querry about his reasons for coming to Africa and about the ways in which he is willing to serve, Doctor Colin shows the "logical" way of looking at the fragments. Rycker shows another way: the false "moral" view of all pieces as either black or white. Rycker cannot accept any view of Querry except one of two equally false extremes, the saint who has come to devote his life to the lepers or the sinner who has come to seduce Rycker's child-wife. Parkinson offers the "popular" view, a slick magazine picture tagged with clichés and meaningless quotations. Even the fathers fail to agree on the way to look at this life represented by the mysterious figure of Querry.

Querry's parable of the Jeweller and the King provides a picture in which most of the parts of his life have been fitted together. Yet even this story is not an accurate account of Querry's own career as architect, husband, and lover. Although he is attempting to follow the suggestion in the epigraph of *Journey without Maps* ("If I could look back [over my whole life], as we look at the child's map when it is put together . . ."), Querry as an artist shifts the parts of experience into his own version of reality, telling Marie, "You mustn't draw close parallels" (p. 196). The Jeweller's story is a transformed version of Querry's career. It is also incomplete, as untidy as life itself, and lacking a satisfactory conclusion. Querry spins his tale only until "the whisky is gone."

The incompleteness of Querry's parable is Greene's reaffirmation of the artist's self-imposed limitation, his refusal to transform fiction into philosophy. Once the enchantment of the fiction is over, Querry returns to the familiar irritations, as Greene himself had emerged from his travels to find waiting for him tenements, lawsuits, and nagging reporters. The fictional spell is over; yet no one is quite the same. Querry has not made his story into a parody of confession (in the way that Scobie thought of confession as "shift[ing] my burden"—*HM*, p. 219), although he does feel a sense of freedom and release. He has not given the listening Marie a "message"—he has only tried to tell her a bedtime story. Yet his entertainment has effects far beyond Querry's intention: by talking to Marie he finds out something about himself. Unfortunately he also adds to her romantic self-deceptions: ironically Querry's pseudo-Confession is a prelude to his death.

Querry tells a "fairy story" about a boy who lived "once upon a time" in the "deep country" (reminiscent of Greene's childhood in "wild jungle country"). The boy's parents taught him about their King, an omniscient Being who rewarded and punished his subjects in ways that were not immediately apparent. The boy grew up and married; his only child died. Then he quarreled with his wife; but there was no evidence that the King punished him for his conduct. He enjoyed "a great deal of fun" with many women; and one of them gave him the money with which he became a jeweller. Yet his first ambition had been to carve statues, as large and important as the Sphinx. The Jeweller grew richer and richer; he continually refined his work. But "nobody ever made him suffer"; he grew bored. There were times when "just for a change he would

have welcomed feeling the pain of the punishment that the King
must all the time have been inflicting on him."

The Jeweller continually traveled, but "he always came to the
same place where the same things happened: articles in the paper
praised his jewellery, women cheated their husbands and went to
bed with him, and servants of the King acclaimed him as a loyal
and faithful subject." Many people were perplexed that so "good"
a man should have enjoyed quite so many women—but they
learned to explain it as "love," to them "the highest of virtues." The
Jeweller became self-satisfied, really believing that he loved a great
deal better than all the so-called good people. He became rich. He
was "a master technician." And then he discovered that he did not
love, that he was bored, and that he had come to an end of his profession. His latest mistress, Marie, killed herself. His work became
increasingly frivolous. Finally, he lost his (intellectual) belief in
the King. In the resulting "total vacancy" the Jeweller suspected the
King's punishment; the problem was complicated "to the point of
absurdity." Nevertheless, he found it "difficult to leave a profession."

It is of course tempting to read Querry's tale as some sort of
confession by Graham Greene. The Jeweller's career sounds like
a satiric version of Greene's, a commentary on the spiritual journey
that underlies Greene's own aesthetic explorations. As a boy, the
Jeweller would not accept his parents' story of the King who lived
far away yet "knew everything that went on everywhere." From his
remarks in the opening pages of *The Lawless Roads* and in his essays, it is clear that Greene himself was dissatisfied with the God
pictured by his parents' Church of England tradition. The Jeweller's
proof that "the King existed by historical, logical, philosophical and
etymological methods" echoes and perhaps parodies Greene's declaration of "intellectual if not emotional" belief in Roman Catholic
teaching (*JM*, p. 4).

The parable also repeats ideas expressed by Greene's earlier
heroes. Fowler had reflected, "It's a strange poor population that
God has in his kingdom, frightened, cold, starving . . . you'd think
a great King would do better than that" (*QA*, p. 56). Arthur Rowe
in *The Ministry of Fear* had believed as a child that "God is good,
the grown-up man or woman knows the answer to every question,

there is such a thing as truth, and justice is as measured and fault-less as a clock" (p. 68). The Jeweller is related very closely to the central figure of "A Visit to Morin" (1957). For Morin had asked, "Can you find anything more inadequate than the scholastic arguments for the existence of God?" (p. 25).[23] Like the Jeweller, and like Querry ("I gave up the sacrament before I gave up the belief"—p. 247), Morin had lost his belief but not his faith. He suffered from a terrible paradox: "As long as I keep away from the sacraments, my lack of belief is an argument for the church. But if I returned and they failed me . . ." (p. 24). Yet Morin obviously remained closer to God than such "believers" as the villain Lime of *The Third Man*. The Catholic Lime sold black market penicillin, bringing death and insanity to soldiers, civilians, and children, yet he claimed: "I still *believe*, old man. In God and mercy and all that. I'm not hurting anybody's soul by what I do" (p. 126). Another "believer" was Driver in "When Greek Meets Greek," whose dishonesty showed the emptiness of his "I believe in religion" (*21S*, p. 187).

The way in which the Jeweller's public willfully misunderstands his work and his motives is reminiscent of Greene's own problems with Catholic readers and critics.[24] People have always insisted that the Jeweller is a good man; his public demanded "eggs with crosses"; even his "trifles" were regarded seriously, and he was called a "moralist." When his jewels became less popular, the people who disliked popular success were pleased and wrote books with such subtitles as "The Art of Fallen Man" or "The Jeweller of Origi-

23. In view of Greene's sense of humor, it is worth noting that the troublesome priest in the leper colony is Father Thomas, a true disciple of Aquinas. Morin's resemblance to Greene is even closer than the Jeweller's: he refuses to accept the common view of himself as a theologian (see n. 24, below); he has been accused of Jansenism; and his eyes are "like those of a man caught in some great catastrophe which it is his duty to record, but which he cannot bear to contemplate for any length of time" (cf. Newman's "aboriginal calamity," used in the epigraph of *The Lawless Roads*). But of course Morin is not Greene; Greene did not "write away" his belief.

24. In asserting that he is not "a writer of Catholic novels, but a writer who in four or five books took characters with Catholic ideas for his material," Greene told how he had found himself "hunted by people who wanted help with spiritual problems. . . . Not a few of these were priests themselves" (*SC*, p. 13n5). A useful survey of Greene's encounters with critics is Donald P. Costello, "Graham Greene and the Catholic Press." An earlier study is William Birmingham, "Graham Greene Criticism: A Bibliographical Study."

nal Sin." Coming to "the end of his profession," a common stage for Greene's heroes, the Jeweller tried to discourage his admirers, to "show them how his mind had changed" by cutting a few more stones "as frivolously as he knew how." This is suspiciously like Greene himself, ironically referring to "one more worthy and boring" thesis written by a student for a baccalauréate (SC, p. 19). Querry tells of those "who claimed to know and love the King" writing about the Jeweller—a thinly veiled allusion to the interminable Catholic commentary on the "Catholic writer" Greene. When Querry adds, "People declared that he was a moralist and that these were serious satires on the age," he might be referring to comments on Greene's exercises in self-mockery, *The Complaisant Lover* and *Our Man in Havana.*

Many of the Jeweller's satirical views sound like Greene's. Querry's parable tells of servants sleeping in a haystack: "The girl was more beautiful with her virginity gone and afterwards married the foreman, but that was only because the punishment was postponed. . . . The King was the King of the Dead, too, and you couldn't tell what terrible things he might do to them in the grave." Here Querry echoes Greene's references to the "popular" fables of God: the vague "One" of the crematorium, who will make everything "right" in the hereafter; the wise but terrible Judge; and the bland Being who watches over Ida Arnold's contemporaries (although Ida herself is not content to leave punishment to God, since she regards her own sense of "Right" as more pressing). Querry is adding to Greene's many attacks on those who preach pious platitudes about the rewards of virtue and the punishment of sin, examples of the condition described in "Across the Bridge": "A human being's capacity for self-deception, our baseless optimism that is so much more appalling than our despair" (21S, p. 87). Greene himself is obviously aware of the realities behind Querry's satire, for he has repeatedly used the incident of the pregnant adolescent as an example of tragic lost innocence among the poor.

Rich and exquisite jewels are appropriate symbols of art which is blind to all except material values and appearances.[25] In selecting

25. Cf. Bendrix' dream of "factitious" jewels (EA, p. 169), and Scobie's loss of integrity associated with diamond smuggling.

the jeweller-craftsman, Greene ironically places man in the mechanistic universe where the only God is a superior Watchmaker. The boredom of the jeweller never satisfied with his work is the boredom of today's successful man (even the successful artist) continually seeking pleasure in new things, living in a world devoid of spiritual values. Yet this Jeweller eventually longs for punishment and pain, the conditions of spiritual rejuvenation in Greene's novels, and a source of spiritual benefit according to Catholic teaching.

The Jeweller's "progress" from exquisite eggs to elegant navel-jewels and finally to "Letters of Marque" designed for "the man who has everything" is an ingenious symbolic pun on man's spiritual beginning, middle, and end; for Greene has frequently written about "cellophane-wrapped" and "chromium-plated" contemporary treatments of sex. A golden coat-of-mail is the finest achievement of a culture with such odd values. It marks the "adult" in a civilization where innocence has become an ingenious egg and the badge of an unconquered virginity has been replaced by a jeweled toad for vain adolescents.

In the final analysis, however, the Jeweller is not an allegorical equivalent of Greene.[26] The Jeweller's story is only partly Querry's, varying in minor details as well as describing a different career. Certainly Greene is not applying to himself Querry's description of the Jeweller: "None of these people knew . . . [that] our hero had made a startling discovery—he no longer believed all those arguments, historical, philosophical, logical and etymological that he had worked out for the existence of the King. . . . [His heart] was calloused with pride and success. . . . He had deceived himself just as much as he had deceived others." Greene takes a perverse pleasure in telling interviewers: "Oh! vous savez, je suis un catholique très, très relâché. . . . Non, je ne vais pas à la messe tous les dimanches. . . . Oui, mon attitude religieuse a changé depuis l'époque de *La*

---

26. Nor is Querry himself to be identified with Greene, although he repeats many of Greene's own comments. His "boredom of the bush" (p. 34) is like Greene's "boredom" in the Liberian forest. He even says that "the subject of a novel is not the plot" (p. 50), repeating Greene's view in "Books in General" (October 2, 1954) that the "plot of a novel catches the attention, but the subject lies deeper." Like Fowler, Bendrix, and Morin, Querry sometimes speaks with Greene's voice; but like them he remains different from his creator.

Puissance et la Gloire, l'élément émotionnel tend à disparaître."[27] His recent novels and short stories are much more ironic in their view of men and of Catholicism than the earliest work.[28] Yet there is absolutely no evidence to support some commentators' claims that Greene himself is now "burnt-out."

When Querry describes the Jeweller's heart as being calloused with pride and success or asserts that his problem is "complicated to the point of absurdity," and that his sense of vacancy is "perhaps what people meant by pain," he is describing a universal malady, not Greene's personal spiritual anguish.

Throughout his novels, Greene has been mapping the world in which such sickness is common, while developing his own artistic perceptions. His growth can be measured by setting the trite plot, the awkward diction, and the strained metaphors of *The Man Within* or the confused identities of "A Day Saved" (1935) against the economical presentation of the confused man within Querry. Originally "X"—the unknown quantity sought by the psychologist in "Analysis of a Journey"—the character of Querry appropriately emerges from an actual journey into the Congo. He becomes a man literally going beyond the end of the river to find himself.

In view of Greene's repeated emphasis on the distinction between novels and apologetics, his insistence that a writer does not have a "Message," and that the writer avoids providing the answers to his questions, it would be foolish to draw an oversimplified meaning from Querry's parable. The story of the Jeweller and the King is no more a complete "answer" than Doctor Colin's "atlas" of lep-

27. Quoted by Tanneguy de Quénétain, "Faut-il brûler Graham Greene?" p. 123.

28. For instance, Greene treats humorously the mission fathers of *A Burnt-Out Case* and their predecessor Father Donnell in "Church Militant" (1956). Comparison of the implicit Catholicism of *The Quiet American* or the "dramatic expression [of] various types of belief, half-belief, and non-belief" in *A Burnt-Out Case* with the recurrent candles, statues, and agonized Christ-figures in *Rumour at Nightfall* or *The Name of Action* is instructive. The richness of Greene's own perception of the meaning of Roman Catholicism is further suggested in the difference between the lovers' meetings in dark churches in those two early novels and the terrible encounter of Sarah and Bendrix in *The End of the Affair.* In the early novels, the church provided a variety of romantic-emotional "agonies" for the participants; but for Sarah and for Bendrix the nearness of God intensified their awful feeling of separation from each other.

rosy, which pictures the disease without offering a cure. Yet the parable does have a universal application; the boy's doubts and the man's difficulties are those of all men who have been puzzled by the demands of their religion and by the difference between belief and faith. Querry's tale distinguishes the man who believes, i.e., who "knows" the teachings of his church, assents to propositions, and accepts symbols, from the man with faith—the man who knows God.

Querry's own discovery is no more than the recurrent question of today's thoughtful novelist: "This is Absurd, or else. . . ." Rather than clutching a Catholic thesis and fitting his novels to the simplified and often false morality of the blindly pious, Greene in his novels explores all the regions of man's failures and doubts. Each of his stories is a chart suggesting the questions of one segment of the battleground. In *It's a Battlefield,* the question is one of Biblical simplicity: "Thou shalt not kill, neither shalt thou commit adultery" —but the problem is one of increasing complexity for Conrad and Milly Drover. Continually interpreting the clichés of belief in terms of the verities of faith, Greene shows the emptiness of such terms as "good" and "pity" and "love" when they are not related to Good and Mercy and Love. Yet he never loses sight of the fiction. In "Les paradoxes du christianisme" he said: "Nous ne saurions trouver meilleure illustration du paradoxe chrétien essentiel, la co-existence du mal avec le bien omnipotent et omniscient, Dieu et son ombre, la tentation dans le désert devenue pour jamais sacramentelle dans la vie de l'homme, comme l'Euchariste." He also spoke of "le besoin de connaître et le besoin de trouver une réponse simple" as being "deux tendances profondes et souvent en conflit, de la nature humaine." These are the thoughts underlying his fiction, giving his characters "solidity," in contrast to the "cardboard" characters he finds in novels written without regard to "eternal values" (*LC*, pp. 69–73).

Dramatizing the struggle of man in an Absurd universe, Greene maintains a sense of Divine power and personal commitment that continually suggests a promise without ever slipping over into pious homily. When Greene declared that he would never write another novel (in *In Search of a Character,* as well as in the *Réalités* interview already cited), he was not saying that he was exhausted as the Jeweller was. Greene was only suggesting that he had brought his perceptions to their finest point, that he had succeeded in asking the most important Question of all. In spite of the smells and mutilations of the leper colony, in spite of the physical and spiritual deformities of the white men, in spite of the strange involvement of God's priests with bandages and bidets, there is a question of hope for man's future. Doctor Colin's last angry remark expresses that promise: there will be no more mutilations. There will only be the echoes of Querry's laughter, that odd gaiety "under the shadow of the Cross."

Chapter **8** EXPLORING "UNDER THE
GARDEN": WE ARE ALL
COMEDIANS

G REENE'S ASSERTION that *A Burnt-Out Case* would be his
"last" novel may be discounted. He is still preoccupied
with the artistic quest, still using the map metaphor, and still stress-
ing the importance of the "moral" dimension in character creation,
although his subsequent work has been in lighter vein. As in *Our
Man in Havana*, Greene seems to enjoy laughing with the reader
over shared memories of the old Greene territory. Occasionally macabre details mar short stories of the 1960s. Father Christmas
(Santa Claus) is beheaded by a helicopter in "Dear Dr. Falkenheim," for instance. Henry's nerve-wracking speculations about the
care of "The Over-night Bag" (its contents: "my wife's" [dead]
baby) are further embellished with memories of "a little toe in the
marmalade," an object that Henry placed "very conspicuously at
the edge of the plate." The "gaiety of despair" in *The Comedians*
sometimes sounds closer to hysteria, and the farcical adventures of
lesbians and homosexuals in *May We Borrow Your Husband? and
Other Comedies of the Sexual Life* at times are too consciously
"clever." All of these, however, are but steps on the way to that un-
abashed romp of 1970, *Travels with My Aunt*.

Beneath this tale of banker Henry Pulling's *Travels* into new
regions, though, the reader discovers Greene's familiar themes.

159

Once again, the experiences of travel and of crossing boundaries—geographical, psychological, and aesthetic—provide metaphors for the exploration of the artistic self and the discovery of sharpened sensibilities. *Travels with My Aunt* invites the reader's laughter, yet it offers additional pleasures to the reader who has first examined "Under the Garden." Perhaps the finest expression of Greene's own years of exploring the theory and practice of the craft of fiction, this 59-page story was first published in his *A Sense of Reality*. It offers explicit commentary on the lifetime of aesthetic discovery that Greene has so often tied to actual journeys. And it can even serve as an extended footnote to all Greene's work, for it is a mythic rendition of his recurrent themes of lost childhood, of a universal "journey without maps," and a quest for "the heart of the matter," enriched by episodes, characters, and symbols made familiar in earlier contexts.

As far back as 1936, Greene had written of "legend, figures which will dramatize the deepest personal fantasy and deepest moral consciousness of a man's time: this is the only thing worth attempting."[1] In "Under the Garden" he has provided his own form of legend, with the figures of Javitt and Maria dramatizing both personal fantasy and moral consciousness.

At first, the reader sees little evidence of the questing artist in a boy's record of exploring a dark passage that has hieroglyphics on its wall. Rather than tracing a path to the creative process, Wilditch appears to discover only the way to a world smelling unpleasantly of cabbage and watched over by a dirty old woman saying, "Kwahk." Moreover, the lord of this underworld seems unimpressive: a big, white-bearded old man sitting on a lavatory seat. Yet Javitt's words include many of Greene's own statements about the novelist's task. Like Greene, he looks at the familiar world with an unconventional eye. In addition, he and Maria are prototypes of Power, the supernatural force whose loss from the modern world Greene has so frequently mourned.

Wilditch "goes back," as Greene himself followed ancestral threads in Africa. Wilditch goes to the scene of boyhood vacations, to a time before he had learned that "imagination was usually a

1. "Legend," *Spectator*, April 24, 1936.

quality to be suppressed." Like Greene, he tries to discover a lost vision as he journeys to a world of childhood. It is worth noting, too, that A.E.'s "Germinal," from which Greene takes the much-quoted lines on "the lost boyhood of Judas," opens with "Call not the wanderer home as yet." Its final verse suggests "Let thy young wanderer dream on: / Call him not home. / A door opens, a breath, a voice, / From the ancient room, / Speaks to him now. . . ."

The ancient room to which Wilditch wanders in "Under the Garden" gives new depth to Greene's theme of the artist as wanderer, explorer, map-maker. Although Greene writes, "It was plain that the young Wilditch's talents had not been for literature," the adult Wilditch is well aware that an author must "order and enrich experience." Like his creator Greene, Wilditch examines his original experience, translating the childhood vision from the perspective of years spent wandering in quest of Beauty.

Like the narrator of "The Innocent," working out and re-interpreting a childhood memory as he lay in bed beside a pickup, Lola, Wilditch revisits the scenes of innocence, remembering and re-forming the child's experience in order to re-interpret the present. In "The Innocent," the narrator recognizes the distortions introduced by the cynicism of adult perception (the child's "uniquely beautiful" picture seemed to the adult more like "an ugly drawing on a lavatory wall"). Wilditch finds the meaning of *his* experience not in terms of a lavatory scrawl but in a tin chamberpot flecked with yellow paint. Even as he perceives its meaning, Wilditch recalls that the child found the "golden po" uniquely beautiful (again recalling the "beauty" of the drawing in "The Innocent").

Describing the early formative years of a writer, Greene has spoken of the "innocent eye dwelling frankly on a new unexplored world, the vistas of future experience at the end of the laurel walk."[2] The vistas at the end of Wilditch's laurel walk eventually open the way to his years of experience traveling in search of Beauty (Javitt's daughter): "The purpose of life had suddenly come to me as it must have come to some future explorer when he noticed on a map for the first time an empty space in the heart of a continent" (p. 48).

2. "Books in General," *New Statesman*, July 18, 1953.

Again, Wilditch's words clearly echo those in *Journey without Maps*. Wilditch entering the heart of darkness below the tree resembles Greene, who described himself as "a complete amateur at travel in Africa . . . with no idea of what route to follow or the conditions he would meet" (*JM*, p. 46). Greene further referred to his African journey as "a smash-and-grab raid into the primitive"—an amusing foreshadowing of Wilditch's experience with the treasure, which reminds him of a display in a jeweller's window.

Other details of Wilditch's life similarly parallel Greene's, and remind us of Greene's comparison of the romantic storybook world to actual exploration: Both belong to "the region of the imagination —the region of uncertainty, of not knowing the way about."[3] Wilditch tries to discover the truth of memories of a dark territory "under the garden," the world of Javitt's mysterious Power, a world oddly touched by traces of civilization. He reads a story that he had written down when he was a boy (although it was published six years after the original action). Noting discrepancies, Wilditch wonders whether the boy had forgotten or was "afraid" to remember (reminiscent of Greene's insistence that the novelist must "face his fears"). Yet Wilditch clings to the "fact" that he dreamed. Concluding "a dream too was an experience," he begins to write an account of what he had found—or dreamed he had found—when he first descended into the darkness under the garden.

Here are hints of Greene's comments on the effects of Africa and its ancient Power upon the unconscious mind of the writer: its inexplicable quality of "darkness," its geographical "heart" also suggesting an essential mystery ("the heart of things"), and compre-

---

3. *The Lost Childhood and Other Essays*, p. 15. Sometimes, Greene seems to be deliberately teasing the reader with autobiographical mystery, as he has so often done in interviews and fiction. Wilditch recalls roots of a tree in Africa: he seems to describe the shrine for a fetish in Greene's own memories. He talks of his child being unable to come to England because of the color bar: Greene has an unpublished early story dealing with the embarrassment of a colored child. George describes his brother as "a restless man . . . travels . . . rumors of Africa"; Wilditch's restless life of travel suggests Greene's accounts of his own wanderings, especially the comments in Tanneguy de Quénétain's "Faut-il brûler Graham Greene?" Wilditch's story opens with some of Greene's personal symbols, including a map-like x-ray and a child's cry of fear at the prospect of a dentist inflicting pain.

hension of himself in nature and in Time.[4] That might well be a description of Wilditch's journey, even as Wilditch's journey echoes Greene's other comparisons of journey and dream. Recalling the details of his adventure, Wilditch says: "Absolute reality belongs to dreams and not life. . . . What seems is" (p. 51).

Wilditch travels away from the false "reality" of his mother's world, where poetic imagination had to be "rigidly controlled." Allusions to "mysteries," to "puzzles," and to "religious" feeling recall Greene's own fictions. Finally, the mystery of Wilditch's garden cannot be suppressed. He must re-examine the dark hidden roots of dream-reality, where the treasures of language and of thought have not yet been contaminated by the clichés of popular culture or dulled by the stock responses typified in brother George's lack of understanding of "what might lie underneath the garden."

Wilditch is in flight from the fictional "reality" that Greene sees as a mirror of Mrs. Dalloway's face, reflected dully through her thoughts of shop windows in Regent Street. As he travels into the realm of darkness, without maps, Wilditch, too, can discover the heart of things for himself. The boundaries of dream and reality are as uncertain as Greene's various geographical frontiers. We are never quite permitted to discover the source of Wilditch's story, in spite of Greene's careful separation of adult re-creation and childhood vision (through the device of shifting from a third-person narrative to Wilditch's). For even as Artist-Wilditch separates his "corrected" version from the schoolboy fiction, he repeatedly comments on the impossibility of separating dream from life: "A dream can only contain what one has experienced, or, if you have sufficient faith in Jung, what our ancestors have experienced."[5]

4. "Analysis of a Journey," *Spectator*, September 27, 1935.
5. Perhaps Greene's myth refers (at least obliquely) to Jung's opinion of religious failure in the West, the vision of God's underground counterpart, the nameless subterranean God. Javitt's name is secret, and he sits upon a throne-like lavatory seat: one visualizes Jung's God and wonders whether Greene alludes to Jung's notorious dream (symbolizing the ruin of religion in the image of God letting fall a turd upon the roof of Basel Cathedral). Jung's ritual phallus might well be the enormous shadow of one-legged Javitt. But Greene's darkness is not Freud's; Jung's vision is not Greene's, and Greene does not share Jung's confidence in fantasy as a successor to Christian faith. Greene's various comments on psychoanalysis show damaging effects on creative power in the psychoanalytical quest for our dark center.

Wilditch's story becomes an exercise in creative map-making for the reader. As Greene has said in another context, "The writer's task is the correct setting of a question." The writer must stimulate the reader to wonder. He must create a world of sympathy (for "gray and black characters alike"); communicate mood or atmosphere, as Wilditch communicates the cabbage odor and the strange routine of the dark underground passage; and suggest moral values without ever sinking to pious homily, as Javitt's pronouncements demand reweighing of conventional commandments. The writer must avoid sentimentality—hence the detachment of Wilditch's viewpoint, the repeated references to his "story," and the attempts to separate the primary reaction from later judgment and rewriting of experience.

Arthur Rowe in *The Ministry of Fear* also "found" himself through experiences in a garden, although he too at first had "the wrong map." Like Rowe and like Greene's own childhood psychoanalyst, Wilditch pieces together fragments of the past, examining these fragments of a puzzle in a manner that suggests the epigraph of *Journey without Maps*. Faced with death, Wilditch discovers the richness of restored perceptions: "Curiosity was growing inside him like the cancer." The artist, though, is alive again—as Querry was "revived."

Other characters in Greene's world find enlightenment in dark places. The enlightenment may be religious—as in *The Power and the Glory*, where the dark prison cell brings to the whisky priest an awareness of "the convincing mystery—that we were made in God's image" (p. 129). Yet Greene's use of "the heart of darkness" and "the heart of the matter" is usually no more than "the hint of an explanation." Greene writes of another mystery: "J'ai toujours été préoccupé par le mystère du péché, il a toujours été à la base de mes livres."[6] Neither God nor sinner can claim exclusive rights to this dark center, however. Like Bendrix' discovery, it may be the transformation of hate into love—or like Wilditch's, the discovery of the existence of Beauty.

"Beauty" sprung from a one-legged old man on a lavatory seat and a dumb hag in faded blue and sequins is as ambiguous a term

6. "Propos de table," p. 127.

as others in Greene's fiction. The questions raised by Greene's use of such labels as "justice" in *It's a Battlefield*, "belief" in *The Third Man*, "faith" in "A Visit to Morin," or "love" in *The End of the Affair*, are asked again by Javitt. Javitt's use of language stresses the need for new words and different meanings. His riddles challenge young Wilditch, while he takes such familiar terms as "white elephant stall" at a garden fête and converts the words to "royal beasts" and "man's fate." Such wordplay is perhaps symbolic of the linguistic traps awaiting writers. It also reminds us how often we "read" a novel (or life) on the basis of primary meanings, only later—and perhaps in another context—perceiving true meanings and ironic implications. In Javitt's world, Time itself has "a different meaning"; the world's time is unrelated to that of the dark underground, and the ruins of time become transformed into phallic pillars.

Javitt challenges Wilditch's conventional use of language with practical, cryptic, and even poetic comment—although the boy does not immediately understand. This advice is "stored in [Wilditch's] memory like a code uncracked which waits for a clue or an inspiration." Javitt, the dirty old man on a lavatory seat, is the New Muse. Behind this role, however, lies Javitt's resemblance to the ancient Power Greene identifies with the creative force. He is also clearly associated with concepts of godhead, and like the Hebrew Yahweh he has another name—one too sacred to be spoken.

Javitt's symbolic value is continually hinted, whether in his knowledge of "the first name of all," in his resemblance to a crucifix, or in his promise of forgiveness "seventy times seven." Lest we are tempted to confuse Javitt with God himself, however, we are told of his resemblance to an old tree trunk. Thus he is set back in the fictional world of *A Burnt-Out Case*, through an implied resemblance to the natural man, Deo Gratias, the leper who helped to restore the dulled perceptions of artist Querry.

The parable of the Jeweller in *A Burnt-Out Case* describes an artist whose treasures had been reduced from great cathedrals to golden letters of marque. But the treasure in "Under the Garden" is a symbol of promise, in spite of the adult Wilditch's "scepticism of middle-age" and his comparison of the jewels with the artificial display of a cheap store window. It would, however, be a mistake to limit the treasure to religious meaning, although the setting is an egg-shaped hall, where the swinging lamp resembles a censer, Javitt makes ceremonial preparations, and Maria dons a hat.

To dismiss these or the sacramental golden po as Greene's whimsy, as further examples of his too rarely recognized sense of humor, is no more satisfactory than to read them as a religious riddle. Taken as symbols of artistic quest and discovery, however, they do contain additional hints of Greene's literary intentions. Javitt chides the boy: "You think you can just take a peek and go away." This suggests a criticism of the superficial writer. It is also an allusion to the attitude of so many of Greene's critics. In the interview "Propos de table avec Graham Greene," he observed: "Quant aux incroyants, ils ne sont pas scandalisés, mais montrent une incompréhension presque totale, même les critiques les plus intelligents. Ils sont si loin de toute vue chrétienne de l'homme qu'ils ne peuvent entrer dans mon univers." These critics and other writers tend to "take a peek" at the varying worlds created by the questing author, but Greene wants them to enter his fictional universe and share his exploration of the mapless "gray and black" territory of contemporary life.

The keeper of the key to Javitt's treasure, the literary inspiration, is Maria. She is Woman—"sister, wife, mother, daughter. . . . What difference does it make?" Her name places her in the complex family of Greene's characters called Anne Marie.[7] Her appearance suggests the mysterious Power, the power Greene felt in

7. Anne-Marie in *The Name of Action* and Querry's woman in *A Burnt-Out Case* (Parkinson calls her Anne: Querry says she was Marie). Ann alone is a recurrent name (see Ch. 6n11), while Greene's Maries range from the whisky priest's woman to Marie Rycker (whose remarks on conception scarcely identify her with the Madonna), and to such minor characters as the Customs Officer's daughter in *Travels with My Aunt* ("minor" in only a limited sense, since she provides the heavenly future that Henry Pulling anticipates). It would be tedious to name all of the Maries, Annes, and Roses in Greene's fiction—yet it is worth noting that these three Christian names (Mary, Virgin or Magdalene; Anne, Mother of Mary; and Rose, the symbol of Christ's pain) are frequently at the center of Greene's stories. In a personal communication Greene has pointed out that he uses the same Christian names frequently, "not because of any resemblance between the characters, but simply because there are very few women's names which seem to me to belong to human beings. . . . So one falls back over and over again on the true and classical Christian name."

Africa and recalled in terms of a witch that haunted his childhood. Like the witch-voiced Mrs. Baines in "The Basement Room" and the dark devils of Greene's African villages, Maria inspires fear in Wilditch. Yet it is her force which ultimately propels him back into the real world. She forces Wilditch back to the world where he must interpret the clues provided by the oracular Javitt.

Javitt's riddles provoke thought: Maria's actions rouse primitive instincts. Once again, Greene hints at the dual nature of the artist's inspiration. This duality is further stressed in what Wilditch calls "a strange balance"—the continual tension between fear and happiness or laughter. Javitt tells Wilditch to "Forget your mother and your father too" and "Forget all your schoolmasters teach you." Like Greene, he is urging the fresh vision, the "disloyalty" to emotional and ideological clichés of his time—the difficulties Greene discussed in *Why Do I Write?* Javitt also admonishes, "Be disloyal. It's your duty to the human race. . . . Be a double agent—and never let either of the two sides know your real name. The same applies to women and to God. They both respect a man they don't own, and they'll go on raising the price they are willing to offer. Didn't Christ say that very thing. . . . The obedient flock didn't give the shepherd any satisfaction or the loyal son interest his father" (pp. 44–45).

In spite of such hints of Greene's Catholic contexts, Wilditch notes that the odd adventure-dream always "kept coming back to ordinary life with simple facts." As in Greene's own works, the story must keep its characters in *this* world, its narrative set in a recognizable "actual" scene, its plot related to "the way men really act" instead of being confined to individual "waves"—the thoughts and fantasies of the kind of "cardboard" characters that Greene scorns. Instead of sentimentalized sex and violence, the tired phrases of popular fictions, Javitt offers Beauty spawned by Maria in the dark room, and the monkeys' view of death as an "accident." Javitt's conversations with Wilditch further suggest the kind of author-reader dialogue Greene advocates.

Like Javitt, Wilditch sometimes speaks in Greene's own voice or assumes his creator's familiar mannerisms. His brother George describes Wilditch as a "restless man" and adds terms reminiscent of Greene's allusions to his own restlessness and need to travel.

Wilditch's curiosity about the world of darkness under the tree echoes Greene's own interest in Africa's creative heart of darkness. When Wilditch hears of Beauty, he becomes like an explorer noticing a blank place on the map. When he finally becomes "achingly tired as though at the end of a long journey," he repeats Greene's own experiences in *Journey without Maps,* and an idea found in contexts as varied as *The Lawless Roads, The Man Within,* and *Our Man in Havana.*

The story suggests a myth through which Greene can express his preoccupation with the mystery of Faith, the difficulties of belief, the loss of "mystique" from today's religious life. Javitt, "less interested in conversation than in the recital of some articles of belief," is indeed the ancient oracle, guardian of the treasure. Appropriately, the jewels are hidden—even the boy must wait for the privilege of revelation—for as Greene had written thirty years earlier in *Stamboul Train,* "We have been for a thousand years in the wilderness of a Christian world, where only the secret treasure is safe."

Wilditch's growing curiosity may be a question of fiction or of faith, but eventual judgment depends on experience. Although language may have sent Wilditch in search of Beauty, "it was only years later, after a deal of literature and learning and knowledge at second hand," that he could record a "true" version of his story.

Entrance to Wilditch's childhood fantasy is made by way of the real world (here enriched by Greene's personal symbolism). We are permitted to read the child's adventure story, a somewhat inadequate fiction, and we return with the artist to the dark sources of imaginative power and inspiration, the mystery of jewels concealed in the most literally "seedy" atmosphere of all Greene's fiction. It is clear, though, that Wilditch could not remain in the underground world of canned sardines and cabbage broth, lavatory seats and old newspapers. Although his first glimpse of the treasure had made him feel that he must give up "all the riches of the world, its pursuits and enjoyments," he had to return to "the world he knew." In that world he could record for his dull brother George and his faithless Mother the world of mystery and imagination "under the garden."

Javitt challenges the boy: "Haven't I given you a kingdom here of all the treasures of the earth and all the fruits of it" (p. 46), echoing the King in Querry's parable. He adds, "You go and defy me with a spoon laid the wrong way," hinting again at the obedience demanded by God, an obedience not always understood by the suffering Catholic heroes of Greene's earlier fiction. Wilditch then writes, "For all [Javitt's] freedom of speech and range of thought, I found there were tiny rules which had to be obeyed." That these rules include the method of folding a newspaper and the placement of a spoon does not preclude a serious interpretation.

On the other hand, the satirical hints of these rules, of the golden po's "sacramental" quality, of Javitt finding portents in tea leaves, should not be taken as evidence that Greene has begun to satirize religious belief or that he is mocking the spiritual dimension of his fictional world. The story is but an extension of that observation in "An Indo-China Journal": "Under the enormous shadow of the Cross it is better to be gay."

Such a gay, lighthearted attitude helped guide Greene's charming self-mockery in *Loser Takes All, Our Man in Havana,* and *The Complaisant Lover.* It provided the mature perception of Absurd Man's return to wholeness in *A Burnt-Out Case.* It also led to the play *Carving a Statue* (1964), in which we are asked to enjoy this gay farce of life under a slightly different shadow—the enormous shadow of an incredible "block of stone," a recalcitrant figure of God. The sculptor-father ignores his own son, for "God doesn't love. He communicates, that's all. He's an artist" (p. 56). With this example, the sculptor-artist inevitably finds in his own life incredible problems of communication. He also feels, "I'm tied enough already [to God]" (p. 70).

The words and actions in this strange sculptor's studio suggest that we are moving in a familiar landscape, even carrying a hint of Querry's first ambition: for the Absurd artist Querry had once wished only to carve statues. In *Carving a Statue* we find ourselves "on the main Brighton road" again, with tins of salmon providing the nourishment, and hints of figures we have met before. Once again, the concepts of suffering, pain, and pride are up for examination. Farcical figures with cigars, however, cannot distract us from the context of suicide and sudden death, while the sculptor's son offers ironic perceptions of a lost childhood. Ultimately, though, the artist-father, following Greene's view of the closeness of farce and tragedy, asserts, "This comedy has got to end or I shall turn serious" (p. 60).

In *The Comedians* (1966), Greene offers an odd trio of Brown:Jones:Smith—"three names, interchangeable like comic masks in a farce" (p. 24). The narrator, Brown, at the opening of the novel is "returning without much hope to a country of fear and frustration" (p. 46). He is responding to a postcard sent by his mother, another wanderer and a "true" comedian who later dies in finely theatrical fashion, consoled by her black lover. Echoing Greene's view of the need for gaiety beneath the shadow of the Cross, Brown also says: "When I was a boy I had faith in the Christian God. Life under his shadow was a very serious affair. . . . Now that I approached the end of life it was only my sense of humour that enabled me sometimes to believe in Him. Life was a comedy, not the tragedy for which I had been prepared, and it seemed to me that we were all driven by an authoritative practical joker towards the extreme point of comedy. . . . 'I laughed till the tears came'" (pp. 33–34). Brown, born in Monte Carlo, educated by the Jesuits, expressing a sense of emptiness, assuring the reader he has forgotten how to be "involved" (p. 198), is closely related to other Greene figures, while the novel's epigraph, with the words "who seems / Most kingly is the King," shows Greene determined to add yet another postscript to his story of Querry.

The novel opens with an ambiguous reference to "the international road which [Jones] failed to cross in a country far from home," and Jones says, "We seem to be sailing towards a strange country" (p. 44). Paradoxically, the ambiguities of this novel, however, are too explicit. Narrator Brown continuously injects the word "ambiguous"—attributing the quality to characters as varied as Jones (his language, his supposed military rank, his history, his clothes) and the spic-and-span Negro, Fernandez, whose conversation consists of "polite" and "ambiguous" monosyllables, and who sheds unexplained and terrible tears during the shipboard entertainment.

In contrast to the mystery of Querry and the uncertainty of

Wilditch's search beneath the garden, the ambiguities of *The Comedians* lack both the suspense of Greene's early entertainments and the true sense of exploration that distinguishes so much of his work. A seagull, the Palace of Chance, allusions to childhood nightmares and terrors: these pieces of the puzzle do not help the reader to reconstruct "the meaningful whole" of earlier map-making ventures, although many details are reminiscent of the self-parody in *Our Man in Havana.*

Brown comments that Smith "had been born with peace in his heart instead of the splinter of ice" (p. 268), taking us back to the world of Raven in *This Gun for Hire.* Jones is discovered in "an attitude of prayer" (p. 293): but he has just vomited. Moreover, some of the jokes, as in the short stories of the 1960s, ring rather hollow after thirty years of repetition. Cynical touches appropriate to the narrator's character preclude the subliminal effect that similar allusions had in the context of *Our Man in Havana.*

Once more there are dreams. Once more there are mocking allusions to Greene's critics. The narrator refers to a cashier as "a Manichean like myself" (p. 89). Martha comments, "It's a dark Brown world you live in" (p. 250), echoing the critics' view of Greene-land. There is a gap in the street "like a drawn tooth" (p. 21), we see "the wink of gold teeth" and "a raw wound." The "complaisant" husband is now Ambassador Pineda rather than the dentist, but the narrator likens himself to a dentist putting in a temporary filling. Brown also observes that cuckolding a member of the diplomatic corps is an act belonging "too closely to the theatre of farce" (p. 112)—another echo of Greene's comments on *The Complaisant Lover.* Doctor Magiot tells Brown: "You've lost [your faith]" (p. 256). But Brown is not a priest, in spite of Martha's suggestion that he is a "prêtre manqué."

In *The Comedians,* these sly allusions and Greene's familiarly ingenious metaphors alike are often lost in the exaggerations of the farcical stage, as when the narrator tells us: "As other boys fought with . . . masturbation, I fought with faith" (p. 64). Readers of this novel may occasionally even feel that Greene is cheating. We comedians have been here too often before. The triangle of Martha, her husband, and her lover is a distorting-mirror image of Bendrix,

Henry, and Sarah in *The End of the Affair* or of the plans for three-way domesticity at the end of *The Complaisant Lover*. Greene's view of American "innocence" seems to have mellowed into a relatively sympathetic picture of Smith, the vegetarian candidate-for-president, although "Reality could not touch him" (p. 170). Yet Greene's collaboration in the movie version featuring Elizabeth Taylor and Richard Burton—especially when compared with Noel Coward's role and the lighthearted antics of the *Our Man in Havana* film—emphasizes the oddly contrived impression created by much of *The Comedians*. The monogrammed pajamas of Mother Brown's black lover are a sly borrowing from *The End of the Affair*: but this is a secondhand costume, no longer as amusing as when Hawthorne wore them and we laughed at their "royal" air.

Brown is a stranger in the country of *The Comedians*—the darkness and black magic of Haiti here replacing the darkness "farther back" and the black magic of Africa. The political context and Haitian setting may also be read as variations of the old Indo-China conflict, with the two angles of vision in *The Quiet American* shifted to include all of us, since now "We are all comedians." Nor is Haiti exceptional, in spite of the horrors of Papa Doc and his Tontons Macoute. Haiti is "A small slice of everyday taken at random" (p. 141).

The pressures of laughter are as relentless as the political. The reader is never permitted to discount "the confused comedy of our private lives" (p. 33) or to ignore the various contexts of laughter, whether it comes "at the wrong moment" or denotes a proper "laughing matter." Brown's mother was an "accomplished comedian" (p. 82). In contrast Martha is distinguished from other members of the cast (there is continual reference to "role-playing"). Generally, Martha is "no comedian," for she "never claimed to like a thing she disliked or to love something to which she was indifferent," and she has "kept the virtue of innocence" (p. 151). Innocence, however, is apt to be an ambiguous label in Greene's maps. In *The Comedians*, Brown speculates on the quality common to saint and rogue alike: "innocence perhaps" (p. 213). And when her husband interrupts the love-making of Brown and Martha, she too is described as a comedian.

The Comedians ends with the narrator being summoned to his first assignment—a job with Mr. Fernandez, the undertaker across the border from Haiti. Martha is due to follow her Ambassador husband to another country, and Jones is dead, a lifetime of role-playing capped by a memorial at the spot where he failed to cross a frontier. Jones' death has occurred offstage, although in Brown's dream Jones played a final scene in which he had trouble with his lines—lines that provoked laughter. This is a fitting conclusion to a novel set in an atmosphere of "the gaiety of despair" (p. 108). We are only a step away from the after-the-atom-bomb "Arcadia" of the story "A Discovery in the Woods," where childhood was "lost" indeed, and the grotesque mutilations had gone far beyond those of Querry's leper colony.

Greene takes a perverse delight in the continued use of his own private symbols, although at various times he has denied every one of his own statements of intention and of critical interpretations both of the man and his "message." He has even asserted that the symbols of his fictions are nonexistent (e.g., in his comments on *Carving a Statue*). But *Travels with My Aunt* makes no denials and no false claims. It is as playful as *Our Man in Havana,* and as rich with familiar Greene details set in even more startlingly unfamiliar contexts.

As the story opens, Henry is attending his mother's cremation. Enter Aunt Augusta Bertram, an inveterate traveler, well past seventy but vigorously enjoying her black companion—rather wickedly named Wordsworth, with hints of his manner of providing the Aunt's "Intimations of Immortality" and of his namesake's lines on Innocence. Instead of comforting the bereaved nephew, Aunt Augusta tells him that the woman whose ashes he is planning to place on a suitable plinth in his dahlia garden was not his "real" mother at all. Henry's sense of reality is thus disturbed at the outset, and the reader has been given new wordplay on the old concept of a "mystery."

Henry is introduced as a pretty dull fellow, a man who had intended to spend the rest of his life walking the paths of his garden. He has never looked much beyond its dahlias, and rather than enjoying the world through childhood's "undimmed window of the innocent eye,"[8] he has peered across a banker's desk. Henry at first assures his aunt that he has "never had the opportunity" to travel (p. 16), and when she suggests "a little trip or two," assumes she refers only to a seaside excursion. Yet before long he initiates a journey: most appropriately, to Greene's ever recurrent Brighton.

Later, Henry suggests a journey to Boulogne, to visit his father's grave, as he learns to travel in Aunt Augusta's "world of the unexpected and the unforeseen event" (p. 185). Eventually, Henry prepares to "pass the border into my aunt's world where I had lived till now as a tourist only" (p. 230). As he learns to face his fears in the true aesthetic-explorer fashion, moreover, Henry ceases to speak of his aunt's "theatrical career." Instead, he casually imagines her "dancing in the reception room of the brothel" (p. 152). At the end of the novel, bringing his "aunt" news of her companion's fate he says straightforwardly, "Mother, Wordsworth's dead."

Considering, too, that Wordsworth had poured his (supposed) mother's ashes down the drain and substituted marijuana, Henry is remarkably well disposed toward Aunt Augusta's friend. It is, however, Wordsworth's significant gesture that starts Henry on his travels, following an encounter with the policeman who wants to take "just a tiny pinch" of mother (to see whether the "ashes" are mother or marijuana). Wordsworth's action precipitates Henry on a romp through territory that the reader finds delightfully familiar.

Cremation, voyage, and dream have their function in *Travels with My Aunt*. As in other Greene adventures, men wearing shabby macintoshes appear. Henry, Maria, Anne-Marie, Rose, Bertram— we have heard these names before. Here, too, is Visconti, a man from Aunt Augusta's past. But he is known as "Viper"—a sly reference to Greene's longstanding literary joke, his supposed literary debt to *The Viper of Milan*, underscored by Aunt Augusta's confession that her "career really started" in Milan (p. 76).

Reading of *Travels with My Aunt*, we recall earlier visits to far shores and journeys up distant rivers. Greene's mocking hostility to the Englishman's best friend continues—now transformed into a church for "doggies," conducted before the novel opens by one of Auntie's friends and including "the last sacrament [offered] in the

8. "The Turn of the Screw," *Spectator*, June 20, 1941.

form of a ritual bone" (p. 109). Once more there are allusions to wounds and pain, to dentists and teeth, and to borders both actual and symbolic. As in *The Comedians,* events are seen sometimes in theatrical terms—a hotel resembles a stage set, Aunt Augusta's lines are reminiscent of some written by "a Haymarket author."

The reader is not required to excavate beneath Henry's garden, however. When Henry writes "My garden called" (p. 7), he is thinking of dahlias and a lawnmower left out in the rain. He is not seeking the solution to Wilditch's mystery, although he ultimately unravels the threads leading to his true mother's identity. Differences in tone and attitude now separate the seemingly familiar characters and events from their prototypes. Aunt Augusta, for instance, with her taste for cream cakes, good drinks, and lively companions, may seem like a cousin of Ida in *Brighton Rock.* Yet we are a lifetime away from the heartless "justice" that provided "fun" for Greene's earlier and perverse mother-image. Aunt Augusta asserts: "Never presume yours is a better morality" (p. 97). And Henry himself bears little resemblance to an earlier character who had spent "all his adult years behind the counter of a bank." That man, the patient of "Dream of a Strange Land," found that his last journey led only to the mystery of a casino in an unfamiliar landscape and a despairing death.

In contrast, Henry Pulling's journeys are through territory in which Greene's familiar landmarks have become signposts to frank laughter. Like other travelers, Henry needs something "to sustain [him] for a long voyage" (p. 152): not spiritual comfort, but mince pies! The symbolic "golden po" of "Under the Garden" is transformed into "a tiny po with a whistle in the handle," a favor hidden in Henry's Christmas cracker. An uncle died "on his travels"—but these were only journeys from room to room of an old house near Milan. Each shift to a new bedroom was designed "to make life last longer" (p. 48), while the uncle's death as he struggled in vain to reach his last room (the lavatory) is an extended pun on Greene's theme in *The Living Room* and on the lavatory he included in that play in defiance of the Lord Chamberlain's ban.

Catholicism, childhood, and violence continue to provide theme and metaphor in *Travels with My Aunt.* Aunt Augusta variously de-

scribes herself as "a half-believing Catholic" (she is a convert) and
as "really" a Roman Catholic ("Only I just don't believe in all the
things they believe in," p. 135). Henry hears Visconti say, "Any
Catholic knows that a legend which is believed has the same value
and effect as the truth" (p. 241). But Henry himself prefers "the
more poetic aspects of Christianity" (p. 153). At the end of the
novel, he is content to quote Browning: "God's in his heaven— /
All's right with the world!" At this moment he is looking forward to
marrying Maria, the daughter of the chief of customs, next year
"when she is sixteen."

Scholarly discussions of the Hound of Heaven, of Greene's "Existential" heroes, and of Divine Mystery seem remote indeed from
this world. In *Travels with My Aunt*, variations on Greene's familiar
theme of innocence include the innocence of Henry's virgin
"Mother"; the "clumsy innocence" of the ironically named Wordsworth; and advice that Henry "plead innocence"—to a possible
charge of smoking marijuana. A wine tastes "like an evil medicine
of childhood" (p. 199), but the bitter taste of Greene's schooldays
has vanished. We meet another character who has "lost his way,"
but we are not invited to mock this American's taste in food or his
innocence. Henry rather than the American is the one who has been
protected "by a hygienic plastic screen." It is true that O'Toole's
daughter, like other Greene characters, is seen as "a small pain"
(p. 112) and compared with cancer. But for mockery we are invited to substitute admiration directed toward O'Toole's ingenious
project: "I count while I'm pissing" (p. 182), a meticulous record of
time and duration and of honest admission that "I forgot to count."

At one point, Henry Pulling comments that "physical violence,
like the dentist's drill, is seldom as bad as one fears" (p. 210), recalling Greene's favorite cluster of images. As in the earlier period
of self-mockery, these allusions provide subliminal commentary on
Greene's fictional preoccupations. But the old terrors have been
outgrown, as on the Orient Express. Once again we are on our way
to Istanbul, but the fearful pursuit of *Stamboul Train* is over. Shorn
of its old romantic associations, the train carries Henry into the
world of farcical smuggling, in which Aunt Augusta conceals bul-
lion in a candle; and the melodramatic encounter with musical

comedy agents and policemen is typified by Colonel Hakim, whose double appears on the cover of the Aunt's pornographic novel.

Old words have new meanings, and the tone is set by Henry Pulling himself. For surely this name hints that Greene is, in the English idiom, pulling the reader's leg. Henry assures us that he has never been "a spirit-drinker" (p. 188), although he regards "a shabby whisky-drinker" as more trustworthy than a well-dressed drinker of beer (p. 10). But the traveling Aunt is both a whisky drinker and one who has lived in Brighton. It is the Aunt rather than Henry who has a taste for detective stories ("I don't share my aunt's taste in that direction," p. 126), and she has been much influenced by the "Viper."

Henry himself is clearly related to Greene's other questing artists and heroes, although the familiar symbols have largely comic effect in the context of Henry's travels. We do, however, find familiar themes underlying Henry's restorative adventures, as he crosses new boundaries, both physical and psychological. Like so many of his fictional predecessors and like Greene himself, Henry journeys through strange territory without maps. His guide is unreliable: Aunt Augusta is at best an ambiguous source of information, in spite of assurances that there is always an element of truth in her stories.

Slowly, Henry learns to look at the world in new ways, to discount convention and cliché. He shares his creator's attitudes, as when he quotes a book on Dickens, on the author not being "attached" to characters (p. 143). He is also a comic counterpart of many of Greene's characters and even of Greene himself. It is fitting if we allow Henry the last word—his ironic use of Browning (perhaps another punning allusion to the old Greene man): "God's in his heaven— / All's right with the world!" With these words, concluding *Travels with My Aunt,* Henry Pulling is not expressing the piety that Greene has been mocking through a lifetime of essays, stories, and novels. He is recognizing the delights awaiting those who break out of restraining clichés of language and of life alike. After a lifetime of map-making, Greene acknowledges in Henry's fictional discovery that even under the shadow of the Cross this world is indeed a rather delightful place after all.

APPENDIX A

In *Land Benighted,* Barbara Greene says that she agreed to go with Graham Greene when he asked her at a wedding "after a glass of champagne" (p. 1). She only knew him slightly before the journey to Liberia (p. 17). Her description of him is scarcely flattering:

> His brain frightened me. It was sharp and clear and cruel. I admired him for being unsentimental, but "always remember to rely on yourself," I noted. "If you are in a sticky place he will be so interested in noting your reactions that he will probably forget to rescue you." For some reason he had a permanently shaky hand. . . . Physically he did not look strong. He seemed somewhat vague and unpractical, and later I was continually astonished at his efficiency and the care he devoted to every little detail. Apart from three or four people he was really fond of, I felt that the rest of humanity was to him like a heap of insects he liked to examine, as a scientist . . . coldly and clearly. He was always polite. He had a remarkable sense of humour and held few things too sacred to be laughed at. . . . He was continually tearing down ideas I had always believed in, and I was left to build them up anew. It was stimulating and exciting. . . . He was the best kind of companion one could have for a trip of this kind. I was learning far more than he realised (pp. 6–7).

Later, she describes Greene on the trek, with men crowded around him joking and laughing, "while he, like a benevolent father, would smile kindly upon them" (p. 68). He also grew a beard that never got past "the untidy beach-comber stage" (p. 49). On the last stages of the journey, Greene joined Barbara and Victor Prosser in singing the Liberian national anthem. Barbara by that time had become very irritated about Greene's socks continually wrinkling down around his ankles; he in turn was infuriated by her very short and baggy shorts.

Such tidbits provide some amusing information about the man who went on the journey; they do not tell us much about the writer or about the true purpose of his journey. Yet *Land Benighted* does show how different the experience seemed to Barbara, who lacked Greene's artistic purpose. She tends to record their journey in two ways, neither of them very close to Greene's. Many of her descriptions are tinged with romantic associations: a route no white people had walked, a Freetown bar that resembles a Somerset Maugham setting but "with no action," the strange adventures her friends expected her to have in Liberia. But for the most part Barbara's account gives more "facts" about the natives, the missionaries, and the route than we find in Greene's "analysis" of the journey.

Barbara Greene tells of Amadu's dignity, a quality that kept the cousins courteous toward each other (p. 8); although Greene late in *Journey without Maps* says, "It was to my cousin's credit that we never let our irritation with each other out into words" (*JM*, p. 266), for most of the journey he seems scarcely conscious of her presence. In Barbara's account, Lamina was "like a little Cockney street urchin . . . affectionate and lovable," who used to decorate her bed with blossoms during their trek.[1] Sometimes her descriptions are both clearer and less kind than her cousin's. For instance, she describes a woman missionary at Zorzor as resembling unbaked dough: a large white lump with black currants for eyes, "shapeless" and "podgy," yet with "a big heart" (pp. 81–84). She

1. Greene does write of his men (Amedoo, Laminah, and Souri): "Our relationship was to be almost as intimate as a love affair; they were to suffer from the same worn nerves; to be irritated by the same delays; but our life together, because it had been more perfectly rounded, seemed less real" (*JM*, p. 51).

tells more than Greene does of Amadu's illness at Bolahun; she also makes it quite plain that Greene himself was considerably more sick than one would gather from his own narrative.

Although Greene occasionally speaks of going "up" to a village, or refers to a ring of hills, his *Journey without Maps* is more concerned with inner reflections and with interpretations than with simple observations. In contrast, his cousin tells of the train puffing and panting up the hill to Pendenibu; she describes travel on the rough and hilly road beyond the frontier, where she and Greene scrambled up and down, "sometimes on all fours" (p. 17). She is more explicit about the dirt of the huts and the problems of bed, bathroom, and breakfast. Moreover, she adds all sorts of inconsequential details, including their craving for sugar, and Greene's obsession with such heavy food as steak and kidney pudding.

Since her book was published two years after *Journey without Maps*, it is not surprising that Barbara sometimes echoes her cousin's phrasing about seediness, rats, and civilization. Occasionally, she repeats a passage so closely that her variations from Greene's text emphasize their difference in purpose and outlook. Quoting Mark's letter, she includes phrases not in Greene's version (e.g., "I beg you and Miss or Madam," p. 25); Greene had suppressed the unnecessary reference to his female companion. Similarly, she adds to the account of the chief and his daughters at Djiecke the girl's remark: "My fadder says you very fine woman" (pp. 105–6). Oddly, Barbara saw this scene as "almost overpowering in its atmosphere of sex and drunkenness," whereas Greene found an atmosphere of "sex and relaxation" (*JM*, p. 197).

Barbara writes, "With a dreamlike inconsequence we would aim first for one village, then for another, always hoping that we were pointing our footsteps in the right direction" (p. 97); she says that the uncertainty of names and distances "made our whole adventure as unsubstantial as a shadow, and gave it the magic quality of a fairy tale" (p. 98). Yet in contrast to Greene's exploration of magic, of lost childhood, and of civilization "farther back," her "dreamlike" and "fairy-tale" journey is invariably a very direct account. Not only did Barbara dispose of preparations for the journey and the voyage to Africa in five pages; she also reached the Liberian frontier by page 15. Greene did not arrive until page 83 of his narrative. She writes with similar despatch at the end of the journey. Again her description—of continual drinking in Monrovia—bears little resemblance to Greene's memories. To Greene, the town was "more pleasant" than Freetown, its social life "more human and kindly than in an English colony" (*JM*, p. 292).

Continually on the journey Barbara sees Greene ahead of her on the path, comments on his behavior, observes the state of his health. Greene had only rarely referred to her, and then in such neutral terms that one might well miss the fact that his companion was a woman. He speaks of "the other woman" passenger on the voyage out, but once he and Barbara are on the journey he never seems to notice the cousin to whom he was once "grateful" (p. 10) for sharing the journey and about whom he was simply "anxious" (p. 149) when she became lost. At the end of *Journey without Maps*, back in England, Greene says nothing of Barbara, although according to her account he actually left her sitting alone on a railway platform in the rain, waiting for a train to London (p. 204).

APPENDIX B

The Bear Fell Free is an odd, very short story published in 1935. In its eighteen pages of narrative, Greene tries to present a group of lives in the jigsaw puzzle form suggested by the epigraph of *Journey without Maps*, in Holmes' analogy of the child's dissected map. Primarily, the story gives the fragments of Anthony[1] Farrell's experience: brief references to a gray-haired mother; to his friends Baron, a man wearing horn-rimmed glasses and carrying boardschool (i.e., free day school instead of proper Public School) memories, and Carter, a believer in being true blue, in the old school and the old battalion, in reunions, in "voting national"; to a girl named Jane who gave Anthony the plush bear of the title "because we are just crazy about each other," but who sleeps with both Baron and Carter.

The actual narrative comprises only a few dozen words: Anthony Farrell uses the money he has won in the Irish Sweepstakes to throw a party from which he takes off in a newly purchased plane on a solo flight to New York. Only the bear returns. Greene tells of "rearranging the pieces." He presents fragments of the various characters' thoughts interspersed with fragments from the past

---

1. Cf. Anthony Farrant, the immature hero of *England Made Me.*

(Carter going "over the top," seeking his friends dead in the trenches), future (Baron and Carter at the church door after Farrell's crash), and present (the moments before and during Farrell's flight).

Baron consciously and patiently, "like a child beginning a puzzle all over again," sets out the pieces of Farrell's money, won without labor by the accidental turn of a wheel, his own dreams of political success, and the sour taste of "the final soapsud." Yet the pieces Baron produces and the pieces Greene provides fail to make the final picture come clear. Greene writes: "All the pieces spread on the table: the marquee, Mrs. Farrell running, S.O.S. to shipping, not seen over Ireland, food tickets, the Irish sweep, Baron in his bath, leaving Buckingham Palace." These fragments are followed by twelve lines of unpunctuated and generally unidentifiable thoughts: "Reserve me a place on innumerable pieces, but no pieces ever mislaid . . . Christ eternally dying for a jigsaw piece."

Time is fragmented also. A description of the bear with a strand of seaweed coiled round one ear—after the crash and the rescue of the bear have been reported—is followed by an earlier moment, when Farrell bought his ticket: "Farrell bought a sweep ticket at the local pub, had another bitter. Carter lifted up his feet from the mud and wept for Davis [i.e., a memory of World War I]. Baron sorting out the muddle patiently, like a child with a jigsaw puzzle, died in his bath [i.e., a leap forward in time to the story's conclusion]."

Conflicting and confusing thoughts appear in seemingly unrelated sequence. Someone thinks: "It was great of young Farrell," but we are not sure whether these words are to be read as part of the adjacent speech by Baron, "No patience for mistakes. . . . So much to do." Jane's acceptance of Carter's phone call telling of Farrell's death (she says, "We were so crazy about each other") is followed by a fragment of movement: "She ran back to bed, naked, laughing, adorable," telling someone—perhaps Baron—"I've got such a lech for him, darling." Relatively straightforward dialogue is interspersed with interior monologue, especially of Farrell's drunken and brief thoughts in the plane. The vocabulary ranges from a simple shorthand to "flocculent" cloud and "steatopygous" women.

Odd as these bits and pieces may be, they are very familiar
Greeneana. The house shadows look like piano keys along the front
—a recurrent image. Carter is an omnipresent character (often a
villain—as noted), women fly to the party and land "like cockroaches," Carter wears an old school tie (Lancing), there are "birth
and death simultaneously," we hear a baby's birth cry, there is a suicide. But the total effect is one of unsuccessful experiment. Because of its very limited printing (250 copies), critics have largely
ignored *The Bear Fell Free* in spite of these significant elements.
Yet the final paragraph hints at the direction of the novels that followed *Journey without Maps*:

> Birth and death simultaneously tainted with each other. Guilt
> and suicide in the maternity ward, guilt and suicide in the
> trenches, in Jane's flat guilt and suicide. Patient serious Baron,
> tasting from the first of the final soapsud. . . . Money for
> nothing wrenched from Mrs. Farrell's womb, sherry circulating
> through the broken neck [Farrell's], unbearable agony of the
> cracked skull in Jane's bed. Prayers no good for something
> already happened, memory no good with no past, hope no good
> with no future, love no good with no end and no beginning.
>   The teddy bear fell free.

That final release suggests the larger reality of Greene's fictional
world, while the fragments of the narrative might well be drawn
from many of his novels.

BIBLIOGRAPHY OF WORKS CITED

GRAHAM GREENE: NOVELS, SHORT STORIES, POEMS, AND PLAYS

Dates in parentheses following earlier short stories are those given as "dates of writing" in the 1960 Heinemann edition of *Twenty-One Stories*.

BOOKS AND ARTICLES CONSULTED

"Across the Bridge" (1938). Based on Greene's Mexican journey, this story is set in a border town; it tells of a pursuit in which a "sentimental" detective is the dangerous one. In *19S* and *21S*.

"Alas, Poor Maling" (1940). One of the few stories in which Greene uses his experiences in World War II, this tells of Maling's "tragedy"—a peculiarly sensitive stomach that picks up and transmits sounds ranging from a Brahms Symphony to an air-raid alert. In *19S* and *21S*.

"Awful When You Think of It." The narrator's whimsical encounter with a baby aboard a train ("Even as a baby we carry the future with us. . . .")—a laughing baby who communicates in bubbles! In *MWB*.

Babbling April. Oxford: Basil Blackwell, 1925. This collection of poetry was Greene's first published book. Includes autobiographical poems (e.g., the "suicidal" experiences recorded in his essay "The Revolver in the Corner Cupboard") and anti-romantic verses (e.g., two men making grand gestures appear to the distant observer to be engaged in a romantic duel; on closer examination, the speaker finds that they are merely "like dogs using a wall").

"The Basement Room." "Conceived on a cargo steamer on the way home from Liberia to relieve the tedium of a voyage" (i.e., in 1935), according to a note in *The Third Man and The Fallen Idol* (p. 145). *Twenty-One Stories* gives the date of writing as 1936, although the story was first published in *The*

187

Basement Room and Other Stories (1935). The butler Baines has been on the seedy coast of Africa; the boy Philip is a child lost in England (for the first time Greene quotes the lines from "Germinal" on "the lost boyhood of Judas"). Although Greene rewrote the story for the film "The Fallen Idol," the version published in *The Third Man and The Fallen Idol* does not differ from the text in *19S* and *21S*.

The Basement Room and Other Stories. London: Cresset Press, 1935. Includes "The Basement Room," "Brother," "A Chance for Mr. Lever," "A Day Saved," "The End of the Party," "I Spy," "Jubilee," and "Proof Positive." Greene dates some of these stories 1936 in *21S* and the volume 1936 in a note to *19S*.

The Bear Fell Free. London: Grayson and Grayson, 1935. Two hundred and eighty-five copies were printed, two hundred and fifty of them for sale.

"Beauty." *Esquire*, April 1963, p. 60. A "perfect" dog and its owner, an "old sterile thing . . . calling for lost Beauty." (Hints of Greene's running attack on dogs, although the narrator asserts, "I was wholly on his side.") In *MWB*.

"The Blessing." *Harper's Magazine*, March 1966, pp. 91–94. Weld (a reporter), an archbishop blessing tanks ("blessing" is "when you want to love and you can't manage it" and Weld has "never known a blessing save a life"; also, "we bless what we hate"). Weld seems "in a simple landscape, yet one where every path led into a maze . . ." and there are allusions to a holy war, superstition, pious man.

"The Blue Film" (1954). Indo-China, a marked hero, and other recurrent elements, including Carter. In *21S*.

Brighton Rock. London: Heinemann, 1938. First published in the United States as an "entertainment," but later restored to "novel" classification. All quotations in text are from Heinemann 1950 reprint.

"Brother" (1936). Political action, Paris setting, and a couple reminiscent of Anthony and Kate Farrant in *England Made Me*. In *The Basement Room, 19S*, and *21S*.

A Burnt-Out Case. London: Heinemann, 1961. (French edition: *La Saison des Pluies*, since there is no French phrase for the "burnt-out" leper.)

Carving a Statue. London: Bodley Head, 1964. First performance at the Haymarket Theatre, London, September 17, 1964.

"The Case for the Defence" (1939). Related to *It's a Battlefield*, and other early stories of confused identity. One twin brother has apparently committed murder; after the acquittal, one of the men is pushed under a bus. The narrator asks, "Divine Vengeance?" In *19S* and *21S*.

"Chagrin in Three Parts." "Shabby" narrator, a "voyeur" (cf. Greene's description of himself) observing two women embarking on a lesbian encounter. The elder (a widow whose husband crowed like a cock ["après seulement deux coups"—but "jamais trois"] three times a week) is about to console the younger (whose husband performed three times a day, only "toujours d'une façon classique"). In *MWB*.

"A Chance for Mr. Lever" (1936). Based on Greene's journey through Liberia and on one of his fellow passengers on the African voyage. In *The Basement Room, 19S*, and *21S*.

"Cheap in August." The surprisingly tender encounter of Mary Watson, English wife of an American professor, in off-season Jamaica, and an old man, reminding her in turn of a hippo and of Neptune, but also making her think of "the remote future, after God knew what catastrophe." In *MWB*.

"Church Militant." *Commonweal*, January 6, 1956, pp. 350–52. A short story about religious orders in Kenya. "The Little Sisters of Charles de Foucauld" are pious ladies who refuse nursing duty; they will only empty slops or work like African women. The narrator is an "outsider" and a journalist. Father Donnell is a joke-loving priest, resembling those on Greene's Congo journey.

The Comedians. London: Bodley Head, 1966.

The Complaisant Lover. London: Heinemann, 1959. First performed at the Globe Theatre, London, on June 18, 1959.

The Confidential Agent. London: Heinemann, 1939. All quotations in the text are from *Three by Graham Greene.*

"A Day Saved" (1935). One of Greene's early stories about identity. A man responds to many names, none of them clearly his own. In *The Basement Room, 19S,* and *21S.*

"Dear Dr. Falkenheim." *Vogue,* January 1, 1963, pp. 100–101. Written in the form of a letter to a psychoanalyst, this story picks up a number of Greene's familiar themes—even the "chromium-plated" world of the United States, which here changes to Canada. The narrator's son, Colin, witnessed the death of Father Christmas (beheaded by a helicopter in the midst of a group of children). The boy grows up unable to stop believing in Santa Claus ("'Of course he's real,' he says, a bit like an early Christian, 'I saw him die'").

"The Destructors" (1954). Horrible children plot to demolish an old man's house; it falls to the sound of a lorry driver's laughter. In *21S.*

"A Discovery in the Woods." *Rogue,* March 1963, pp. 68–72, 76–78. Children explore strange territory in a world apparently devastated by atomic blast long ago. They are all deformed; they kiss a "cross," not knowing its significance. In *SR.*

"Doctor Crombie." Another of Greene's stories examining "innocence." Here, an "image of innocence" is the peaceful afternoon spent by the narrator as a boy with his school doctor. The adult and the "innocent" have different interpretations of "playing with oneself," but the narrator does indeed develop cancer (to the doctor, the result of "sexual congress"). In *MWB.*

"Dream of a Strange Land." *Saturday Evening Post,* January 19, 1963, pp. 44–47. A story assembling Greene's recurrent leper, doctor, casino, teeth, "deep country," a shabby patient with frayed cuffs, a man who had worked "on the coast," patient and doctor "lost." The patient feels as though he had missed the path; the sound of a revolver, hinting of death, and talk of suicide provide additional echoes of Greene's "The Revolver in the Corner Cupboard." In *SR.*

"A Drive in the Country" (1937). This story foreshadows some of the details in *Brighton Rock.* Fred drives his "immature" unnamed girlfriend out into the country and tries to persuade her to join in a suicide pact. She does not; after the incident, "she was quite free from pain." In *19S* and *21S.*

The End of the Affair. London: Heinemann, 1951.

"The End of the Party" (1929). *London Mercury,* July 1932, pp. 238–44. Greene's first story of twins—two children at a party where one of them dies while "Peter wondered with an obscure self-pity why it was that the pulse of his brother's fear went on, when Francis was now where he had been always told there was no more terror and no more darkness." In *The Basement Room, 19S,* and *21S.*

England Made Me. London: Heinemann, 1935. Quotations in the text are from Heinemann Uniform Edition, 1947.

The Heart of the Matter. London: Heinemann, 1948. Quotations in the text are from the Heinemann Uniform Edition, 1951.

"The Hint of an Explanation" (1948). *Commonweal,* February 11, 1949, pp.

438–42. The narrator is an "Agnostic" recounting a story heard on a railway journey: the baker Blacker had tried to bribe a boy to steal a consecrated wafer—an example of "the corruption of children"—but the boy became a priest who remembers "that Thing weeping for its inevitable defeat." In the American edition of *19S*, and in *21S*.

"I Spy" (1930). An early story in which a child is faced with the mystery of adult experience (two men escort his father away in the dark). In *The Basement Room*, *19S*, and *21S*.

"The Innocent" (1937). A short story based on Greene's visit to Berkhamsted (see "Twenty-four Hours in Metroland"). The narrator is held by "the smell of innocence" which contrasts with the cheap perfume of the pickup he is traveling with. Walking through the town in which he grew up, the man thinks of the past: "It was like a map which had got wet in the pocket and pieces had stuck together . . . there were whole patches hidden." In *19S* and *21S*.

"The Invisible Japanese Gentlemen." *Saturday Evening Post*, November 20, 1965, pp. 60–61. Though present, the Japanese of the title serve only as a comment on the girl whose editor has apparently praised the "powers of observation" in her first novel. She has not even seen these eight men, but the narrator (also a writer) has observed the girl as she discusses the future with a young man (also, characters are "matching miniatures, but what a contrast in fact they were"). In *MWB*.

It's a Battlefield. London: Heinemann, 1934. Quotations in the text are from the Heinemann Uniform Edition, 1959.

"Jubilee" (1936). A brief tale of an encounter between "frayed" Mr. Chalfont and "vulgar," "cheerful," "overblown" Amy, who clearly foreshadows Ida Arnold. In *The Basement Room*, *19S*, and *21S*.

The Labyrinthine Ways. New York: Viking, 1940. First American edition of *The Power and the Glory*. The 1946 American edition resumed the original title.

The Little Horse Bus. London: Parrish, 1952. Greene's other children's books are *The Little Fire Engine*, *The Little Steam Roller*, and *The Little Train*. John Atkins in *Graham Greene* (London, 1957) quotes Greene as saying that these books were written during the flying bomb raids of 1944 "for fun and relaxation" (p. 175).

"A Little Place Off the Edgware Road" (1939). Craven is a man in "frayed" clothes who is obsessed with "the toothache of horror"; he goes to an old movie house and encounters a man already dead. In *19S* and *21S*.

The Living Room. London: Heinemann, 1953. First performance, Wyndham's Theatre, London, April 16, 1953. Quotations in the text are from the American edition (New York: Viking Press, 1954).

Loser Takes All. London: Heinemann, 1955. Also published in *Harper's*, October 1955–January 1956. An entertainment "originally written for the films."

"The Lottery Ticket" (1938). In this short story, set in Vera Cruz, "the action dictated by hate was like an action of love." In the English edition of *19S* only.

The Man Within. London: Heinemann, 1929. Quotations in the text are from the Heinemann Uniform Edition, 1959.

"May We Borrow Your Husband?" *The London Magazine*, November 1962, pp. 5–30. The narrator is a middle-aged writer, William Harris ("a professional novelist" working on a biography of Rochester—the subject of one of Greene's own *Spectator* reviews), witnessing the seduction of a young honeymooning husband by a pair of homosexual interior decorators, Stephen and

Tony. There are mocking references to "the ecclesiastical rules," "innocence almost unbearable," a character named Colin, and other familiar Greene tidbits, as well as the "air of innocence" of the young couple in "this sad little comedy." In *MWB*.

May We Borrow Your Husband? and Other Comedies of the Sexual Life. New York: Viking, 1967. Includes "May We Borrow Your Husband?," "Beauty," "Chagrin in Three Parts," "The Over-night Bag," "Mortmain," "Cheap in August," "A Shocking Accident," "The Invisible Japanese Gentlemen," "Awful When you Think of It," "Doctor Crombie," "The Root of all Evil," and "Two Gentle People."

"Men at Work" (1940). *New Yorker,* October 25, 1941, pp. 63–66. A satirical account of civil servants during the early months of World War II. In *19S* and *21S*.

The Ministry of Fear. London: Heinemann, 1943. Quotations in the text are from *Three by Graham Greene*.

"Mortmain." *Playboy,* March 1963, pp. 77, 110, 136–37. The title echoes an earlier comment on the Roman Catholic confession freeing the sinner from the mortmain of the past (*EA,* p. 56). Philip Carter, a forty-two-year-old writer, has just married young Julia; his former companion shows a "deadly kindness"—little notes scattered around the apartment they used to share, even under the mattress, giving Julia advice. In *MWB*.

The Name of Action. London: Heinemann, 1930. Greene will not permit reprinting. Although this story was written some years before Greene's journey to Liberia, the hero has a sense of "dangerous walking in a hazardous place" (p. 22). Anne-Marie looks like someone who has completed a long journey (p. 336). Chant remarks that "men have always tried to solve the mystery of God, whether by mathematics or by prayers . . ." (p. 286; cf. Bendrix' words). A Christ figure seems to Chant to represent "the God who, like an eagle, tears the hearts of men out with doubts, terror, mystery and what is strangely called divine unrest" (cf. the Prometheus statue in "Dream of a Strange Land," and the Judas-Prometheus analogy in *The Power and the Glory*).

Nineteen Stories. London: Heinemann, 1947. The stories of *The Basement Room and Other Stories,* with the addition of "Across the Bridge," "Alas, Poor Maling," "The Case for the Defence," "A Drive in the Country," "The Innocent," "A Little Place Off the Edgware Road," "The Lottery Ticket," "Men at Work," "The Second Death," and "When Greek Meets Greek," as well as the unfinished novel "The Other Side of the Border." The American edition omits "The Lottery Ticket" and substitutes "The Hint of an Explanation."

"The Other Side of the Border" (1936). Based on Greene's journey to Africa in 1935. In *19S* only.

Our Man in Havana. London: Heinemann, 1958. An entertainment. Quotations in the text are from the American edition (New York: Viking Press, 1958).

"The Over-night Bag." A macabre tale with various bizarre details, and ironies and mysteries related to this bag carried from Nice to London. Its owner (another Henry) is en route to his mother's, and the bag supposedly contains a baby's body ("My wife's baby," carefully so distinguished). In *MWB*.

"The Palace of Chance." *The Reporter,* December 2, 1965, pp. 41–42. Fragment of *The Comedians,* including the narrator's "only love affair . . . which ended without pain or regret."

The Potting Shed. London: Heinemann, 1957. First performance, January 29,

1957, at the Bijou Theater, New York. Quotations in the text are from the American edition (New York: Viking Press, 1957).

The Power and the Glory. London: Heinemann, 1940. Quotations in the text are from Heinemann Library Edition, 1959.

"Proof Positive" (1930). An early life-after-death story in which a man who "must have been dead a week" testifies to the spirit outliving the body, but "all he had certainly revealed was how, without the body's aid, the spirit in seven days decayed into whispered nonsense." In *The Basement Room, 19S,* and *21S.*

The Quiet American. London: Heinemann, 1955.

"The Root of All Evil." *Saturday Evening Post,* March 7, 1964, pp. 56–58. The narrator recounts his Protestant father's story linking "secrecy" and "sin." Here, "the heart of the mystery" involves farcical disguises, misread as transvestitism; a father is hostile to fairy stories (cf. the mother in "Under the Garden"); and as the result of "curiosity" death comes from a falling chamber-pot. In *MWB.*

Rumour at Nightfall. London: Heinemann, 1931. Greene will not permit further reprints (there was one in 1933). The novel preceded his Liberian journey, but Greene uses the map metaphor: Crane "never consented to leave another mind unmapped. He must always be affixing labels and symbolic figures in the manner of the old cartographers with 'Here are fears. Here Superstitions dwell. Here Purity. And here lust reigns.'" Refers to God betraying Judas, "waiting for his coming." Quotations are from the American edition (New York: Doubleday, 1932).

"The Second Death" (1929). In *19S* and *21S.*

"The Secret." Original title of "Two Gentle People" when it appeared in *Vogue,* January 1, 1967, pp. 94–95.

A Sense of Reality. New York: Viking, 1963. Includes "A Discovery in the Woods," "Dream of a Strange Land," "Under the Garden," and "A Visit to Morin."

The Shipwrecked. New York: Viking, 1935. American edition of *England Made Me.*

"A Shocking Accident." A boy has "re-created" his Father (a "restless" author) just as "man re-creates God," but his romantic response to news of his father's death is deflated by the reality: "A pig fell on him." Following Jerome to the moment when his fiancée repeats Jerome's childhood response ("What happened to the pig?"), Greene again examines the "comic," "death without pain," and "fear." In *MWB.*

"Special Duties" (1954). In *21S.*

Stamboul Train. London: Heinemann, 1932. Greene's first entertainment. In the United States, published as *Orient Express.*

"The Third Man." *American Magazine,* March 1949, pp. 142–60.

The Third Man and The Fallen Idol. London: Heinemann, 1950. Quotations in the text are from the 1953 reprint. (Although written as a film, the published version of the story differs from the movie *The Third Man.*)

This Gun for Hire. New York: Doubleday, 1936. (In England, *A Gun for Sale.*) Quotations are from *Three by Graham Greene.*

Three by Graham Greene. New York: Viking (n.d.). The three entertainments: *This Gun for Hire, The Confidential Agent,* and *The Ministry of Fear.*

Travels with My Aunt. New York: Viking, 1970.

Twenty-One Stories. London: Heinemann, 1954. This volume contains the same stories as the 1947 Heinemann edition of *Nineteen Stories,* but omits

"The Lottery Ticket" and "The Other Side of the Border" and adds "The Hint of an Explanation," "The Blue Film," "Special Duties," and "The Destructors."

"Two Gentle People." Marie-Claire and Henry, a middle-aged couple on a park bench ("modesty and disillusion gave them something in common") enjoy a delicately rendered encounter and dinner. They separate—she to hear once more her husband in an adjoining room with his latest homosexual partner, and he to return to his demanding wife Patience ("fond of Coca-Cola"), concluding with an unvoiced, mild protest against "the condition of life." In *MWB*. Also published as "The Secret."

"Under the Garden." In *SR*.

"A Visit to Morin." *The London Magazine,* January 1957, pp. 13–25. In *SR*.

"When Greek Meets Greek" (1941). *Illustrated London News* (Supplement), November 20, 1941, pp. 1–4. Driver, a man who "believes" in religion, enrols his son (a youth with a scar, serving a prison term) in a correspondence course for a degree at an institution that is actually "a swindle called St. Ambrose's College, Oxford." In *19S* and *21S*.

GRAHAM GREENE: TRAVELS, ESSAYS, AND CRITICISM

Many of the essays noted below, including those reprinted in *The Lost Childhood* (*LC*), also appear in Graham Greene's *Collected Essays* (London: Bodley Head, 1969).

"Analysis of a Journey." *Spectator,* September 27, 1935, pp. 459–60.

"At Home." Essay on wartime violence, in *The Lost Childhood.*

"Before the Attack." *Spectator,* April 16, 1954, p. 456. Dated January 5, Hanoi and Dien Bien Phu, this despatch from Indo-China includes a big woman with a desire to help (a sort of female Pyle), a scarred priest, and a description of bodies in a canal.

"The Blind Eye." *Spectator,* July 1, 1938, p. 13. The stowaway incident included in *The Lawless Roads.*

"A Boat-load of Politicians." *Spectator,* December 6, 1935, pp. 938–39. The Liberian launch incident of *Journey without Maps.*

"Bombing-Raid." *Spectator,* August 18, 1939, p. 249. Included in *The Lost Childhood and Other Essays* as "Bombing Manœuvre," pp. 186–88.

"Books in General." *New Statesman and Nation,* June 21, 1952, p. 745.

"Books in General." *New Statesman and Nation,* July 18, 1953, p. 76.

"Books in General." *New Statesman and Nation,* October 2, 1954, p. 411.

"Boy Loses Girl." *Spectator,* January 27, 1939, p. 141.

"The Catholic Temper in Poland." *Atlantic Monthly,* March 1956, pp. 39–41.

"The Cinema." *Spectator,* January 10, 1936, p. 50.

"The Cinema." *Spectator,* January 17, 1936, p. 91.

"The Cinema." *Spectator,* March 20, 1936, p. 512.

"The Cinema." *Spectator,* April 10, 1936, p. 664.

"The Cinema." *Spectator,* May 1, 1936, p. 791.

"The Cinema." *Spectator,* May 8, 1936, p. 835.

"The Cinema." *Spectator,* June 12, 1936, p. 1080.

"The Cinema." *Spectator,* June 10, 1938, p. 1056.

"The Cinema." *Spectator,* June 17, 1938, p. 1096.

"The Cinema." *Spectator,* November 11, 1938, p. 807.

"The Cinema." *Spectator,* April 14, 1939, p. 632.

"The Cinema." *Spectator,* April 21, 1939, p. 668.

"The Cinema." *Spectator*, May 5, 1939, p. 760.

"The Cinema." *Spectator*, December 1, 1939, p. 776.

"The Cinema." *Spectator*, February 16, 1940, p. 213.

"Congo Journal." Published in *In Search of a Character*.

"Convoy to West Africa." In *The Mint*, edited by Geoffrey Grigson. London: Routledge, 1946. Greene's journal of his wartime voyage to Sierra Leone was reprinted with only minor changes in *In Search of a Character*.

"The Dark Backward: A Footnote." *London Mercury*, October 1935, pp. 562–65. An essay on the ways in which novelists deal with the passage of time: Henry James, Elizabeth Bowen, Ford Madox Ford.

"A Day at the General's." *Spectator*, April 15, 1938, p. 670. Greene's description of his visit to General Cedillo, included in *The Lawless Roads*.

"Death in the Cotswolds." *Spectator*, February 24, 1933, p. 247. The Charlie Sykes (Seitz) episode included in *Journey without Maps*.

"Devil-Blacksmith." *Spectator*, March 6, 1936, pp. 393–94. An incident from Greene's African journey, included in *Journey without Maps*.

"The Dictator of Grand Bassa." *Spectator*, January 17, 1936, pp. 89–90. In the *Spectator* essay, Greene refers more often to the color and the American origin of the Dictator than in *Journey without Maps*.

"The Domestic Background." One of Greene's reviews dealing with Joseph Conrad, reprinted in *The Lost Childhood*, pp. 100–101.

"Edwardian Inferno." *Spectator*, February 16, 1934, p. 240. Reprinted as part of Greene's essay on "Frederick Rolfe" in *The Lost Childhood*.

"The Entertainments of A. E. W. Mason." *New Statesman and Nation*, October 4, 1952, p. 381.

"The Escapist." *Spectator*, January 13, 1939, pp. 48–49. The episode of K on the German liner returning from Mexico, reported in *The Lawless Roads*; it includes another reference to the "map" of life—"The pieces of the jigsaw slowly came together, making a picture of escape."

"A Few Pipes: Extract from an Indo-China Journal." *The London Magazine*, December 1954, pp. 17–24. Greene's report of his experiences with opium includes some dreams that may have provided ideas for *The Quiet American*; for instance, Greene made a bargain with the Devil—something to do with a girl "with whom I was apparently living." Another dream, of architectural squares, perhaps suggested Querry's occupation in *A Burnt-Out Case*.

"Fiction." *Spectator*, February 10, 1933, p. 194.

"Fiction." *Spectator*, June 16, 1933, p. 880.

"Fiction." *Spectator*, June 30, 1933, p. 956.

"Fiction." *Spectator*, September 22, 1933, p. 380.

"Fiction." *Spectator*, October 20, 1933, p. 538.

"Fiction." *Spectator*, May 18, 1934, p. 786.

"Fiction." *Spectator*, June 1, 1934, p. 864.

"Fiction." *Spectator*, June 29, 1934, p. 1010.

"Fiction." *Spectator*, July 27, 1934, p. 144.

"Ford Madox Ford." *Spectator*, July 7, 1939, p. 11. Compares Ford's method in his later books with the "method Conrad followed more stiffly and less skillfully." Reprinted in *The Lost Childhood*, pp. 89–91.

"Fragment de journal: le grand bombardement du mercredi 16 avril 1941." In Victor de Pange, *Graham Greene*, pp. 117–22.

"François Mauriac." A review of Mauriac's *La Pharisienne*, discussing Mauriac's other works, and pointing out the importance of the "religious sense" in novels. Reprinted in *The Lost Childhood*, pp. 69–73.

"Frederick Rolfe: Edwardian Inferno, From the Devil's Side, [and] A Spoiled

Priest." Greene's three-part essay on the proximity of Good and Evil, the resemblance between saint and sinner, reprinted in *The Lost Childhood*, pp. 92–97.

"The General and the Spy: Extract from an Indo-China Journal." *The London Magazine*, August 1954, pp. 26–29. Datelined Saigon, December 31, this report describes an occasion when Greene and a friend were under suspicion as members of the British Secret Service.

"Great Dog of Weimar." *Spectator*, November 8, 1940, p. 474. In this report on a "talking" dog, Greene explains his attitude toward dogs: "I have always suspected dogs: solid, well-meaning, reliable, they seem to possess all the least attractive human virtues." Reprinted in *The Lost Childhood*, pp. 168–70.

"In Search of a Character." *Harper's*, January 1962, pp. 66–74. These extracts from "Congo Journal" omit most of Greene's references to sex.

In Search of a Character. New York: Viking Press, 1962. Two African journals: "Convoy to West Africa" and "Congo Journal."

"Indo-China." *New Republic*, April 5, 1954, pp. 13–15. A despatch in which Greene discussed the differences between British and American participation in Indo-China and referred to the "American dream" of a third force.

"An Indo-China Journal." *Commonweal*, May 21, 1954, pp. 170–72. A critical description of Vandenburg; and comparison of European and Vietnamese Mass.

"The Job of the Writer." *The Observer*, September 15, 1957, p. 3 (Greene on his role as novelist and as reporter).

Journey without Maps. London: Heinemann, 1936. Only the first edition was dedicated: "To my Wife: 'I carry you like a passport everywhere,'" from William Plomer's "Visiting the Caves." Quotations in the text are from the Heinemann Uniform (reset) Edition, 1953, except where reference is made to the Compass Books Edition (New York: Viking Press, 1961), which generally follows the first rather than the reset edition. In the Uniform Edition the section originally entitled "Pa Oakley" becomes "Daddy," and "Signed Aronstein" is replaced by "No Screws Unturned." The principal omission from the reset edition is Greene's encounter with colonial protocol and color prejudice.

"Last Act in Indo-China." *New Republic*, May 9, 1955, pp. 9–11; and May 16, 1955, pp. 10–12.

"The Last Word." In *The Old School*. Greene's description of Berkhamsted School.

The Lawless Roads. London: Longmans, 1939. Quotations in the text are from the Heinemann Uniform Edition, 1955.

"Legend." *Spectator*, April 24, 1936, p. 766. Book reviews, including Stephen Spender's *The Burning Cactus* and Katherine Anne Porter's *Flowering Judas*.

"The Lesson of the Master." *Spectator*, April 26, 1935, p. 698. An essay on James' fictional world of corruption and violence. Reprinted in *The Lost Childhood*, pp. 49–50.

"Lettre de Graham Greene." *Dieu Vivant* 17 (1950): 151–52. A letter in which Greene qualified the remarks he had made during "Propos de table avec Graham Greene"; he pointed out the difficulties of an interview, especially his embarrassment at talking about his books, and his attempt to cut the interview short with an abrupt half-truth.

"London Diary." *New Statesman and Nation*, November 22, 1952, p. 593. Miscellaneous commentary (including political) and references to the "sad pleasure" of looking at old diaries.

"The Lost Childhood." Title essay written for the collection *The Lost Child-hood and Other Essays*, pp. 13–17. Greene gives an account of his boyhood reading and his discovery of evil, referring to his childhood as "fourteen years in a wild jungle country without a map."

The Lost Childhood and Other Essays. London: Eyre and Spottiswoode, 1951. Most of these essays appeared first in *The Spectator, New Statesman and Nation, London Mercury*, and other periodicals.

"Men and Messages." *Spectator*, August 19, 1938, pp. 310–11.

"Mr. Maugham's Pattern." *Spectator*, January 14, 1938, p. 59.

"A Note on Hans Andersen." *Spectator*, December 8, 1933, p. 854. Greene notes Andersen's "Artist's parallel to the Catholic ideal of the acceptance of pain for a spiritual benefit."

"A Novelist's Notebook." *Spectator*, October 1, 1937, p. 557.

The Old School: Essays by Divers Hands. Edited by Graham Greene. London: Jonathan Cape, 1934.

"Les paradoxes du christianisme." *Dieu Vivant* 18 (1951): 35–42. An important essay on the association of Good and Evil, the closeness of God and the Devil, and the country in which the Christian dwells, "un pays de bri-gandage, entre le Bien et le Mal."

"Pigs, Be British." *Spectator*, March 23, 1934, p. 455. One of Greene's earliest humorous essays, a "review" of Walt Disney's book of *The Three Little Pigs*, in which Greene makes some sly comments on the differences between Eng-lishmen and Americans and comments on the peculiarly British qualities of the pig: "Honest, a little stupid, commercially-minded, perhaps, but with a trace of idealism in his love affairs."

"Propos de table avec Graham Greene." *Dieu Vivant* 16 (1950): 127–37. Transcript of a conversation between Greene, Père Jouve, and Marcel Moré, datelined "Paris, déjeuner du 20 décembre 1949." Greene discusses *The Heart of the Matter*, denies various so-called influences on his work, and at-tempts to explain the presence of evil and of Catholicism in his novels.

"Rebel Manqué." *Spectator*, January 12, 1934, p. 56.

"Remembering Mr. Jones." *Spectator*, September 17, 1937, pp. 469–70. A re-view of an edition of Conrad's *Prefaces*, noting the differences between these and the Prefaces of James as well as describing Conrad's "residual" Catholicism. Reprinted in *The Lost Childhood*, pp. 98–99.

"The Revenge." *Commonweal*, January 14, 1955, pp. 403–4. Greene recalls an encounter in December 1951 at Kuala Lumpur with "Watson," one of a pair of bullies (the other was Carter) who had "tortured" him during their years at Berkhamsted School. Greene even suggests, "The past lost some of its power—I wrote it out of me. . . . I wondered . . . whether I would ever have written a book if it had not been for Watson and the dead Carter."

"The Revolver in the Corner Cupboard." In *The Saturday Book*, edited by Leonard Russell, pp. 135–38. London: Hutchinson, 1946. Greene's descrip-tion of playing Russian roulette after he had been "wrung dry" by psycho-analysis; he concludes, "The war against boredom had to go on." In *The Lost Childhood*, pp. 173–76.

"Short Stories." *Spectator*, May 22, 1936, p. 950.

"The Soupsweet Land: Return to Freetown, Sierra Leone." *Holiday*, August 1968, pp. 40–41. A quarter of a century later, Greene recalls his wartime mis-adventures; comments on the significance of childhood; and revisits the fa-miliar scenes (including several used in *The Heart of the Matter*). He con-cludes: "I felt the guilt of a beachcomber *manqué*: I had failed at failure. How could they tell that for a writer as much as for a priest, there is no such thing as success?"

"Strike in Paris." *Spectator,* February 16, 1934, pp. 229–30.

"Subjects and Stories." In *Footnotes to the Film,* edited by Charles Davy. London: Lovat Dickson, 1938. Greene draws a parallel between cinema and novel, and states the only true subject for a film: "Life as it is and life as it ought to be." Quotes Ford Madox Ford on the poetic quality of James and Conrad (i.e., their "power to suggest human values"). Praises as "proper" popular use of film the work of Chaplin and of Laurel and Hardy.

"Theatre." *New Statesman and Nation,* September 13, 1947, p. 208.

"Three Travellers." *Spectator,* December 8, 1939, p. 838.

"To Hope Till Hope Creates." *New Republic,* April 12, 1954, pp. 11–13. A report from Saigon, in which Greene advocated independence for Indo-China.

"The Turn of the Screw." *Spectator,* June 20, 1941, p. 657.

"Twenty-Four Hours in Metroland." *New Statesman and Nation,* August 13, 1938, p. 250. A description of Berkhamsted, giving details Greene also used in *The Lawless Roads* and in "The Innocent."

"Two Capitals." *Spectator,* October 20, 1933, pp. 520–21. One of Greene's earliest journeys, perhaps providing some of the details of setting for *England Made Me.*

"Vive le Roi." *Spectator,* July 22, 1938, pp. 139–40. An essay in which Greene expressed "pity for the human race" and gave an ironic view of "civilization" through the eyes of African troops in Paris. Reprinted in *The Lost Childhood,* pp. 177–79.

"Voyage in the Dark." *Spectator,* September 16, 1938, p. 437. An incident later included in *The Lawless Roads.*

"The Waste Land." *Spectator,* June 7, 1935, p. 986.

"West Coast." *Spectator,* April 12, 1935, pp. 620, 622.

"What is an English Film?" *Spectator,* June 5, 1936, p. 1036.

Why Do I Write? London: Percival Marshall, 1948. An exchange of views between Elizabeth Bowen, Graham Greene, and V. S. Pritchett.

Books and Articles Consulted

Anon. "Shocker." *Time,* October 29, 1951, pp. 98–104. Profile-Interview, illustrated.

Atkins, John. *Graham Greene.* London: John Calder, 1957.

Birmingham, William. "Graham Greene Criticism: A Bibliographical Study." *Thought* 27 (Spring 1952): 72–100.

Breit, Harvey. "In and Out of Books." *New York Times Book Review,* January 20, 1957, p. 8.

Camus, Albert. *Le Mythe de Sisyphe.* Paris: Gallimard, 1942.

Clurman, Robert. "In and Out of Books." *New York Times Book Review,* August 26, 1956, p. 8.

Costello, Donald P. "Graham Greene and the Catholic Press." *Renascence* 12 (1959): 3–28.

de Pange, Victor. *Graham Greene.* Paris: Éditions Universitaires, 1953.

de Quénétain, Tanneguy. "Faut-il brûler Graham Greene?" *Réalités,* décembre 1962, pp. 123–25. A slightly different article appeared in the English edition of *Réalités* (see Guy Martin).

De Vitis, A. A. "The Entertaining Mr. Greene." *Renascence* 14 (Autumn 1961): 8–24.

Evans, Robert O. "Existentialism in Greene's *The Quiet American.*" *Modern Fiction Studies* 3 (1957): 241–48.

Greene, Barbara. *Land Benighted.* London: Geoffrey Bles, 1938.

Kunkel, Francis L. "The Hollow Man." *Renascence* 14 (Autumn 1961): 48–49.

Lewis, R. W. B. *The Picaresque Saint.* New York: Lippincott, 1956 (1959 ed.).

Martin, Guy. "The Heart of the Graham Greene Matter." *Réalités,* December 1962, pp. 60–63.

Mauriac, François. "La Puissance et la Gloire." *Renascence* 1 (Spring 1949): 25–27.

Rostenne, Paul. *Graham Greene: Témoin des temps tragiques.* Paris: Juilliard, 1949.

Shuttleworth, Martin, and Raven, Simon. "The Art of Fiction III: Graham Greene." *The Paris Review,* 3 (Autumn 1953): 24–41.

Smith, George D., ed. *The Teachings of the Catholic Church.* London: Burns, Oates, and Washbourne, 1948.

Stratford, Philip. "Unlocking the Potting Shed." *Kenyon Review* 24 (Winter 1962): 129–43.

Note: For an excellent bibliography, the reader is directed to Philip Stratford, *Faith and Fiction: Creative Process in Greene and Mauriac* (University of Notre Dame Press, 1964), a volume that appeared after all of my material on the works up to and including 1963 had been completed.

INDEX

"Aboriginal calamity" (quoted), 53, 128, 153n

Absurdity and the Absurd Condition, 1, 3, 4, 14, 71, 72, 100n, 114, 116, 117, 120, 127, 130, 131, 133, 134, 136, 141, 141n, 142, 142n, 143, 152, 156–58 passim, 169

Accident, death as, 167

Accidents of transubstantiation, 38n. See also Communion; Eucharist; Mass

Acky, 40, 115n, 146n

"Across the Bridge," 154

Adam's wound, 38n

Adolescence, 27, 55, 64, 80, 82, 90, 102, 116, 141, 148, 154, 155; in Mexico, 2, 53, 55, 56, 57, 71, 79n; religious, 102

Adolescent characters: Cholmondeley, 34, 39–40, 41; in The Complaisant Lover, 128; Pemberton, 84, 88; Pyle, 87n, 112, 113; Rowe, 87n; Wilson, 84, 87, 87n. See also Cruelty; Giggling; Pinkie; Romance

Adult, contemporary, 3, 80, 102, 155; perceptions of, 16, 17, 34, 89, 128, 161; sentimental responses of, 17;

"wholeness," 82. See also Absurdity; Laughter; Maturity; Suffering

A.E. (George William Russell). See "Germinal"

Aesthetic sense, 23n, 26, 29, 102, 116, 134, 147, 152, 160. See also Boredom; Journeys

Africa, 2, 5–32, 40, 57, 61–62, 63, 78, 124, 131–38, 141n, 160; beauty of, 7, 13, 20–21, 23n, 24, 29, 56, 58n, 134, 135, 136; comparisons with American and European "civilization," 12, 15, 19, 22, 23–25, 23n, 26, 27–29, 31, 134, 136; comparisons with Mexico, 56–58 passim, 58n, 61–62; emotions ("purer" terrors, etc.), 12, 19, 21–22, 31, 45, 56, 105, 116, 136; Greene's "fixation," 2, 131; imagination and perception in, 1, 2, 4, 6, 7, 12, 19, 23, 27–28, 31, 32, 51, 82, 132, 162, 167; religious values, 2, 14–15, 19, 27, 32, 51, 107, 136; self-understanding, 14, 18, 19, 29–30, 31, 133, 134, 135; as setting, 28n, 34, 34n, 133, 133n, 135; symbolism, 2, 6–8, 8n, 9, 11, 12, 14, 15,

Fell Free, 184. *See also* Question, novelist's
Diaries: Conrad, 137; Marie, 145*n*; Querry, 144; Sarah, 91, 92, 94, 144; Scobie, 88
Dickens, Charles, 177
Digby. *See* Rowe, Arthur
"A Discovery in the Woods," 149*n*, 173
"Disloyalty," writer's, 52*n*, 167
Dogs, 16–17, 98, 126, 126*n*, 174–75
Donner, Etta (*Hinterland Liberia*), 15
"Dream of a Strange Land," 121, 127*n*, 139*n*, 142, 175
Dream(s), 9, 18, 25, 30, 31, 35, 79*n*, 81, 99, 126*n*, 132, 138*n*, 155*n*, 162, 163, 163*n*, 171, 173, 174; as source of Greene's plots, 18. *See also* Fantasy
"A Drive in the Country," 129
Driver, 153
Duogobmai, 13, 21, 22, 26

Eliot, T. S., 4*n*, 7, 7*n*, 31
The End of the Affair, 3, 9, 10, 36, 38*n*, 43, 77, 78, 80, 85–86, 86*n*, 90–96, 97*n*, 99, 108, 112, 121, 124, 125, 127, 129, 139, 139*n*, 143*n*, 144, 148, 155*nn*, 156*n*, 164, 165, 171, 172
"The End of the Party," 6, 44*n*, 98*n*
England, Church of. *See* Anglicans
England and the English, 7, 19, 22, 23*n*, 24, 25, 26, 29, 34, 51*n*, 56, 57, 58, 61, 62, 102, 102*n*; British Empire, 102*n*
England Made Me, 6, 9, 10, 22, 34*n*, 37, 38*n*, 93, 111, 115, 115*n*, 119, 127*n*, 129*n*, 139*n*
Entertainments, 5, 32, 35*n*, 40, 42, 51–52, 63, 77, 78, 81, 120, 121, 139*n*, 171. *See also The Confidential Agent; Loser Takes All; The Ministry of Fear; Our Man in Havana; Stamboul Train; The Third Man; This Gun for Hire*
"The Entertainments of A. E. W. Mason," 35*n*
Epigraphs, 6, 10–11, 13, 53, 78, 119, 138*n*, 139*n*, 151, 153*n*, 164, 170, 183
Episcopalians, 15, 29

"Epitaph for a Play," 100*n*, 119
Equation, Bendrix', 36, 86, 86*n*, 92, 96; "God of formulas," 124
Escape, 38*n*, 49, 68
"The Escapist," 61*n*
Essays, Greene's, 4*n*, 33*n*, 34, 40, 44, 106*n*, 130, 137, 146, 152. *See also* Journalist, Greene as; individual titles
Ethical questions. *See* Characters, moral and spiritual dimensions of; Fiction, Greene on
Eucharist, 45, 49, 69, 75, 93, 157. *See also* Communion; Mass
Europe and Europeans, 2, 3, 11, 12, 15, 19, 22–25, 23*n*, 26, 27, 29, 57, 61, 61*n*, 78, 102, 105–7 passim, 134, 136, 141*nn*
Everyman, 79, 108–10 passim, 116
Evil, 27, 31, 39, 42, 44, 49, 53, 58, 59, 61*n*, 69, 74, 127; Jamesian evil, 137; saints and evil, 146*n*. *See also* Goodness
Existentialism, 142, 143*n*, 176
Exploration, psychological, 2, 4, 18, 29–30, 150, 160. *See also* Africa; Psychoanalysis
Explorer: artist and writer as, 1–2, 12, 14, 16, 29, 29*n*, 137*n*, 160, 161, 167; characters as explorers, 79*n*, 103, 111, 116, 150, 159–64 passim, 167, 168, 174; explorer finding God, 78; Greene as explorer, 1–7 passim, 9, 12, 17*n*, 26, 29, 40, 54, 132*n*, 133, 136, 157, 159, 160, 162, 171. *See also* Journeys; Travelers
"Extract from an Indo-China Journal," 101

Fairy story, 35, 35*n*, 36, 41, 78, 81, 120, 123
Faith, 38*n*, 48, 60, 61, 61*n*, 63, 85, 88*n*, 97, 98–99, 108–9, 126, 129, 133, 148, 153, 157, 163*n*, 165, 168, 170, 171. *See also* Roman Catholicism
"The Faith" (section of *The Lawless Roads*), 61*n*
The Fallen Idol, 120, 125. *See also* "The Basement Room"
Fantasy, 35, 122, 160, 163*n*
Farce, farcical episodes, 64, 100*n*,

WITHDRAWN